# Collins Social Studies **Atlas** for The Bahamas

Published by Collins
An imprint of HarperCollins Publishers
Westerhill Road
Bishopbriggs
Glasgow G64 2QT
www.harpercollins.co.uk

First edition 2019

© HarperCollins Publishers 2019
Maps © Collins Bartholomew Ltd 2019

Collins ® is a registered trademark of HarperCollins Publishers Ltd

ISBN 978-0-00-834266-1

10 9 8 7 6 5 4

**MIX**
Paper from responsible sources
FSC
www.fsc.org
**FSC™ C007454**

This book is produced from independently certified FSC™ paper to ensure responsible forest management.

For more information visit: www.harpercollins.co.uk/green

Printed by Bell & Bain, Glasgow, Scotland

All mapping in this atlas is generated from Collins Bartholomew digital databases. Collins Bartholomew, the UK's leading independent geographical information supplier, can provide a digital, custom, and premium mapping service to a variety of markets.
For further information:
Tel: +44 (0) 208 307 4515
e-mail: collinsbartholomew@harpercollins.co.uk
or visit our website at: www.collinsbartholomew.com

If you would like to comment on any aspect of this book, please contact us at the above address or online.

www.collins.co.uk
e-mail: collinsmaps@harpercollins.co.uk

Dates in this publication are based on the Christian Era and the designations BC and AD are used throughout. These designations are directly interchangeable with those referring to the Common Era, BCE and CE respectively.

Collins would like to thank Sally Johnson for her contribution to this atlas. Her help on The Bahamas pages in particular has been invaluable.

This is a photograph of a classroom. You can see most of the room but not all of it. It shows how the desks and chairs are arranged in rows with the teacher and the whiteboard at the front of the classroom. Look at the plan view below to see what you can't see in the photograph.

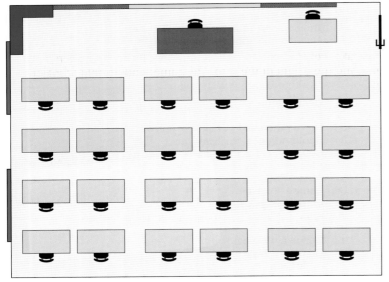

This is a plan of the same classroom. It shows the layout of the room and shows the shapes of the furniture. It is drawn as if you were looking down on it. On a plan we need to use the key to understand what each block of colour means.

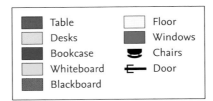

| | | | |
|---|---|---|---|
| Table | | Floor | |
| Desks | | Windows | |
| Bookcase | | Chairs | |
| Whiteboard | | Door | |
| Blackboard | | | |

This is a plan of the whole school. It shows all the rooms in the school. Like the plan of the classroom, the key tells you what each block of colour means.

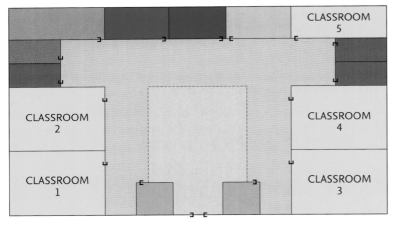

CLASSROOM 5
CLASSROOM 2
CLASSROOM 4
CLASSROOM 1
CLASSROOM 3

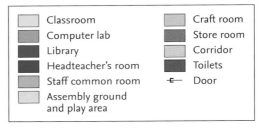

| | | | |
|---|---|---|---|
| Classroom | | Craft room | |
| Computer lab | | Store room | |
| Library | | Corridor | |
| Headteacher's room | | Toilets | |
| Staff common room | | Door | |
| Assembly ground and play area | | | |

This is a map of the area around the school. It includes a larger area than the plan above and shows houses, a church and shops. The individual buildings here are smaller and less detail is given for each.

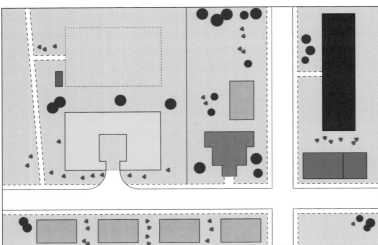

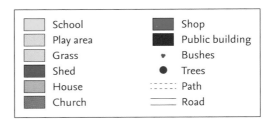

| | | | |
|---|---|---|---|
| School | | Shop | |
| Play area | | Public building | |
| Grass | | Bushes | |
| Shed | | Trees | |
| House | | Path | |
| Church | | Road | |

## Map types

Many types of map are included in the atlas to show different information. The type of map, its symbols and colours are carefully selected to show the theme of each map and to make them easy to understand. The main types of map used are explained below.

**Political maps** provide an overview of the size and location of countries in a specific area, such as a continent. Coloured squares indicate national capitals. Coloured circles represent other cities or towns.

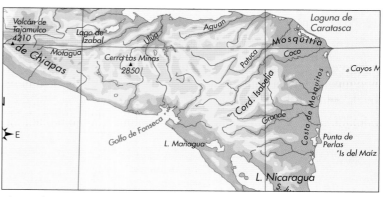

**Physical** or **relief maps** use colour to show oceans, seas, rivers, lakes, and the height of the land. The names and heights of major landforms are also indicated.

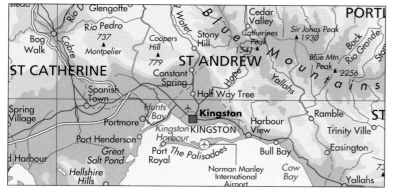

**Physical/political maps** bring together the information provided in the two types of map described above. They show relief and physical features as well as boundaries, major cities and towns, roads, railways and airports.

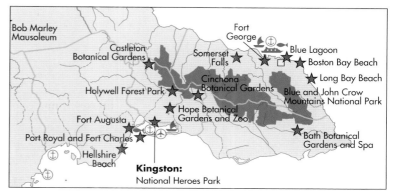

**Features maps** are given for most Caribbean islands in this atlas. They show points of interest, national parks, main resorts, marinas and important ports for fishing, commerce and cruise ships.

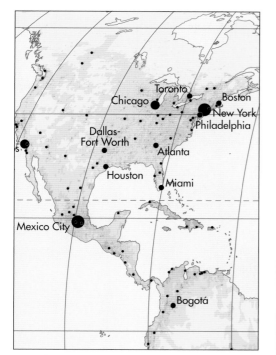

**Distribution maps** use different colours, symbols, or shading to show the location and distribution of natural or man-made features. In this map, symbols indicate the distribution of the world's largest cities.

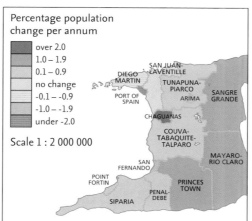

**Graduated colour maps** use colours or shading to show a topic or theme and a measure of its intensity. Generally, the highest values are shaded with the darkest colours. In this map, colours are used to show the percentage change of the population per year in the different areas of local government in Trinidad. It can be seen from this map that the population is increasing in the east of the island, while it is declining in the northwest.

**Satellite images** are recorded by sensors similar to television cameras which are carried aboard satellites. These satellites orbit 500 km above our planet and beam images back to Earth. This is a natural-colour image of Hurricane Sandy, taken on 28 October 2012.

Maps use **symbols** to show the location of a feature and to give information about it. The symbols used on each map in this atlas are explained in the **key** to each map.

Symbols used on maps can be dots, diagrams, lines or area colours. They vary in colour, size and shape. The numbered captions to the map below help explain some of the symbols used on the maps in this atlas.

Different styles of type are also used to show differences between features, for example, country names are shown in large bold capital letters, small water features, rivers and lakes in small italics.

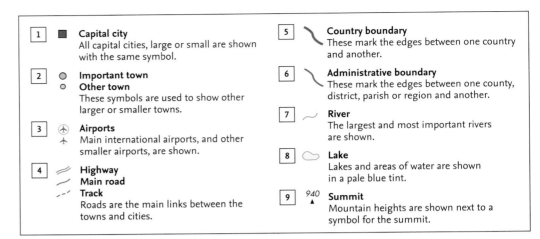

**1** ■ **Capital city**
All capital cities, large or small are shown with the same symbol.

**2** ● **Important town**
   ○ **Other town**
These symbols are used to show other larger or smaller towns.

**3** ✈ **Airports**
Main international airports, and other smaller airports, are shown.

**4** ≈ **Highway**
   — **Main road**
   --- **Track**
Roads are the main links between the towns and cities.

**5** ∖ **Country boundary**
These mark the edges between one country and another.

**6** ∖ **Administrative boundary**
These mark the edges between one county, district, parish or region and another.

**7** ∼ **River**
The largest and most important rivers are shown.

**8** ⬭ **Lake**
Lakes and areas of water are shown in a pale blue tint.

**9** 940 **Summit**
   ▲
Mountain heights are shown next to a symbol for the summit.

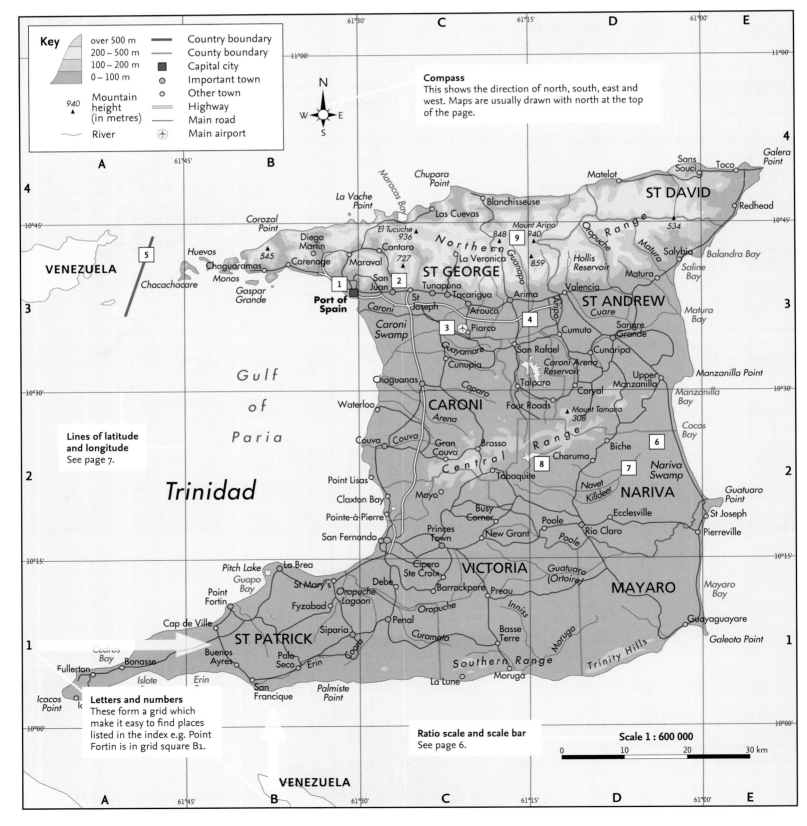

**Key**
- over 500 m
- 200 – 500 m
- 100 – 200 m
- 0 – 100 m
- 940 ▲ Mountain height (in metres)
- ∼ River
- ▬ Country boundary
- — County boundary
- ■ Capital city
- ● Important town
- ○ Other town
- ▬ Highway
- — Main road
- ✈ Main airport

**Compass**
This shows the direction of north, south, east and west. Maps are usually drawn with north at the top of the page.

**Lines of latitude and longitude**
See page 7.

**Letters and numbers**
These form a grid which make it easy to find places listed in the index e.g. Point Fortin is in grid square B1.

**Ratio scale and scale bar**
See page 6.

Scale 1 : 600 000

0    10    20    30 km

## Location maps

These appear on most pages of the atlas. The little map shows you where the area mapped on that page is located in the world.

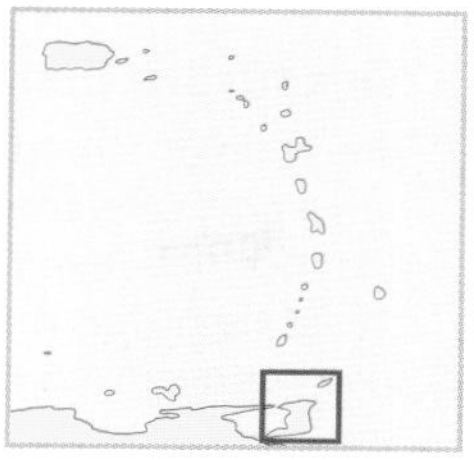

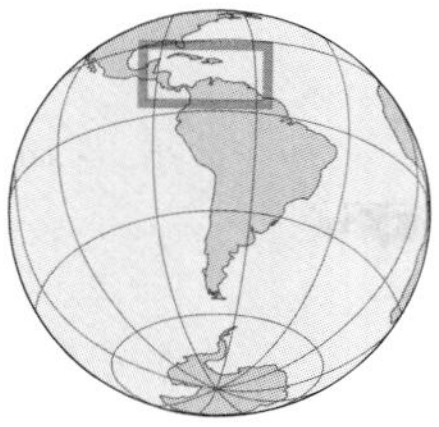

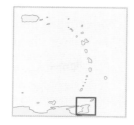

## Photographs

There are many photographs in the atlas. Photos show you what places look like. Some photos show cities and relate to people. Other photos may relate to nature and the landscape.

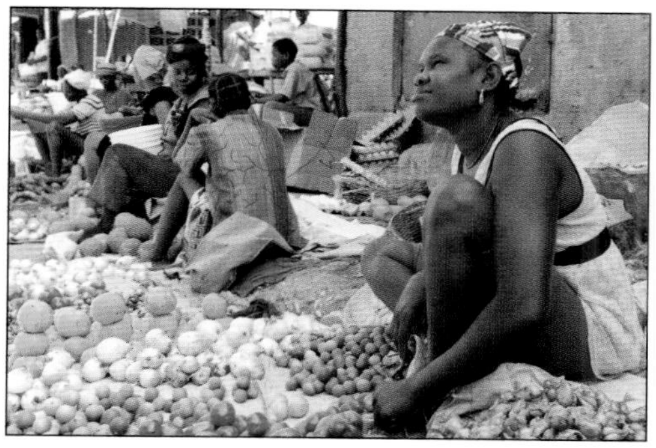

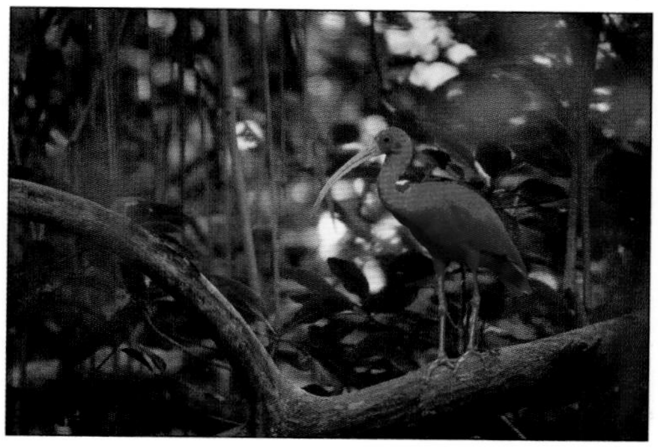

## Map keys

All maps have a key. A map key is a little box next to the map. The key explains all the symbols and colours that are on the map.

**Mining**

- Asphalt
- Gypsum
- Limestone
- Oilfield
- Gasfield
- Oil pipeline
- Gas pipeline

Scale 1 : 1 250 000

**Manufacturing**

- Factories zone
- Cement works
- Chemicals
- Oil refinery
- Metal
- Food processing
- Clothing/textiles
- Electrical goods
- Other light industries

**Features**

- National park
- Point of interest
- Major resort
- Port
- Cruise ships
- Major marina
- Fishing port
- Lighthouse

## Fact boxes

Fact boxes give you extra information about the map or region mapped on the page.

**Caribbean islands facts**

**Population**
41 303 029

**Largest country**
Cuba 110 860 sq km

**Country with most people**
Cuba 11 167 325

**Largest city**
Port-au-Prince 2 481 000

**TRINIDAD AND TOBAGO**

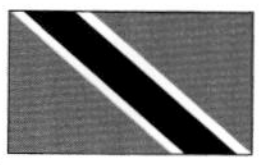

| | |
|---|---|
| **Population** *(2011)* | 1 328 019 |
| **Capital city** | Port of Spain |
| **Area** | 5128 sq km |
| **Languages** | English, creole, Hindi |
| **National flower** | Wild Poinsettia |
| **National bird** *(Trinidad)* | Scarlet Ibis |
| **National bird** *(Tobago)* | Rufous-vented Chachalaca |

## Graphs and tables

Statistical information is shown through a variety of different kinds of graphs (histograms, line graphs and pie charts) and tables.

**Average rainfall**

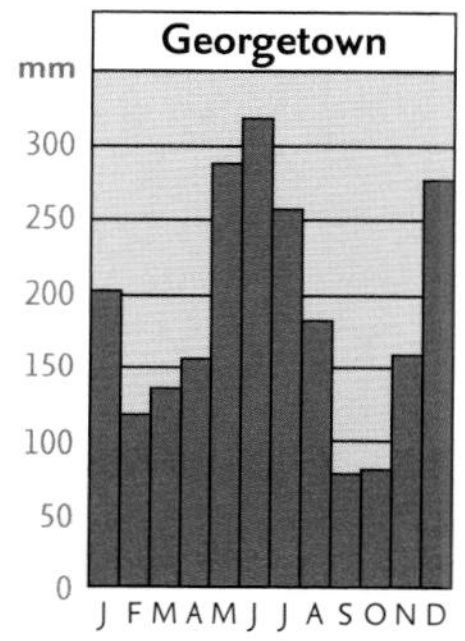


**Population increase, 1960–2011**

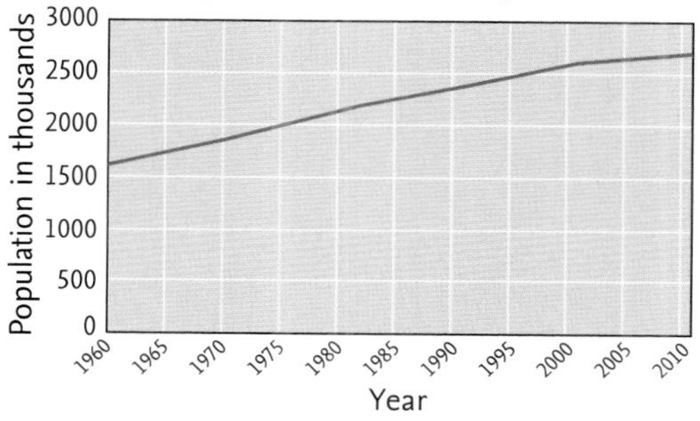


**Urban/rural population, 2011**

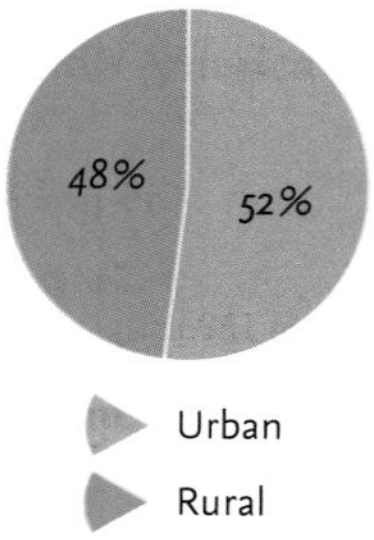


## Text

Bulleted text and photo captions give more detailed information on particular topics of interest for the area featured.

### Mud volcanoes

- Mud volcanoes are a mixture of gas, mud and hot water
- The gas most associated with Trinidad's mud volcanoes is methane
- They are mainly found in the southern half of Trinidad near oil reserves
- There is no eruption of lava but the volcanoes bubble most of the time and generally form a cone of mud and clay

| Island | Area *(sq km)* | Population *(2011)* | Pop. density *(per sq km)* |
|---|---|---|---|
| Trinidad | 4828 | 1 267 145 | 262 |
| Tobago | 300 | 60 874 | 203 |

## Using scale

The **scale** of each map in this atlas is shown in two ways:

**1. The ratio scale** is written, for example, as 1 : 1 000 000. This means that one unit of measurement on the map represents 1 000 000 of the same unit on the ground.
e.g. **Scale 1 : 1 000 000**

**2. The line** or **bar scale** shows the scale as a line with the distance on the ground marked at intervals along the line.

## Different scales

The three maps below cover the same area of the page but are at different scales. Map A is a large scale map which shows a small area in detail. Map C is a small scale map which means it shows a larger area in the same space as Map A, however in much less detail. The area of Map A is highlighted on maps B and C. As the scale ratio increases the map becomes smaller.

**Scale 1 : 3 500 000**

**Map A**

## Measuring distance

The scale of a map can also be used to work out how far it is between two places. In the example below, the straight line distance between Caracas and St George's on the map is 6 cm. The scale of the map is 1 : 10 000 000. Therefore 6 cm on the map represents 6 x 10 000 000 cm or 60 000 000 cm on the ground. Converted to kilometres this is 600 km. The real distance between Caracas and St George's is therefore 600 km on the ground.

**Scale 1 : 10 000 000**

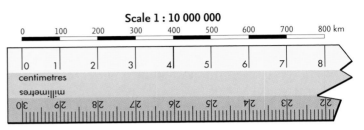

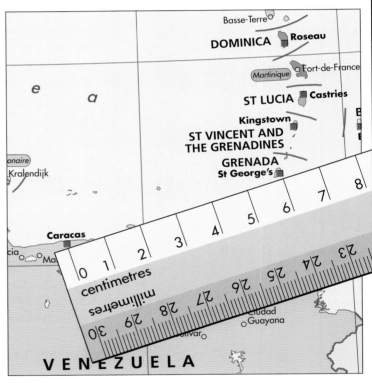

**Scale 1 : 10 000 000**

**Map B**

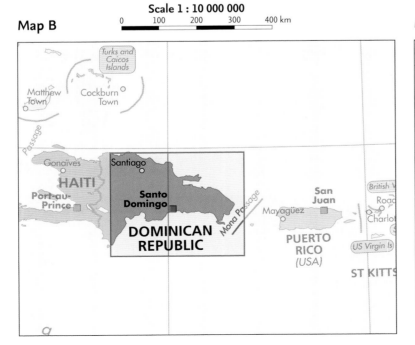

**Scale 1 : 80 000 000**

**Map C**

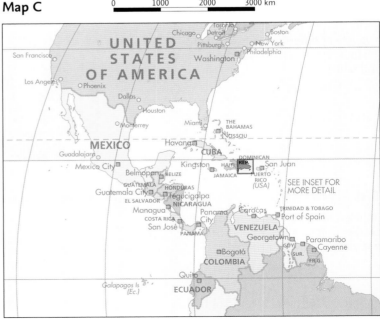

## Latitude and longitude

Lines of latitude are imaginary lines which run in an east-west direction around the globe. They run parallel to each other and are measured in degrees, written as °. The most important line of latitude is the Equator, 0°. All other lines of latitude have a value between 0° and 90° north or south of the Equator. 90° north is the North Pole and, 90° south, the South Pole.

Lines of longitude are imaginary lines which run in a north-south direction between the North Pole and the South Pole. The most important line of longitude is 0°, the Greenwich Meridian, which runs through the Greenwich Observatory in London. Exactly opposite the Greenwich Meridian on the other side of the world, is the 180° line of longitude. All other lines of longitude are measured in degrees east or west of 0°.

When both lines of latitude and longitude are drawn on a map they form a grid. It is easy to find a place on the map if the latitude and longitude values are known. The point of intersection of the line of latitude and the line of longitude locates the place exactly.

The Equator can be used to divide the globe into two halves. Land north of the Equator is the Northern Hemisphere. Land south of the Equator is the Southern Hemisphere. The 0° and 180° lines of longitude can also be used to divide the globe into two halves, the Western and Eastern Hemispheres. Together, the Equator and 0° and 180°, divide the world into four areas, for example, North America is in the Northern Hemisphere and the Western Hemisphere.

1 The globe

2 Lines of latitude

3 Lines of longitude

4 Lines of latitude and longitude

## Time zones

Time varies around the world due to the earth's rotation. This causes different parts of the world to be in light or darkness at any one time.

To account for this, the world is divided into 24 Standard Time Zones based on 15° intervals of longitude (1 hour of time). All places in a time zone have the same time of day. The shapes of some zones have been adjusted so that all of the country or region lies in the same zone.

There is one hour difference between each zone – one hour in the day earlier to the west, one hour later to the east. The local time in another city can be found by counting the number of hours earlier or later than the local time in your own country.

The time at 0° is known as Greenwich Mean Time (GMT) because the line passes through Greenwich in London. Most countries of the Caribbean are either 4 or 5 hours behind GMT.

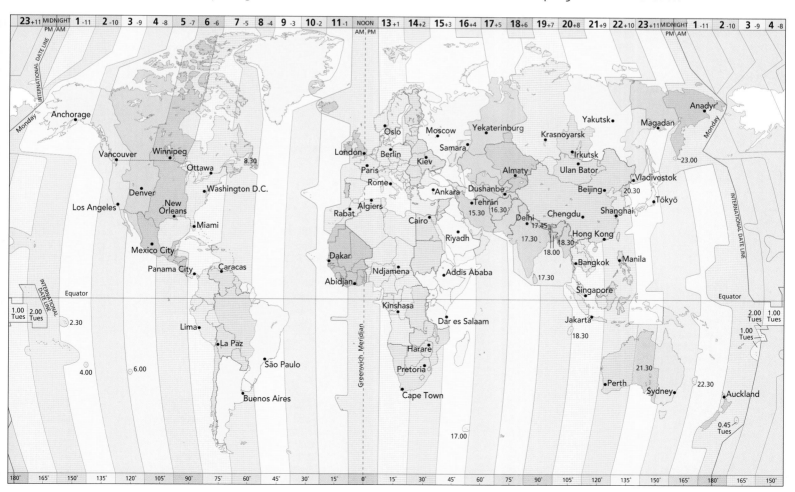

### The Solar System

The Solar System is the Sun and the many objects that orbit it.
These objects include eight planets, at least five dwarf planets and
countless asteroids, meteoroids and comets. Orbiting some of the
planets and dwarf planets are over 160 moons. The Sun keeps its
surrounding objects in its orbit by its pull of gravity which has an
influence for many millions of kilometres.

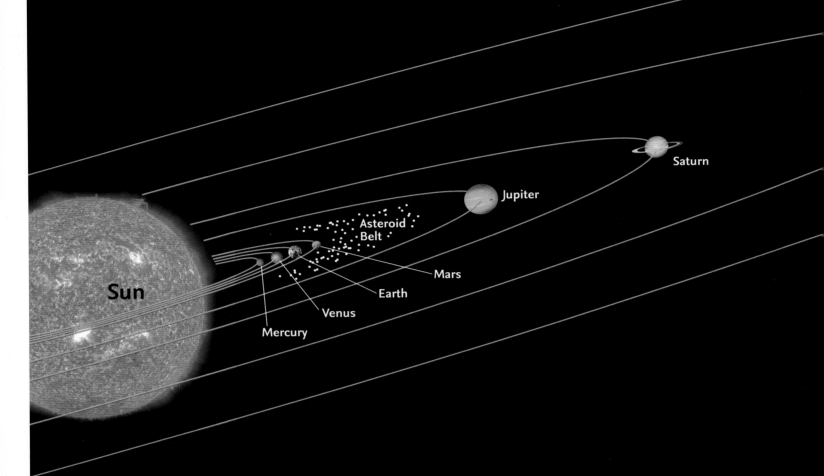

Saturn

Jupiter

Asteroid
Belt

Mars

Earth

Venus

Mercury

Sun

### The Sun

Diameter
1 391 016 km
Circumference
4 370 000 km
Average temperature
5504 °C
Rotation about axis
(measured at its equator)
25 Earth days 9 hours

### The Planets

| | Mercury | Venus | Earth | Mars |
|---|---|---|---|---|
| |  |  | | |
| Diameter | 4900 km | 12 100 km | 12 700 km | 6779 km |
| Circumference | 15 300 km | 38 000 km | 40 000 km | 21 300 km |
| Distance from Sun | 58 million km | 108 million km | 150 million km | 228 million km |
| Length of year | 88 Earth days | 244 Earth days 17 hours | 365 days 6 hours | 687 Earth days |
| Length of day | 59 Earth days | 243 Earth days | 23 hours 56 minutes | 24 hours 37 minutes |

| | Jupiter | Saturn | Uranus | Neptune |
|---|---|---|---|---|
| |  |  |  |  |
| | | |  |  |
| Diameter | 143 000 km | 116 500 km | 50 700 km | 49 200 km |
| Circumference | 450 000 km | 366 000 km | 159 000 km | 154 700 km |
| Distance from Sun | 778 million km | 1427 million km | 2871 million km | 4498 million km |
| Length of year | 11 Earth years 314 days | 29 Earth years | 84 Earth years | 165 Earth years |
| Length of day | 9 hours 55 minutes | 10 hours 39 minutes | 17 hours 14 minutes | 16 hours 7 minutes |

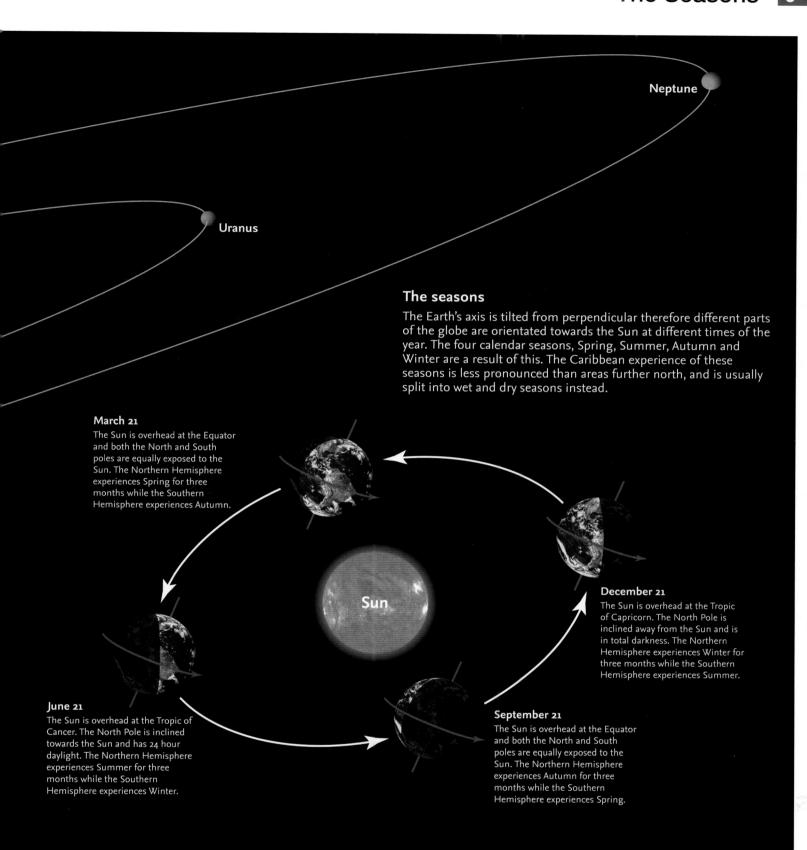

**Neptune**

**Uranus**

## The seasons

The Earth's axis is tilted from perpendicular therefore different parts of the globe are orientated towards the Sun at different times of the year. The four calendar seasons, Spring, Summer, Autumn and Winter are a result of this. The Caribbean experience of these seasons is less pronounced than areas further north, and is usually split into wet and dry seasons instead.

**March 21**
The Sun is overhead at the Equator and both the North and South poles are equally exposed to the Sun. The Northern Hemisphere experiences Spring for three months while the Southern Hemisphere experiences Autumn.

**Sun**

**December 21**
The Sun is overhead at the Tropic of Capricorn. The North Pole is inclined away from the Sun and is in total darkness. The Northern Hemisphere experiences Winter for three months while the Southern Hemisphere experiences Summer.

**June 21**
The Sun is overhead at the Tropic of Cancer. The North Pole is inclined towards the Sun and has 24 hour daylight. The Northern Hemisphere experiences Summer for three months while the Southern Hemisphere experiences Winter.

**September 21**
The Sun is overhead at the Equator and both the North and South poles are equally exposed to the Sun. The Northern Hemisphere experiences Autumn for three months while the Southern Hemisphere experiences Spring.

## Day and night

The Earth turns round on its axis every 23 hours 56 minutes and it is this rotation that is responsible for the daily cycles of day and night. At any one moment in time, one half of the Earth is in sunlight, while the other half, facing away from the Sun, is in darkness. As the Earth rotates it also creates the apparent movement of the Sun from east to west across the sky.

Direction of rotation

**Dawn in the UK**

**Midday in the UK**

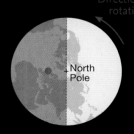

**Dusk in the UK**

**Midnight in the UK**

(The Caribbean will be 4 or 5 hours earlier in the day than the UK at this point.)

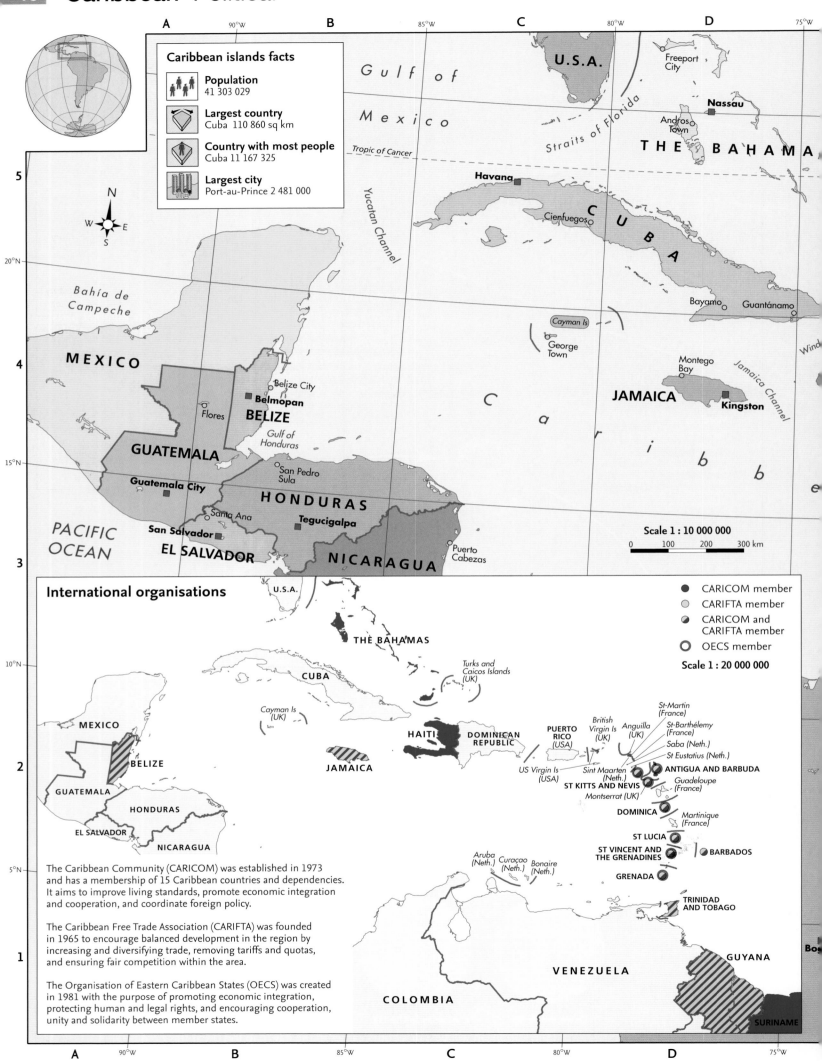

## Caribbean islands facts

**Population**
41 303 029

**Largest country**
Cuba 110 860 sq km

**Country with most people**
Cuba 11 167 325

**Largest city**
Port-au-Prince 2 481 000

A 90°W    B 85°W    C 80°W    D 75°W

5    20°N    15°N    10°N    5°N    4    3    2    1

Gulf of Mexico

U.S.A.

Freeport City

Nassau

Andros Town

THE BAHAMA

Tropic of Cancer

Yucatan Channel

Havana

Cienfuegos

C U B A

Bayamo    Guantánamo

Bahía de Campeche

Cayman Is

George Town

Montego Bay    Jamaica Channel

JAMAICA

Kingston

Wind

M E X I C O

Belize City

Belmopan

BELIZE

Flores

Gulf of Honduras

GUATEMALA

San Pedro Sula

C a r i b b

PACIFIC OCEAN

Guatemala City

Santa Ana

H O N D U R A S

Tegucigalpa

San Salvador

EL SALVADOR

NICARAGUA

Puerto Cabezas

Scale 1 : 10 000 000
0    100    200    300 km

## International organisations

- ● CARICOM member
- ○ CARIFTA member
- ◐ CARICOM and CARIFTA member
- ○ OECS member

Scale 1 : 20 000 000

U.S.A.

THE BAHAMAS

CUBA

Turks and Caicos Islands (UK)

Cayman Is (UK)

HAITI    DOMINICAN REPUBLIC

PUERTO RICO (USA)

British Virgin Is (UK)    Anguilla (UK)

St-Martin (France)
St-Barthélemy (France)
Saba (Neth.)
St Eustatius (Neth.)

MEXICO

BELIZE

JAMAICA

US Virgin Is (USA)    Sint Maarten (Neth.)    ANTIGUA AND BARBUDA

ST KITTS AND NEVIS    Guadeloupe (France)

GUATEMALA

HONDURAS    Montserrat (UK)

DOMINICA    Martinique (France)

EL SALVADOR

NICARAGUA

ST LUCIA

ST VINCENT AND THE GRENADINES    BARBADOS

Aruba (Neth.)    Curaçao (Neth.)    Bonaire (Neth.)

GRENADA

TRINIDAD AND TOBAGO

COLOMBIA    VENEZUELA    GUYANA    Bog

SURINAME

The Caribbean Community (CARICOM) was established in 1973 and has a membership of 15 Caribbean countries and dependencies. It aims to improve living standards, promote economic integration and cooperation, and coordinate foreign policy.

The Caribbean Free Trade Association (CARIFTA) was founded in 1965 to encourage balanced development in the region by increasing and diversifying trade, removing tariffs and quotas, and ensuring fair competition within the area.

The Organisation of Eastern Caribbean States (OECS) was created in 1981 with the purpose of promoting economic integration, protecting human and legal rights, and encouraging cooperation, unity and solidarity between member states.

A 90°W    B 85°W    C 80°W    D 75°W

| Country/territory | Last coloniser | Independence/ Current status | Country/territory | Last coloniser | Independence/ Current status |
|---|---|---|---|---|---|
| Anguilla | UK | British Overseas Territory | Haiti | USA | 1934 |
| Antigua and Barbuda | UK | 1981 | Jamaica | UK | 1962 |
| Aruba | Netherlands | Self-governing Territory | Martinique | France | Department of France |
| The Bahamas | UK | 1973 | Montserrat | UK | British Overseas Territory |
| Barbados | UK | 1966 | Puerto Rico | USA | US Commonwealth |
| Belize | UK | 1981 | Saba | Netherlands | Special Municipality |
| Bonaire | Netherlands | Special Municipality | St-Barthélemy | France | Overseas Collectivity |
| British Virgin Islands | UK | British Overseas Territory | St Eustatius | Netherlands | Special Municipality |
| Cayman Islands | UK/Jamaica | British Overseas Territory | St Kitts and Nevis | UK | 1983 |
| Cuba | USA | 1902 | St Lucia | UK | 1979 |
| Curaçao | Netherlands | Self-governing Territory | St-Martin | France | Overseas Collectivity |
| Dominica | UK | 1978 | Sint Maarten | Netherlands | Self-governing Territory |
| Dominican Republic | Haiti/Spain | 1844/1865 | St Vincent and the Grenadines | UK | 1979 |
| Grenada | UK | 1974 | Suriname | Netherlands | 1975 |
| Guadeloupe | France | Department of France | Trinidad and Tobago | UK | 1962 |
| Guyana | UK | 1966 | Turks and Caicos Islands | UK | British Overseas Territory |
| | | | US Virgin Islands | USA | Unincorporated Territory |

**Key**

— Country boundary
-- Disputed boundary
■ Capital city
○ Important city / town

**Territories**
France
Netherlands
United Kingdom
United States

Turks and Caicos Islands

Cockburn Town

thew

Gonaïves  Santiago

**HAITI**

rt-au-Prince

**Santo Domingo**

**DOMINICAN REPUBLIC**

Mona Passage

Mayagüez

**San Juan**

British Virgin Is

Road Town

Anguilla

Charlotte Amalie

St-Martin

**PUERTO RICO (USA)**

US Virgin Is

Sint Maarten

Saba

St-Barthélemy

**Basseterre**

**ANTIGUA AND BARBUDA**

St Eustatius

**St John's**

**ST KITTS AND NEVIS**

Montserrat

Guadeloupe

Basse-Terre

**DOMINICA**

**Roseau**

Martinique

Fort-de-France

**ST LUCIA**

**Castries**

**BARBADOS**

**Kingstown**

**ST VINCENT AND THE GRENADINES**

**Bridgetown**

**GRENADA**

**St George's**

**ATLANTIC OCEAN**

Scarborough

**TRINIDAD AND TOBAGO**

**Port of Spain**

Aruba

Curaçao

Bonaire

Oranjestad

Willemstad

Kralendijk

**Caracas**

Maracaibo

Barquisimeto  Valencia  Maracay

n

S   e   a

**VENEZUELA**

Ciudad Guayana

Ciudad Bolívar

cuta

San Cristóbal

aramanga

**COLOMBIA**

Georgetown

Paramaribo

**GUYANA**

**SURINAME**

CLAIMED BY VENEZUELA

**BRAZIL**

CLAIMED BY SURINAME

Lambert Conformal Conic projection

**Caribbean islands facts**

| | |
|---|---|
| **Area** | 234 765 sq km |
| **Highest peak** | Pico Duarte 3175 m |
| **Longest river** | Cauto 370 km |
| **Largest lake** | Lago de Enriquillo 265 sq km |

N W E S

Gulf of Mexico

Tropic of Cancer

NORTH AMERICA

Lake Okeechobee
Cape Sable
Florida Keys
Straits of Florida

Bimini Is
Grand Bahama
Little Abaco
Great Abaco
Northeast Providence Channel
New Providence
Eleuthera
Bahama
North Andros
South Andros
Cat I.
Exuma Cays
Exuma Sd
Great Exuma
Islands
Long I.
Crooked
Ackl

C. Catoche
C. San Antonio
Yucatán Channel
Yucatán
Bahía de Campeche
Laguna de Términos
Hondo
Isla de Cozumel
Isla de la Juventud
G. de Batabanó
Arch. de Sabana
Arch. de los Canarreos
Arch. de los Jardines de la Reina
Cuba
Arch. de Camagüey
Cayo Romano
Cayo Sabinal
Golfo de Guacanayabo
Cauto
Sa Maestra
Greater
Little Cayman
Grand Cayman
Cayman Brac
C. Cruz
Pico Turquino 1994
Windward
Jamaica Channel

Caribbean

Ambergris Caye
Belize
Turneffe Is
Victoria Peak
Maya Mts 1120
Sierra Madre de Chiapas
Volcán de Tajumulco 4210
Motagua
Lago de Izabal
Ulúa
Cerro las Minas 2850
Gulf of Honduras
Islas de la Bahía
Islas del Cisne
Jamaica
Blue Mountain Peak 2256
Navassa Island

Aguan
Patuca
Coco
Mosquitia
Laguna de Caratasca
Cayos Miskitos
Cord. Isabelia
Grande
Costa de Mosquitos
Punta de Perlas
I. de Providencia
I. de San Andrés
'Is del Maíz
Golfo de Fonseca
L. Managua
L. Nicaragua
S. Juan
C. Sta Elena

PACIFIC OCEAN

Golfo de Nicoya
Chirripó 3819
Bahía de Coronado
Pen. de Osa
Baru 3475
Golfo de los Mosquitos
Panama Canal
Isthmus of Panama
Golfo del Darién
Golfo de Morrosquillo
Cordillera Occidental
Cordillera Central
Cri
Cauca
Magdalena

Golfo de Chiriquí
Pen. de Azuero
Golfo de Panamá
Isla del Rey
I. de Coiba
Punta Mala

I. de Malpelo
Punta Chirambirá
San Juan
Golfo de Cupica

Punta Reyes

Mangroves are common in and around the Caribbean Sea. These red mangrove roots are providing a nursery and shelter for young fish that will later populate the deeper waters.

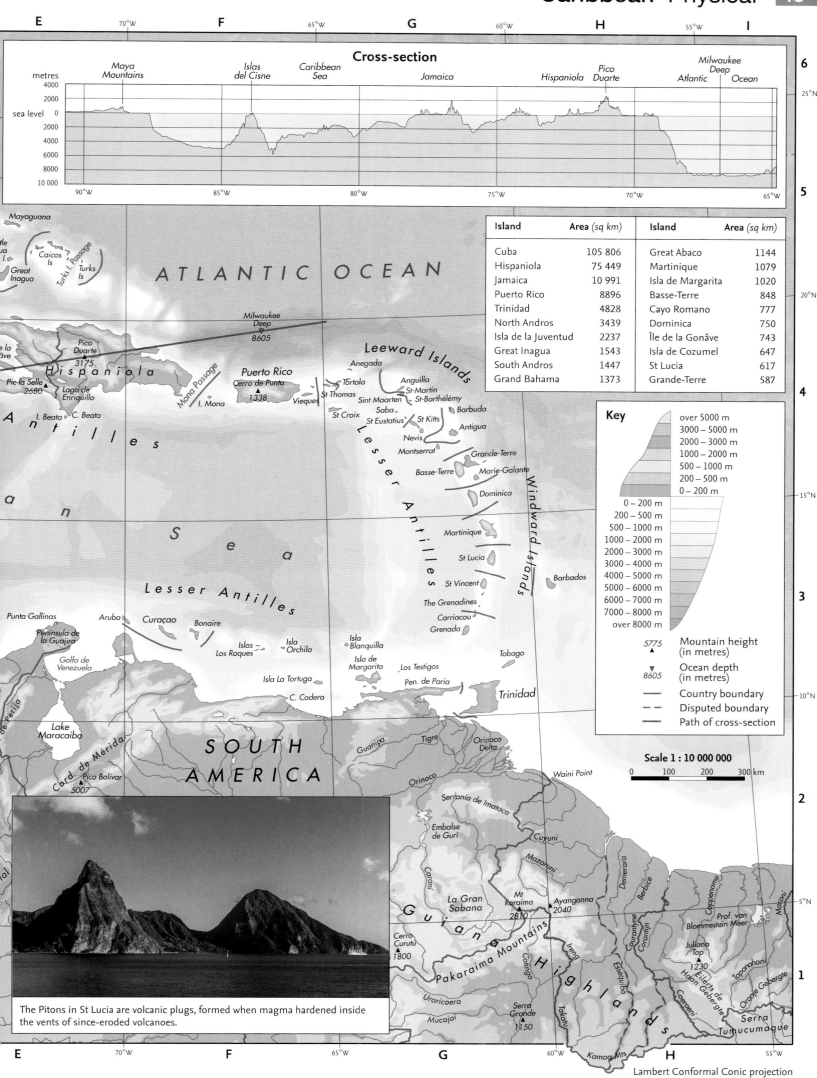

**Cross-section**

metres 4000 2000 sea level 0 2000 4000 6000 8000 10 000

Maya Mountains — Islas del Cisne — Caribbean Sea — Jamaica — Hispaniola — Pico Duarte — Milwaukee Deep — Atlantic Ocean

ATLANTIC OCEAN

Mayaguana, Caicos Is, Turks I. Passage, Turks Is, Great Inagua

Milwaukee Deep 8605

Hispaniola, Pico Duarte 3175, Pic la Selle 2680, Lago de Enriquillo, I. Beata, C. Beata, Mona Passage

Puerto Rico, Cerro de Punta 1338, I. Mona, Vieques, St Thomas, Tortola, Anegada, St Croix, Saba, St Eustatius, St Kitts, Nevis, Montserrat, Sint Maarten, St-Martin, St-Barthélémy, Anguilla, Barbuda, Antigua

Leeward Islands

Grande-Terre, Basse-Terre, Marie-Galante, Dominica, Martinique, St Lucia, St Vincent, The Grenadines, Carriacou, Grenada, Barbados, Tobago

Lesser Antilles, Windward Islands

Greater Antilles, Caribbean Sea, Lesser Antilles

Punta Gallinas, Península de la Guajira, Aruba, Curaçao, Bonaire, Islas Los Roques, Isla Orchila, Isla La Tortuga, Isla Blanquilla, Isla de Margarita, Los Testigos, Pen. de Paria, C. Codera, Trinidad

Golfo de Venezuela, Lake Maracaibo, Cord. de Mérida, Pico Bolívar 5007

SOUTH AMERICA

| Island | Area (sq km) | Island | Area (sq km) |
|---|---|---|---|
| Cuba | 105 806 | Great Abaco | 1144 |
| Hispaniola | 75 449 | Martinique | 1079 |
| Jamaica | 10 991 | Isla de Margarita | 1020 |
| Puerto Rico | 8896 | Basse-Terre | 848 |
| Trinidad | 4828 | Cayo Romano | 777 |
| North Andros | 3439 | Dominica | 750 |
| Isla de la Juventud | 2237 | Île de la Gonâve | 743 |
| Great Inagua | 1543 | Isla de Cozumel | 647 |
| South Andros | 1447 | St Lucia | 617 |
| Grand Bahama | 1373 | Grande-Terre | 587 |

**Key**

over 5000 m
3000 – 5000 m
2000 – 3000 m
1000 – 2000 m
500 – 1000 m
200 – 500 m
0 – 200 m

0 – 200 m
200 – 500 m
500 – 1000 m
1000 – 2000 m
2000 – 3000 m
3000 – 4000 m
4000 – 5000 m
5000 – 6000 m
6000 – 7000 m
7000 – 8000 m
over 8000 m

▲ 5775  Mountain height (in metres)
▼ 8605  Ocean depth (in metres)
Country boundary
Disputed boundary
Path of cross-section

Scale 1 : 10 000 000
0   100   200   300 km

Guanipa, Tigre, Orinoco Delta, Orinoco, Serranía de Imataca, Embalse de Guri, Cuyuni, Mazaruni, Caroni, Waini Point, Demerara, Berbice, Courantyne, Corantijn, Coppename, Maroni

La Gran Sabana, Mt Roraima 2810, Ayanganna 2040, Cerro Curutú 1800, Prof. van Blommestein Meer, Juliana Top 1230, Eilerts de Haan Gebergte, Tapanahoni

Guiana Highlands, Pakaraima Mountains, Uaricoera, Colingo, Ireng, Takutu, Coeroeni, Oranje Gebergte

Serra Grande 1150, Mucajaí, Kamoa Mts, Serra Tumucumaque, Orange Gebergte

The Pitons in St Lucia are volcanic plugs, formed when magma hardened inside the vents of since-eroded volcanoes.

Lambert Conformal Conic projection

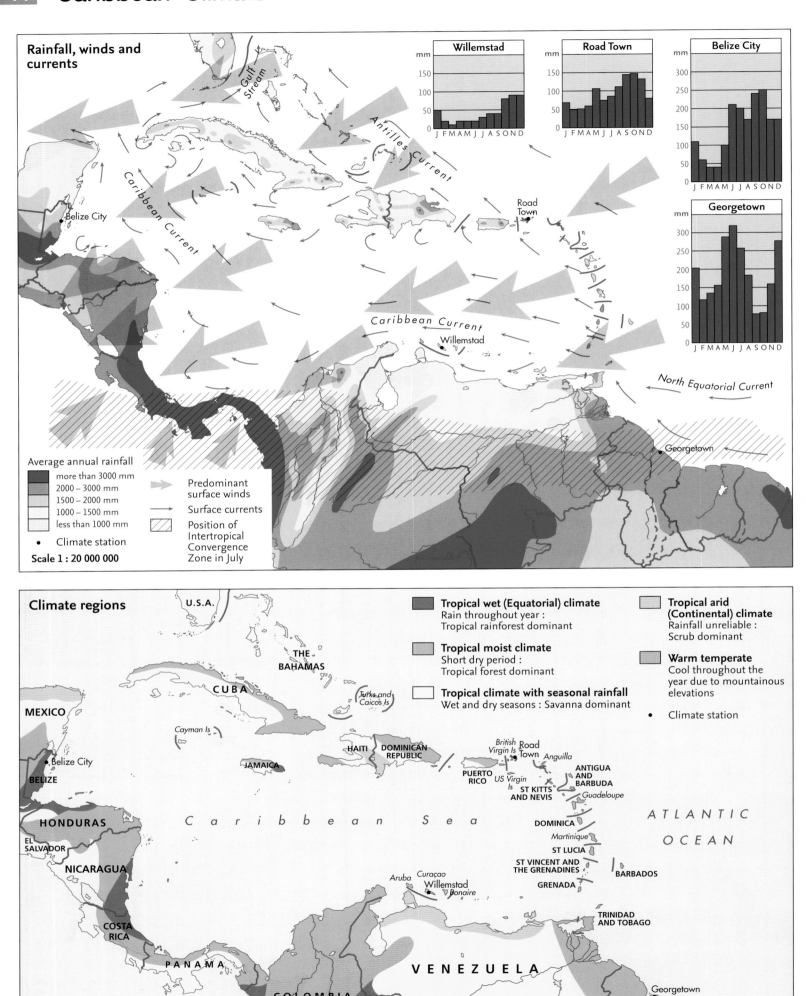

## Rainfall, winds and currents

### Willemstad
mm
150
100
50
0
J F M A M J J A S O N D

### Road Town
mm
150
100
50
0
J F M A M J J A S O N D

### Belize City
mm
300
250
200
150
100
50
0
J F M A M J J A S O N D

### Georgetown
mm
300
250
200
150
100
50
0
J F M A M J J A S O N D

Gulf Stream

Antilles Current

Caribbean Current

Road Town

Caribbean Current

Willemstad

North Equatorial Current

Belize City

Georgetown

**Average annual rainfall**

- more than 3000 mm
- 2000 – 3000 mm
- 1500 – 2000 mm
- 1000 – 1500 mm
- less than 1000 mm
- • Climate station

Scale 1 : 20 000 000

- Predominant surface winds
- Surface currents
- Position of Intertropical Convergence Zone in July

## Climate regions

**Tropical wet (Equatorial) climate**
Rain throughout year :
Tropical rainforest dominant

**Tropical moist climate**
Short dry period :
Tropical forest dominant

**Tropical climate with seasonal rainfall**
Wet and dry seasons : Savanna dominant

**Tropical arid (Continental) climate**
Rainfall unreliable :
Scrub dominant

**Warm temperate**
Cool throughout the year due to mountainous elevations

• Climate station

U.S.A.

THE BAHAMAS

CUBA

Turks and Caicos Is

MEXICO

Cayman Is

BELIZE

Belize City

JAMAICA

HAITI

DOMINICAN REPUBLIC

British Virgin Is

Road Town

Anguilla

PUERTO RICO

US Virgin Is

ST KITTS AND NEVIS

ANTIGUA AND BARBUDA

Guadeloupe

HONDURAS

EL SALVADOR

NICARAGUA

C a r i b b e a n   S e a

DOMINICA

Martinique

ST LUCIA

ST VINCENT AND THE GRENADINES

GRENADA

BARBADOS

ATLANTIC OCEAN

Aruba

Curaçao

Willemstad

Bonaire

TRINIDAD AND TOBAGO

COSTA RICA

PANAMA

COLOMBIA

V E N E Z U E L A

Georgetown

GUYANA

SURINAME

FRENCH GUIANA

Scale 1 : 20 000 000

Hurricanes affecting the Caribbean originate over the warm waters of the Atlantic Ocean or Caribbean Sea. They rotate anticlockwise and always try to move north, but are often forced to travel west or northwest before they can turn. The tracks on the map below show how they do this. Their wind strength declines rapidly once they reach land, but they may still be very wet and cause extensive flooding.

- The most deaths usually occur in the poorest communities
- Heavy rainfall during a hurricane may be more damaging than the wind or storm surge
- Mountainous islands are vulnerable to severe flooding, mudslides and landslides
- Flatter islands suffer much damage from storm surges and coastal flooding
- Many islands are hit by major hurricanes, but those with good preparations and a sound building code rarely have any deaths
- The extent and cost of damage can be excessive even if there are no deaths

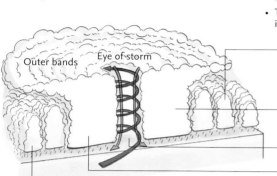

Outer bands  Eye of storm

As the hurricane passes, wind speeds and rainfall decrease and the outer bands bring sunny intervals

After the eye has passed, hurricane-force winds begin immediately from the opposite direction, often accompanied by heavy rain

In the eye of the storm, winds are light and the sky is clear with little rain

Closer to the centre, wind speeds increase to over 100 km/hr, and there may be torrential rain (more than 200 mm/day)

As the hurricane approaches, clouds form and the wind speed increases. The outer bands bring alternate rain showers and sunny intervals

## Hurricane tracks

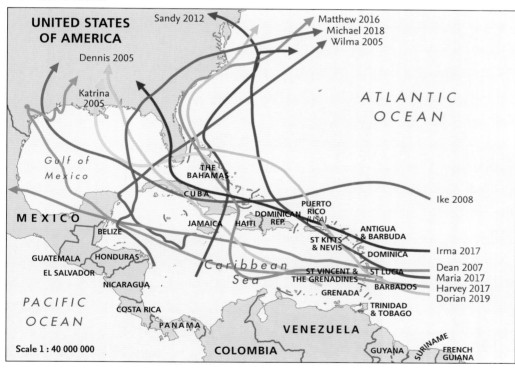

Scale 1 : 40 000 000

## Hurricane risk

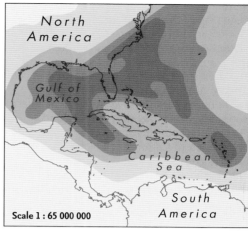

Scale 1 : 65 000 000

Chance of a hurricane during one year

less than 5%   5 – 35%   35 – 55%   55 – 65%   65 – 90%

## Total number of recorded storms for each month over a century

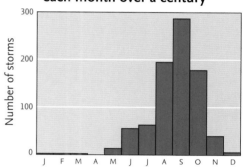

Hurricane Sandy extended over 1000 km and moved very slowly, staying over Cuba, Haiti and The Bahamas for many days and causing much damage.

## Recent hurricanes

| Year | Name | Category | Main countries/territories affected (number of deaths) |
|------|------|----------|---------------------------------------------------------|
| 2005 | Dennis | 4 | Haiti (56), Jamaica (1), Cuba (16), USA (15) |
| 2005 | Katrina | 5 | USA (>1200) |
| 2005 | Wilma | 4 | Haiti (12), Jamaica (1), Cuba (4), Mexico (8), USA (61) |
| 2007 | Dean | 5 | Martinique (3), Dominica (2), Haiti (14), Jamaica (3), Belize, Mexico (13) |
| 2008 | Ike | 4 | Turks & Caicos Is, The Bahamas, Dom. Rep. (2), Haiti (74), Cuba (7), USA (113) |
| 2012 | Sandy | 3 | Jamaica (2), Cuba (11), Haiti (54), Dom. Rep. (2), The Bahamas (2), USA (157) |
| 2016 | Matthew | 5 | Haiti (>500), Dom. Rep. (4), Cuba (4), The Bahamas, USA (47) |
| 2017 | Harvey | 4 | Suriname, Guyana (1), Barbados, St Vincent & Grenadines, USA (76) |
| 2017 | Irma | 5 | Antigua & Barbuda (3), St-Martin/St-Barthélemy (11), Sint Maarten (4), British Virgin Is (4), US Virgin Is (4), Puerto Rico (3), Cuba (10), USA (88) |
| 2017 | Maria | 5 | Dominica (65), Guadeloupe (2), Puerto Rico (2975), Dom. Rep. (5), USA (4) |
| 2018 | Michael | 5 | Honduras (8), Nicaragua (4), El Salvador (3), USA (59) |
| 2019 | Dorian | 5 | The Bahamas (74), Puerto Rico (1), USA (9) |

The Red Cross distributes supplies in Port-au-Prince, Haiti, in the aftermath of Hurricane Sandy.

# Caribbean Earthquakes

The world's major earthquakes occur most frequently at the boundaries of the crustal plates. As all the Caribbean islands are located around the edge of the Caribbean plate they are vulnerable to earthquakes as this plate moves relative to its neighbours. The greatest movement is in the west in Central America, which has the worst earthquakes. Next in severity is the northern boundary, which includes Jamaica and Hispaniola, and the least pressure is exerted in the Eastern Caribbean, which has smaller earthquakes.

The Caribbean islands have around 20 – 30 minor earthquakes a year; they are more common than hurricanes.

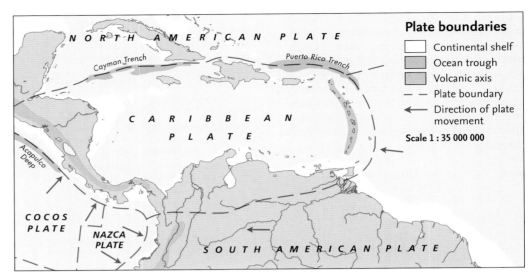

**Plate boundaries**

- Continental shelf
- Ocean trough
- Volcanic axis
- – – Plate boundary
- ← Direction of plate movement

Scale 1 : 35 000 000

## Earthquakes

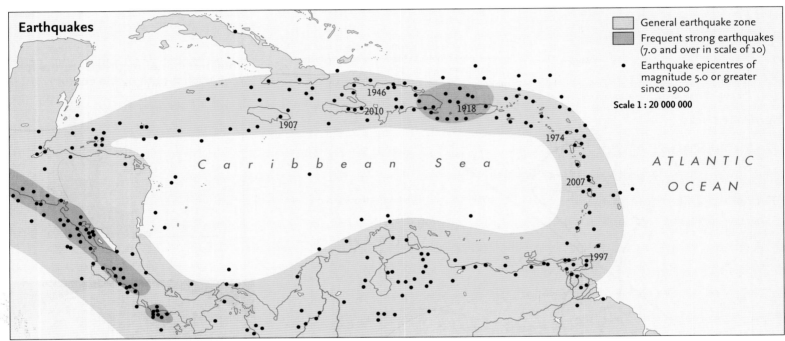

General earthquake zone

Frequent strong earthquakes (7.0 and over in scale of 10)

• Earthquake epicentres of magnitude 5.0 or greater since 1900

Scale 1 : 20 000 000

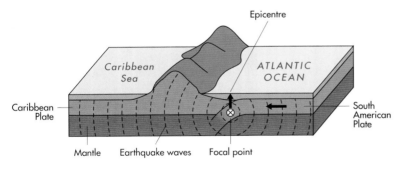

## Major earthquakes

| Year | Location | Magnitude (Richter scale) | |
|------|----------|----------|---|
| 1692 | Port Royal, Jamaica | 7.5 | 2000 dead; also minor earthquakes in 1907 and 1993 |
| 1842 | Cap-Haïtien, Haiti | 8.1 | 5000 dead |
| 1843 | near Guadeloupe | 8.0 – 8.5 | 2000 – 3000 dead on Guadeloupe; English Harbour on Antigua submerged |
| 1907 | Kingston, Jamaica | 6.5 | 800 – 1000 dead |
| 1918 | western Puerto Rico | 7.5 | 118 dead |
| 1946 | El Cibao, Dom. Rep. | 8.1 | 75 dead |
| 1974 | near Antigua | 7.5 | many islands affected; epicentre in Venezuela |
| 1997 | Trinidad and Tobago | 6.5 | 81 dead in Venezuela |
| 2007 | Martinique | 7.4 | 6 dead |
| 2010 | Port-au-Prince, Haiti | 7.0 | 230 000 dead |

Transitional shelter homes being built in large numbers near Port-au-Prince, Haiti, in the aftermath of the devastating earthquake of 2010.

Like earthquakes, volcanoes occur mainly along plate boundaries and the Caribbean is no exception. One difference is that they do not occur along the northern edge of the plate as this is not a collision zone, but they do occur in the west and east. For the same reason that Central America has the largest earthquakes it also has the largest number of volcanoes, and the most active ones. The Eastern Caribbean is a less active plate margin, but the few active volcanoes it does have are extremely dangerous and these, and older dormant volcanoes, are what formed many of the islands.

- Most Caribbean volcanoes are dormant but may erupt in the future
- Volcanic activity, such as sulphur springs and fumaroles, is common on many islands (e.g. Dominica, St Lucia, St Kitts, Montserrat)

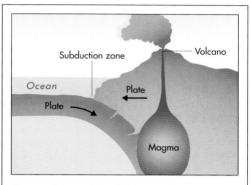

## Formation of Caribbean volcanoes

Wherever two tectonic plates collide a destructive margin is formed. One of these plates will be forced under the other in an area called the subduction zone. Friction (and the increase in temperature as the crust moves downwards) causes the crust to melt and some of the newly formed magma may be forced to the surface to form volcanoes.

The structure of a typical volcano formed in this way is shown below. The increase in pressure as the plate is forced downwards can also trigger severe earthquakes.

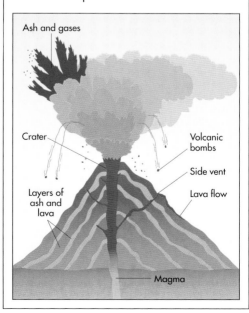

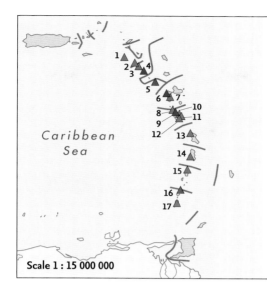

## Volcanoes

▲ Currently active    ▲ Dormant    ▲ Extinct

1 Saba, 1640
2 The Quill, St Eustatius, 250 AD ± 150 years
3 Mount Liamuiga, St Kitts and Nevis, 160 AD ± 200 years
4 Nevis Peak, St Kitts and Nevis
5 Soufrière Hills, Montserrat, 1995 – 2011, 2012
6 Bouillante Chain, Guadeloupe
7 La Soufrière, Guadeloupe, 1977
8 Morne Aux Diables, Dominica
9 Morne Diablotins, Dominica
10 Morne Trois Pitons, Dominica, 920 AD ± 50 years
11 Morne Watt, Dominica, 1997
12 Morne Plat Pays, Dominica, 1270 ± 50 years
13 Montagne Pelée, Martinique, 1932
14 Qualibou, St Lucia, 1766
15 Soufrière, St Vincent and the Grenadines, 1979
16 Kick 'em Jenny, Grenada, 2001
17 Mount St Catherine, Grenada

List gives year of last eruption

Scale 1 : 15 000 000

## Volcanic eruptions

| Year | Volcano | Location | |
|---|---|---|---|
| 1902 (and 1979, minor) | Soufrière | St Vincent | 2000 dead |
| 1902 (and 1932, minor) | Montagne Pelée | Martinique | 30 000 dead |
| 1939 – present | Kick 'em Jenny | off the coast of Grenada | |
| 1977 | La Soufrière | Basse-Terre, Guadeloupe | evacuated, no deaths |
| 1995 – present | Soufrière Hills | Montserrat | southern two-thirds of the island abandoned |

## Montserrat

- In 1995 there were minor eruptions at the summit of Soufrière Hills, and then later in the year more severe eruptions covered parts of Plymouth in ash
- It was decided to evacuate Plymouth at the end of 1995 and although there were attempts to resettle the town, a major eruption in September 1996 destroyed much of the southern half of the island
- In 1997 a further eruption destroyed the rest of Plymouth and the airport, killing 26 people who had not left the area. Ash and sediment covered much of Plymouth
- As volcanic activity has continued to this day, the southern two-thirds of the island has been abandoned and new settlements, and an airport, set up in the northern sector
- The larger part of Montserrat will remain uninhabitable for the foreseeable future. A permanent volcanic observatory monitors the situation around the clock
- The population has declined from about 10 000 in 1995 to about 5000 today

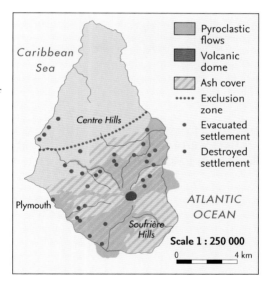

Pyroclastic flows
Volcanic dome
Ash cover
Exclusion zone
Evacuated settlement
Destroyed settlement

Scale 1 : 250 000
0    4 km

A view of the buried town of Plymouth from the sea. In the foreground the ash and sediment has reached the sea. The Soufrière Hills are in the centre background, and the highest point, Chances Peak, is on the right covered in cloud. The South Soufrière Hills are on the far right.

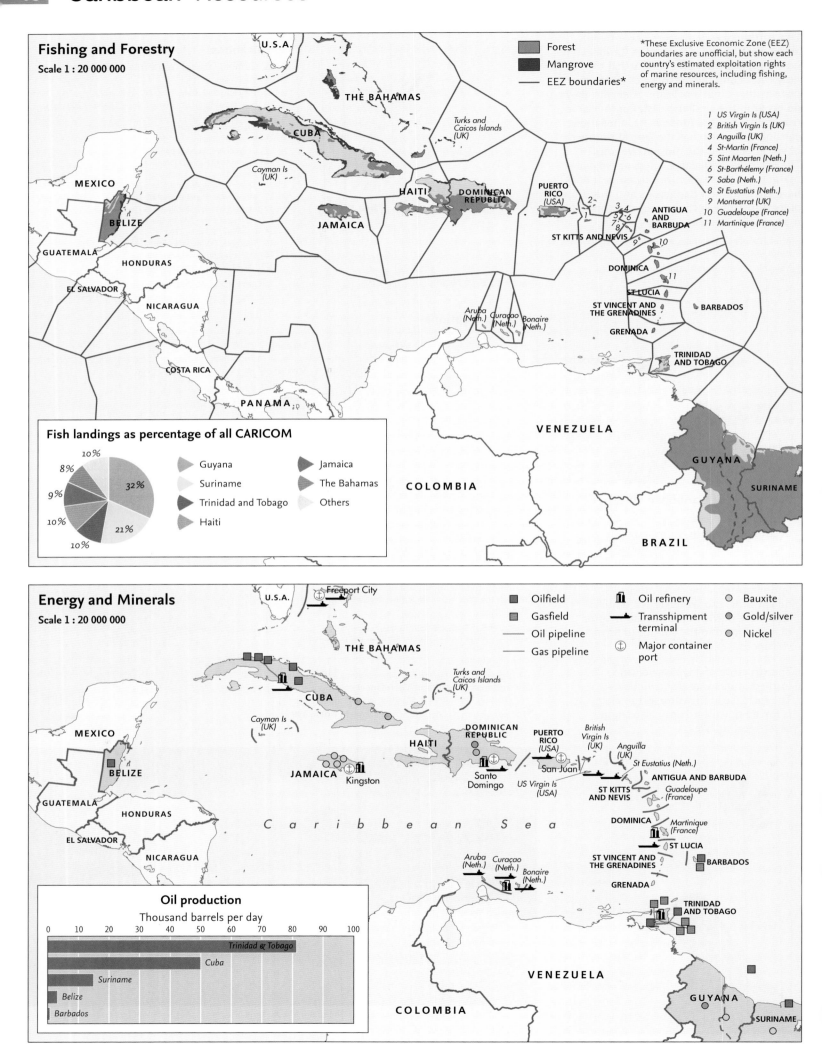

## Fishing and Forestry

Scale 1 : 20 000 000

Legend:
- ☐ Forest
- ☐ Mangrove
- — EEZ boundaries*

*These Exclusive Economic Zone (EEZ) boundaries are unofficial, but show each country's estimated exploitation rights of marine resources, including fishing, energy and minerals.

1 US Virgin Is (USA)
2 British Virgin Is (UK)
3 Anguilla (UK)
4 St-Martin (France)
5 Sint Maarten (Neth.)
6 St-Barthélemy (France)
7 Saba (Neth.)
8 St Eustatius (Neth.)
9 Montserrat (UK)
10 Guadeloupe (France)
11 Martinique (France)

Map labels: U.S.A., THE BAHAMAS, Turks and Caicos Islands (UK), MEXICO, Cayman Is (UK), CUBA, BELIZE, GUATEMALA, HONDURAS, HAITI, DOMINICAN REPUBLIC, JAMAICA, PUERTO RICO (USA), ST KITTS AND NEVIS, ANTIGUA AND BARBUDA, EL SALVADOR, NICARAGUA, DOMINICA, ST LUCIA, ST VINCENT AND THE GRENADINES, BARBADOS, GRENADA, Aruba (Neth.), Curaçao (Neth.), Bonaire (Neth.), COSTA RICA, PANAMA, TRINIDAD AND TOBAGO, VENEZUELA, COLOMBIA, GUYANA, SURINAME, BRAZIL

### Fish landings as percentage of all CARICOM

Pie chart segments:
- 32% Guyana
- 21% (blue segment)
- 10%
- 10%
- 9%
- 8%
- 10%

Legend:
- Guyana
- Suriname
- Trinidad and Tobago
- Haiti
- Jamaica
- The Bahamas
- Others

## Energy and Minerals

Scale 1 : 20 000 000

Legend:
- ☐ Oilfield
- ☐ Gasfield
- — Oil pipeline
- — Gas pipeline
- ⬛ Oil refinery
- ➤ Transshipment terminal
- ⊕ Major container port
- ○ Bauxite
- ◐ Gold/silver
- ● Nickel

Map labels: U.S.A., Freeport City, THE BAHAMAS, Turks and Caicos Islands (UK), MEXICO, Cayman Is (UK), CUBA, BELIZE, GUATEMALA, HONDURAS, EL SALVADOR, NICARAGUA, JAMAICA, Kingston, HAITI, DOMINICAN REPUBLIC, Santo Domingo, PUERTO RICO (USA), San Juan, US Virgin Is (USA), British Virgin Is (UK), Anguilla (UK), St Eustatius (Neth.), ST KITTS AND NEVIS, ANTIGUA AND BARBUDA, Guadeloupe (France), DOMINICA, Martinique (France), ST LUCIA, ST VINCENT AND THE GRENADINES, BARBADOS, GRENADA, Aruba (Neth.), Curaçao (Neth.), Bonaire (Neth.), TRINIDAD AND TOBAGO, Caribbean Sea, VENEZUELA, COLOMBIA, GUYANA, SURINAME

### Oil production

Thousand barrels per day

Scale: 0 10 20 30 40 50 60 70 80 90 100

- Trinidad & Tobago
- Cuba
- Suriname
- Belize
- Barbados

## Population and Language

Scale 1 : 20 000 000

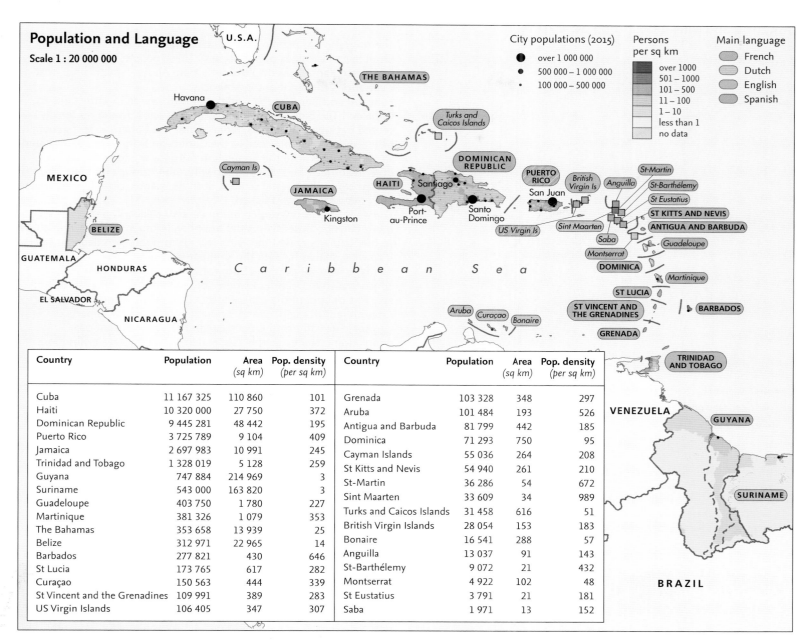

**City populations (2015)**
- over 1 000 000
- 500 000 – 1 000 000
- 100 000 – 500 000

**Persons per sq km**
- over 1000
- 501 – 1000
- 101 – 500
- 11 – 100
- 1 – 10
- less than 1
- no data

**Main language**
- French
- Dutch
- English
- Spanish

| Country | Population | Area (sq km) | Pop. density (per sq km) | Country | Population | Area (sq km) | Pop. density (per sq km) |
|---|---|---|---|---|---|---|---|
| Cuba | 11 167 325 | 110 860 | 101 | Grenada | 103 328 | 348 | 297 |
| Haiti | 10 320 000 | 27 750 | 372 | Aruba | 101 484 | 193 | 526 |
| Dominican Republic | 9 445 281 | 48 442 | 195 | Antigua and Barbuda | 81 799 | 442 | 185 |
| Puerto Rico | 3 725 789 | 9 104 | 409 | Dominica | 71 293 | 750 | 95 |
| Jamaica | 2 697 983 | 10 991 | 245 | Cayman Islands | 55 036 | 264 | 208 |
| Trinidad and Tobago | 1 328 019 | 5 128 | 259 | St Kitts and Nevis | 54 940 | 261 | 210 |
| Guyana | 747 884 | 214 969 | 3 | St-Martin | 36 286 | 54 | 672 |
| Suriname | 543 000 | 163 820 | 3 | Sint Maarten | 33 609 | 34 | 989 |
| Guadeloupe | 403 750 | 1 780 | 227 | Turks and Caicos Islands | 31 458 | 616 | 51 |
| Martinique | 381 326 | 1 079 | 353 | British Virgin Islands | 28 054 | 153 | 183 |
| The Bahamas | 353 658 | 13 939 | 25 | Bonaire | 16 541 | 288 | 57 |
| Belize | 312 971 | 22 965 | 14 | Anguilla | 13 037 | 91 | 143 |
| Barbados | 277 821 | 430 | 646 | St-Barthélemy | 9 072 | 21 | 432 |
| St Lucia | 173 765 | 617 | 282 | Montserrat | 4 922 | 102 | 48 |
| Curaçao | 150 563 | 444 | 339 | St Eustatius | 3 791 | 21 | 181 |
| St Vincent and the Grenadines | 109 991 | 389 | 283 | Saba | 1 971 | 13 | 152 |
| US Virgin Islands | 106 405 | 347 | 307 | | | | |

## Tourism

Scale 1 : 22 500 000

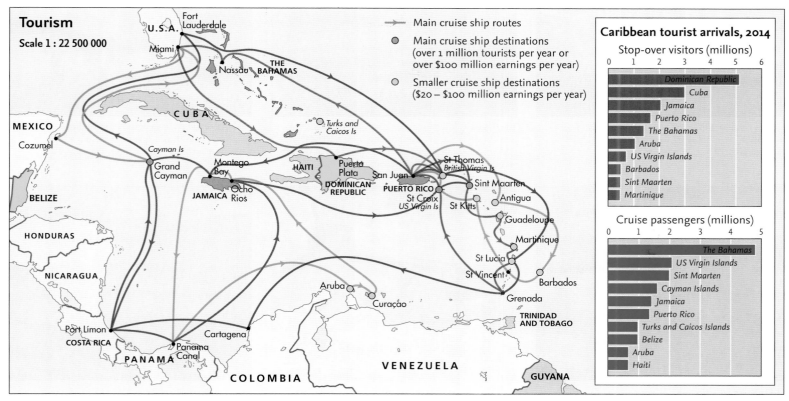

- → Main cruise ship routes
- ● Main cruise ship destinations (over 1 million tourists per year or over $100 million earnings per year)
- ○ Smaller cruise ship destinations ($20 – $100 million earnings per year)

**Caribbean tourist arrivals, 2014**

Stop-over visitors (millions)

0  1  2  3  4  5  6
- Dominican Republic
- Cuba
- Jamaica
- Puerto Rico
- The Bahamas
- Aruba
- US Virgin Islands
- Barbados
- Sint Maarten
- Martinique

Cruise passengers (millions)

0  1  2  3  4  5
- The Bahamas
- US Virgin Islands
- Sint Maarten
- Cayman Islands
- Jamaica
- Puerto Rico
- Turks and Caicos Islands
- Belize
- Aruba
- Haiti

## Amerindian civilisations, 1000 BC – AD 1500

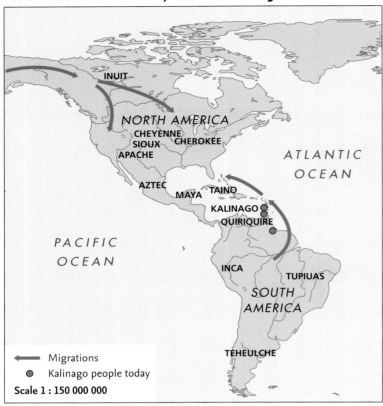

Migrations
Kalinago people today
Scale 1 : 150 000 000

The migration of people from Asia to America across the Bering Strait began about 13 000 years ago. These people, today known as Amerindians, moved southwards from Alaska establishing great civilisations throughout the Americas.

Kalinago and Taino peoples migrated northwards towards Jamaica, Cuba and The Bahamas, and the Lesser Antilles. The Taino mostly settled in Cuba, Hispaniola, Jamaica and The Bahamas. It is generally believed that they migrated to the Caribbean from Venezuela around AD 600-700, because the population outgrew the food supply and other resources; and competition with other groups for land. They settled along the coastal regions of these islands, close to fresh water. They grew cassava and fished.

The Kalinago mostly settled in the Lesser Antilles. The rocky mountains of these islands did not provide much land for agriculture so the Kalinago raided the Taino islands for food. Trinidad and Puerto Rico were shared by both the Kalinago and Taino.

Kalinago who survived the European invasions are now mainly concentrated in Dominica where some 3000 live, with a few hundred spread throughout the other Eastern Caribbean islands. Many Amerindian tribes, including Kalinago, survive today in parts of Guyana, Suriname and French Guiana. Belize's present day population includes people descended from the Maya civilisation.

The Amerindian peoples of the Caribbean are often referred to as 'Arawaks' and 'Caribs'. It is better to use the term 'Taino' instead of 'Arawak' in the Caribbean as 'Taino' distinguishes people in the Caribbean from the Arawakian groups living in South America. Today, we prefer to use the term 'Kalinago' to 'Carib'.

|  | Social life | Economic life | Political life |
|---|---|---|---|
| Tainos | Played a game called batos. Held religious beliefs; believed in multiple gods and kept idols called zemis. | Did hunting, farming, fishing and often traded with other Tainos. Hunted birds, iguanas, conies and other small animals. Planted cassava, sweet potato, pepper and peanuts. | Villages were headed by a cacique whose position was hereditary. All laws and judgements were passed by the cacique who had many privileges. |
| Kalinagoes | Also had idols called moyabas. | Also did farming, hunting and fishing. | Chief was called the oboutou. This position was earned through the demonstration of military skills. |

The El Castillo ruin in the ancient Mayan city of Xunantunich in Belize. El Castillo was probably built around AD 800.

The Caguana Indigenous Ceremonial Park in Puerto Rico is one of the most important Taino archaeological sites in the Antilles. Archaeologists believe that the site was considered sacred by the Taino.

Historians and archaeologists have studied how Amerindians in the Caribbean lived, and a team in Cuba have reconstructed a Taino village.

Archaeologists search for Lucayan artefacts in Samana Cay, northeast of Crooked Island.

We can find traces of Amerindian culture in everyday activities around the Caribbean, such as basket weaving...

...and cassava cultivation.

## European exploration westwards, up to AD 1500

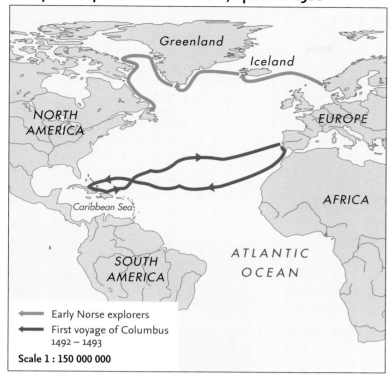

Early Norse explorers
First voyage of Columbus 1492 – 1493
Scale 1 : 150 000 000

## The ancient Silk Road

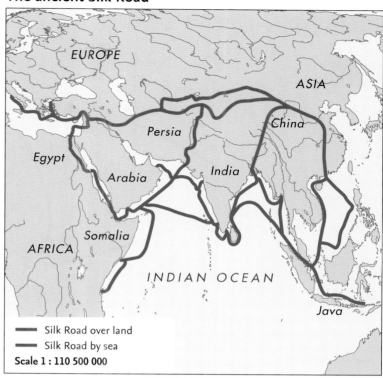

Silk Road over land
Silk Road by sea
Scale 1 : 110 500 000

There is evidence to suggest that there was European exploration of North America before Christopher Columbus. According to the Icelandic Sagas, Vikings first settled in Greenland in the 980s. The only known site of a Viking village in North America outside Greenland is L'Anse aux Meadows in Newfoundland, which may be connected with an attempt by the explorer Leif Ericson to establish the colony of Vinland around 1003. In 1492 Christopher Columbus set sail westwards from Spain. The main aim of his voyage was to try to find a new route to Asia.

The Silk Road to India and China was becoming dangerous and affecting the trade in valuable goods such as spices and silks. People believed that sailing westwards would lead to China, Japan and Indonesia (then called Java). Columbus needed funding for a voyage westwards to try to reach Asia and he approached King Henry VII of England and King John II of Portugal for money before the Spanish monarchs – Ferdinand II of Aragon and Isabella I of Castile – agreed to fund his voyage. Columbus was to claim all new lands for Spain, and in return would be given 10 per cent of all revenues from these new lands.

## Columbus timeline

**1450**

**1451** – Columbus is born in the Republic of Genoa (now part of modern-day Italy).

**1460**

**1485–1491** – Columbus needs money to finance his first voyage westward so he presents his plans to the monarchs of England and Portugal, both of whom refuse to fund his exploration.

**1470**

**1492** – In January Ferdinand and Isabella, the rulers of Spain, agree to fund his voyage. After his preparations are complete Columbus finally sets sail on 3 August 1492.

**1492** – In October Columbus sights one of the islands in The Bahamas. He calls the island San Salvador (which means 'Holy saviour' in Spanish) but the local name was Guanahani. On this voyage Columbus also lands in Cuba and Hispaniola.

**1480**

**1493** – Columbus arrives back in Europe, landing in Portugal in March.

**1493** – Columbus sets off on his second voyage on 24 September. During this voyage, he lands on Marie-Galante and Guadeloupe before travelling northwards and sighting Montserrat, Dominica, Antigua, Redonda, Nevis, St Kitts, St Eustatius, Saba, St-Martin, St Croix, and the chain of the Virgin Islands. He then goes on to land in Puerto Rico and Jamaica.

**1490**

**1496** – Columbus arrives back in Europe, landing at Cadiz in southern Spain in June.

**1498–1500** – Columbus embarks on his third voyage on 30 May 1498. The aim of this voyage is to try to find a continent that King John II of Portugal believed existed to the southwest of the Cape Verde Islands. We know this continent as South America. On this voyage, Columbus lands on Trinidad, explores the gulf that separates Trinidad and Venezuela, sights Tobago, Grenada and St Vincent, and visits Hispaniola.

**1500**

**1502–1503** – Columbus leaves Europe for his fourth and final voyage on 11 May 1502. He lands first at Martinique, then sights St Lucia and explores the coasts of Honduras, Nicaragua and Costa Rica, arriving in Panama in October. He sights the Cayman Islands in May 1503, but is then stranded on Jamaica for nearly a year.

**1504** – Columbus arrives back in Spain.

**1506** – Columbus dies.

**1510**

Christopher Columbus (1451–1506) was Italian, but his great voyages were undertaken for the king and queen of Spain, which ensured the long-term influence of Spain in the Caribbean.

This map is from 1482, before Columbus landed in the Caribbean, and shows the western 'known world' at that time. It illustrates that Europeans didn't know that the Americas and Caribbean existed.

## Triangular Trade route

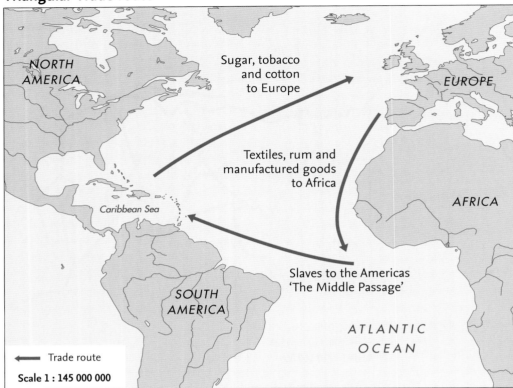

Sugar, tobacco and cotton to Europe

Textiles, rum and manufactured goods to Africa

Slaves to the Americas 'The Middle Passage'

NORTH AMERICA

EUROPE

AFRICA

Caribbean Sea

SOUTH AMERICA

ATLANTIC OCEAN

← Trade route

Scale 1 : 145 000 000

West Africa, showing Senegal and the location of Goree, the largest slave-trading centre between the fifteenth and nineteenth centuries.

The circular fort on the island of Goree off the coast of Senegal.

The **Triangular Trade** was the name given to the trade that operated between Europe and Africa, Africa and the Caribbean and from the Caribbean back to Europe. In Europe, ships were loaded with items such as copper, glass beads, trinkets, cloth, rum, guns and ammunition. The ships then sailed to the west coast of Africa. In Africa, these goods were exchanged for slaves, who were then transported in the same ships to the Caribbean: this was called the **Middle Passage**. On reaching the Caribbean, the enslaved Africans were sold on to plantation owners, and the ships were loaded with cash crops – tobacco, cotton and in particular sugar, often in the form of molasses – to be sent to Europe.

## Enslavement of Africans, 1500 – 1870

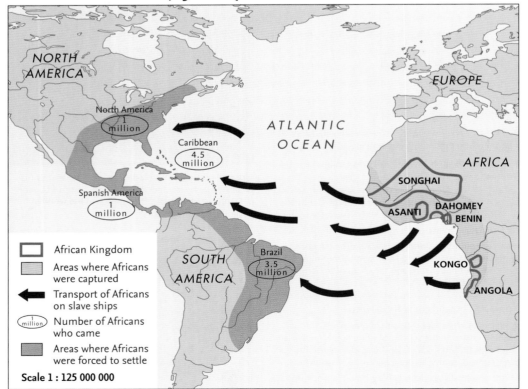

NORTH AMERICA

North America 1 million

ATLANTIC OCEAN

Caribbean 4.5 million

EUROPE

AFRICA

SONGHAI

Spanish America 1 million

DAHOMEY

ASANTI BENIN

SOUTH AMERICA

Brazil 3.5 million

KONGO

ANGOLA

☐ African Kingdom

▢ Areas where Africans were captured

◄ Transport of Africans on slave ships

◯ Number of Africans who came

▨ Areas where Africans were forced to settle

Scale 1 : 125 000 000

This image of a sugar plantation (1852) shows the slave quarters to the left of the plantation-owner's house (centre), with the sugar mill on the right.

One of the most devastating effects of the arrival of Europeans in the Caribbean was on the Amerindian population. Millions of Amerindians were killed in wars and by diseases brought by the Europeans. As a result, there was a need for cheap and reliable enslaved labour to work on the growing sugar, tobacco and cotton plantations.

From the beginning of the sixteenth century Africans were captured and transported across the Atlantic in ships to be sold as slaves in the Americas. Many died on the three-month voyage but 10 million Africans did arrive, with 4.5 million forced to settle in the Caribbean. The majority of African enslaved people were captured in the interior of West African states and then transported on foot to the coastal regions by African slave traders.

## Migration of peoples to the Caribbean, 1830s – 1920s

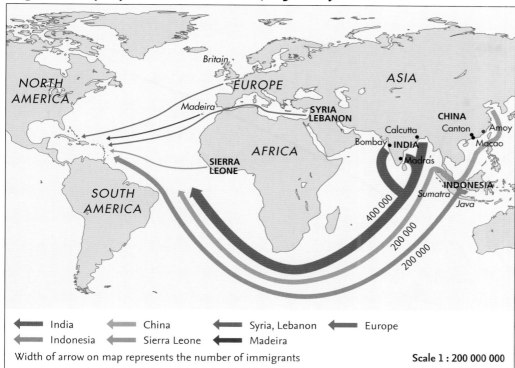

India    China    Syria, Lebanon    Europe
Indonesia    Sierra Leone    Madeira

Width of arrow on map represents the number of immigrants    Scale 1 : 200 000 000

The abolition of slavery in British territory in 1834 led to a frantic search by plantation owners for another source of cheap labour. Labour recruiters started to approach heavily populated and poverty stricken regions in Asia, in particular China, India and Indonesia. People migrated to the Caribbean of their own free will, often as indentured labourers. Under the indentureship scheme, people were given free passage to the Caribbean in return for a set period of work.

The people who migrated to the Caribbean brought with them new religions as well as their languages, cultural practices, industries and food.

## Colonies that recruited immigrants

- Indians
- Indonesians
- Chinese
- Madeirans

Scale 1 : 41 500 000

The larger British colonies of Jamaica, Guyana and Trinidad received the largest number of Asian immigrants, and their legacy and influence are still felt today. More than 400 000 East Indian immigrants entered the Caribbean between 1838 and 1917, and approximately 20 000 Chinese immigrants came between 1852 and 1893.

Doubles – a popular street food in Trinidad of Indian origin – are made with two pieces of fried flatbread filled with curried chickpeas.

The Syrian community in Martinique is about 1 000-strong and has become fully integrated.

Greek migrants from the Aegean Islands introduced sponge-diving to The Bahamas in the late nineteenth century. This was a thriving industry – estimated as the third-largest sponging industry in the world in the mid 1930s – until a fungal infection wiped out most of the sponge beds in around 1938.

The Hindu Temple in the Sea in Trinidad.

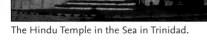

The Keizerstraat mosque in Paramaribo, Suriname.

Cultural dance performance during the East Indian festival of Divali in Chaguanas, Trinidad.

## Emigration from the English-speaking Caribbean

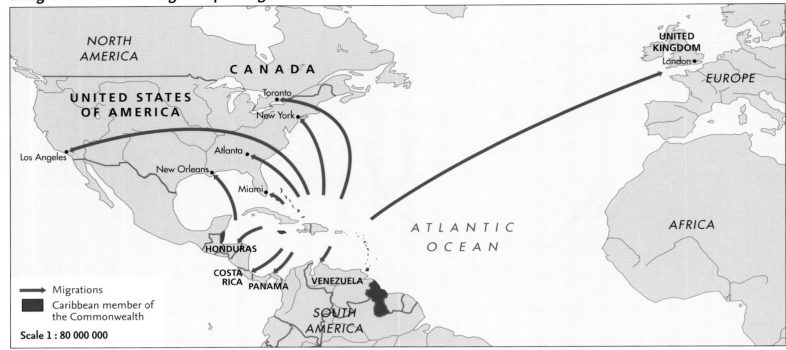

As well as people migrating to the Caribbean, large numbers of Caribbean people have emigrated from the region. From the 1850s to the 1930s migrants from the former British Caribbean colonies moved to Latin America where developments such as the opening of the oilfields in Venezuela and the building of the Panama Canal created new employment opportunities.

From the end of the nineteenth century onwards, Caribbean people started to migrate northwards to the USA and Canada in search of a better life. For example, many Bahamians – struggling under the poor economic climate of the time – made the short trip to Florida to work in agriculture, fishing, turtle-fishing and sponging. Caribbean migration transformed cities in the USA. By around 1896, 40 per cent of people living in Miami were foreign-born blacks, and early twentieth century Caribbean immigration to New York transformed the Harlem area of the city. Many people also travelled during the Second World War to serve in the military and work in countries like the UK and USA. Serious labour shortages in Britain after the Second World War resulted in government recruitment schemes aimed at encouraging Colonial workers to fill this gap. Nearly a million people crossed the Atlantic from the West Indies to take up employment in Britain, with the main migration taking place between 1945 and 1962. The most noticeable impact of the migration of Caribbean peoples the world over is the formation of diaspora communities. These are communities where people from the West Indies converge and form communities reminiscent of their Caribbean homelands. Diaspora communities can be very influential.

One of the first large groups arrived in Britain on board the *Empire Windrush* from Jamaica in 1948.

Looking west along an unpaved Flagler Street, Miami, Florida, circa 1900.

Patricia Scotland was born in Dominica in 1955 but her family migrated to the UK. She studied law and became the first black woman to be made Queens Counsel, the most senior form of barrister. Scotland was made a Baroness in 1997. She is the first woman to become Secretary-General of the Commonwealth of Nations.

The Notting Hill Carnival, held in London at the end of August each year, is an opportunity for the West Indian communities of Britain to celebrate Caribbean carnival music, dancing and food.

The Cuban people of Florida are said to have had a major influence in determining the outcome of every United States presidential election since 2000. Marco Rubio, who is of Cuban origin, is a Republican senator for Florida.

## Impact of colonisation in the Caribbean

### Labour systems

**Encomienda** – a labour system introduced by the Spanish in 1523 to help manage and control the indigenous people. Under this system Taino families were assigned to Spanish settlers called encomenderos. The Taino were required to work for the encomenderos on projects like farming and mining. The encomenderos ensured that the Taino were converted to Christianity. Many Taino families were abused under the system.

**Slavery** – the system of slavery started with the Spanish when their labour force became depleted as the number of Tainos declined. Slavery in the Caribbean was referred to as chattel slavery. This meant that the enslaved had no rights; physical, economic, political or social. Slaves were taken from West and Central Africa.

**Indentureship** – this system involved the use of contracted immigrant labourers after Emancipation. Some migrants came from European countries while others came from places such as Sierra Leone in Africa, and India and China in Asia.

### Social structure

Prior to Emancipation, race was the most significant factor influencing how Caribbean societies were structured. Whites controlled all political and economic power even though they were smallest in numbers. Blacks were the largest in number but remained at the bottom of the social pyramid. They had very few rights and no power.

Following Emancipation, class became the most significant factor by which persons were ranked. Class is determined mainly by wealth but education has played an important role in this.

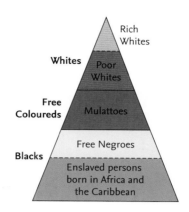

An example of social structure in the islands controlled by the British before Emancipation.

## Movement towards independence

### Timeline

**1935–1938** – Labour riots develop out of the demand for better wages and working conditions; cries for political independence are also stirred.

**1945** – Labour leaders meet in Barbados to discuss both labour and political matters; demands made for minimum wage laws and a British West Indian Federation.

**1947** – Conference held in Montego Bay, Jamaica, to determine how a federation would be achieved.

**1956** – Constitution of the Federation formally agreed; British Caribbean Federation Act passed by the British Parliament.

**1958** – West Indian Federation established; English speaking territories become one political unit. Members include Antigua and Barbuda, Barbados, Dominica, Grenada, Jamaica, Montserrat, St Kitts, Nevis and Anguilla, St Lucia, St Vincent, and Trinidad and Tobago. The capital city is located in Trinidad; Sir Grantley Adams of Barbados installed as prime minister of the Federation.

**1961** – Jamaica withdraws from the Federation; the other countries follow suit. The Federation collapses.

**1962** – Jamaica and Trinidad and Tobago become independent.

**1966** – Barbados and Guyana become independent.

**1968** – The Caribbean Free Trade Association (CARIFTA) is established – Trinidad and Tobago, Guyana, Antigua and Barbados are the first to join.

**1973** – The Bahamas becomes independent.

**1974** – The Caribbean Common Market (CARICOM) is established by the signing of the Treaty of Chaguaramas by the CARIFTA Heads of Government; Grenada becomes independent.

**1978** – Dominica becomes independent.

**1979** – The Grenada Revolution – on 13 March, the People's Revolutionary Army overthrow the Grenada United Labour Party government and install Maurice Bishop as prime minister; St Lucia, and St Vincent and the Grenadines become independent.

**1981** – Antigua and Barbuda, and Belize become independent.

**1983** – St Kitts and Nevis independence; Maurice Bishop, prime minister of Grenada, is assassinated; the United States and other Caribbean forces invade Grenada.

## Some key figures in independence movements

Sir Grantley Adams is one of the National Heroes of Barbados. He was a labour leader and one of the founders of the Barbados Labour Party. He was the first Premier for the island and later became the Prime Minister of the West Indian Federation.

Dr Eric Williams founded the People's National Movement in Trinidad. He was Trinidad's first Premier and helped to secure the country's independence in 1962. Thereafter, he served as Prime Minister until his death in 1981.

Sir Eric Matthew Gairy, national hero and Premier of Grenada from 1967–1974. Sir Gairy became the first Prime Minister when the country became independent in 1974. He was overthrown in a coup in 1979.

George Cadle Price played a key role in Belizean independence and is honoured as the 'Father of the Nation'. He worked tirelessly for independence, serving as the country's first Premier from 1964 when the country gained self-government, and as Prime Minister from independence in 1981 until 1984, and again from 1989–1993.

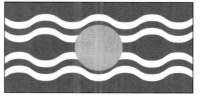

Flag of the West Indian Federation, designed by Edna Manley of Jamaica. The blue represented the Caribbean Sea and the yellow the sun.

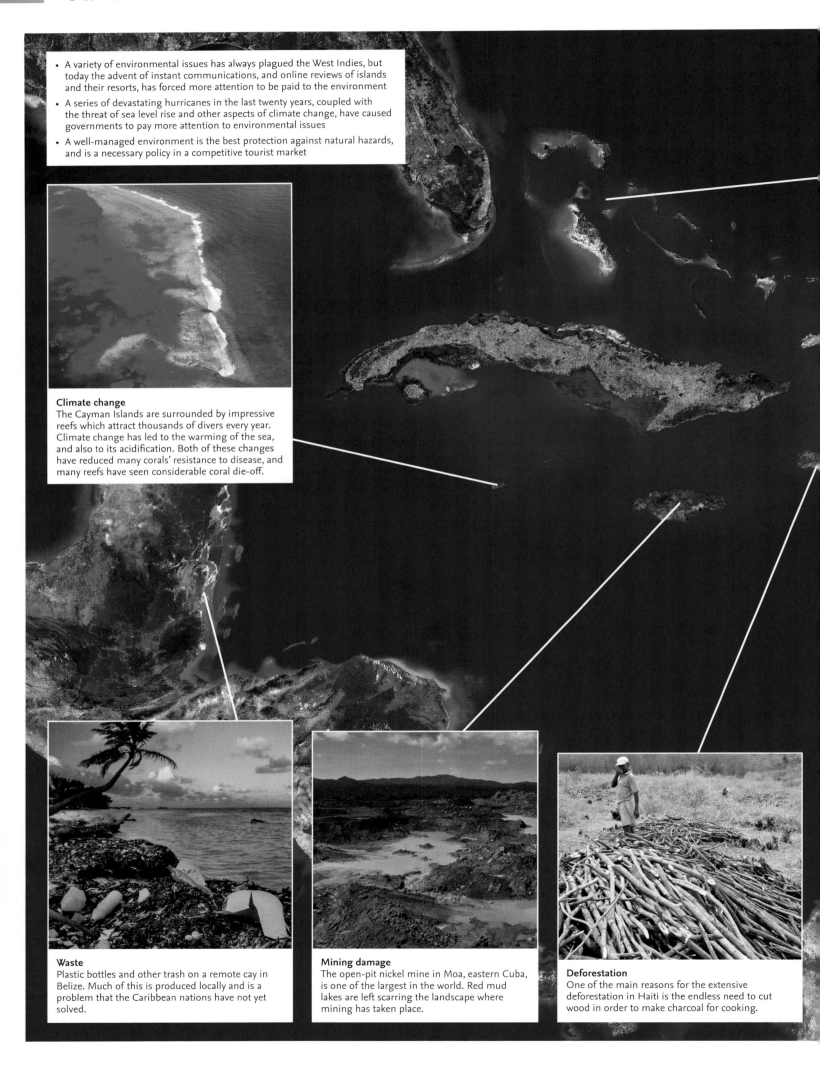

- A variety of environmental issues has always plagued the West Indies, but today the advent of instant communications, and online reviews of islands and their resorts, has forced more attention to be paid to the environment
- A series of devastating hurricanes in the last twenty years, coupled with the threat of sea level rise and other aspects of climate change, have caused governments to pay more attention to environmental issues
- A well-managed environment is the best protection against natural hazards, and is a necessary policy in a competitive tourist market

**Climate change**
The Cayman Islands are surrounded by impressive reefs which attract thousands of divers every year. Climate change has led to the warming of the sea, and also to its acidification. Both of these changes have reduced many corals' resistance to disease, and many reefs have seen considerable coral die-off.

**Waste**
Plastic bottles and other trash on a remote cay in Belize. Much of this is produced locally and is a problem that the Caribbean nations have not yet solved.

**Mining damage**
The open-pit nickel mine in Moa, eastern Cuba, is one of the largest in the world. Red mud lakes are left scarring the landscape where mining has taken place.

**Deforestation**
One of the main reasons for the extensive deforestation in Haiti is the endless need to cut wood in order to make charcoal for cooking.

**Invasive species**

The **cane toad** is a native of South America, but was introduced into the Eastern Caribbean as long ago as the 19th century. It is an omnivore and will eat small animals, as well as being poisonous (including its tadpoles). As recently as 2013 it had invaded The Bahamas.

The **casuarina** (commonly called the Australian pine) is widespread in the Caribbean, where it suppresses the native vegetation and can cause beach erosion. This stand on Paradise Island in The Bahamas has since been removed.

The **lionfish** is an Indo-Pacific species that is a voracious carnivore with poisonous spines. It has invaded the entire Caribbean, probably starting from the US coast, where some are believed to have escaped from an aquarium, then spreading south through The Bahamas. It can be eaten and this is one way of reducing its numbers.

**Endangered species**
Whale-watching is a popular tourist attraction on many Caribbean islands from the Turks and Caicos to Dominica and St Lucia. Unfortunately many whales, like this humpback, are endangered.

**Wind power**
Aruba is blessed with strong winds throughout the year. Power from wind turbines has reduced its energy costs and dependence on oil.

**Coral reef damage**
Coral bleaching is the effect of any disease causing the coral to die and leave a white patch on its skeleton, as seen by this example from Curaçao. This has seriously affected all the Caribbean reefs and the dive tourist industry.

**Carbon dioxide emissions**
Trinidad and Tobago has one of the highest amounts of $CO_2$ emissions per person in the Caribbean – 25 tonnes per person in 2014, compared to the global average of 5. The former Netherlands Antilles is another high emitter; both areas have large oil refineries.

Scale 1 : 5 550 000

0    50    100    150    200 km

**A** 84° **B** 82° **C** 80° **D** 78° **E** 76° **F**

**U.S.A.**
**FLORIDA**

L. Okeechobee

Fort Myers

West Palm Beach

Fort Lauderdale

The Everglades

Miami

Bimini Is

Florida Keys

Straits of Florida

Little Bahama Bank

Freeport City

Grand Bahama

Marsh Harbour

Great Abaco

Northwest Providence Channel

Northeast Providence Channel

**THE BAHAMAS**

Dunmore Town

Eleuthera

Berry Islands

New Providence

Nicoll's Town

**Nassau**

Rock Sound

Arthur's Town

Cat I.

Fresh Creek

Andros

Tongue of the Ocean

San Salvador

Cockburn Town

Exuma Sound

Exuma Cays

Cistern Pt

Great Bahama Bank

George Town

Rum Cay

Port Nelson

Great Exuma

Little Exuma

Long I.

Deadman's Cay

Clarence Town

Island Passe

Crooked

Ragged Island Range

Colonel Hill

Long Cay

Albe Tow

Acklins I.

Crooked

Duncan Town

Salina Pt

Tropic of Cancer

Cay Sal Bank

**Havana**

Matanzas

Cárdenas

Arch. de Sabana

Güines

Pinar del Rio

Colón

Sagua la Grande

Santa Clara

Arch. de Camagüey

Guane

Golfo de Batabanó

Peninsula de Zapata

Cienfuegos

Cayo Coco

C. San Antonio

Cabo Corrientes

Cayos de San Felipe

Arch. de los Canarreos

Sancti Spíritus

Cayo Romano

Isla de la Juventud (Isla de Pinos)

Cayo Largo

**C U B A**

Golfo de Ana Maria

Ciego de Avila

Florida

Nuevitas

Camagüey

Arch. de los Jardines de la Reina

Santa Cruz del Sur

Las Tunas

Holguín

Salado

Golfo de Guacanayabo

Bayamo

Cauto

Manzanillo

Sierra Maestra

Palma Soriano

Niquero

Pico Turquino 1994

Santiago de Cuba

Guantanamo

**G r e a t e r**

Cabo Cruz

Little Cayman

Cayman Brac

**A n t i l l e s**

Windw

George Town

Cayman Islands (U.K.)

Grand Cayman

**C A R I B B E A N**

Montego Bay

Jérémie

South Negril Point

**J A M A I C A**

Port Antonio

Jamaica Channel

Black River

Spanish Town

**Kingston**

Morant Point

**S E A**

HONDURAS

Patuca

Laguna de Caratasca

C. Gracias a Dios

NICARAGUA

Cayos Miskitos

Costa de Mosquitos

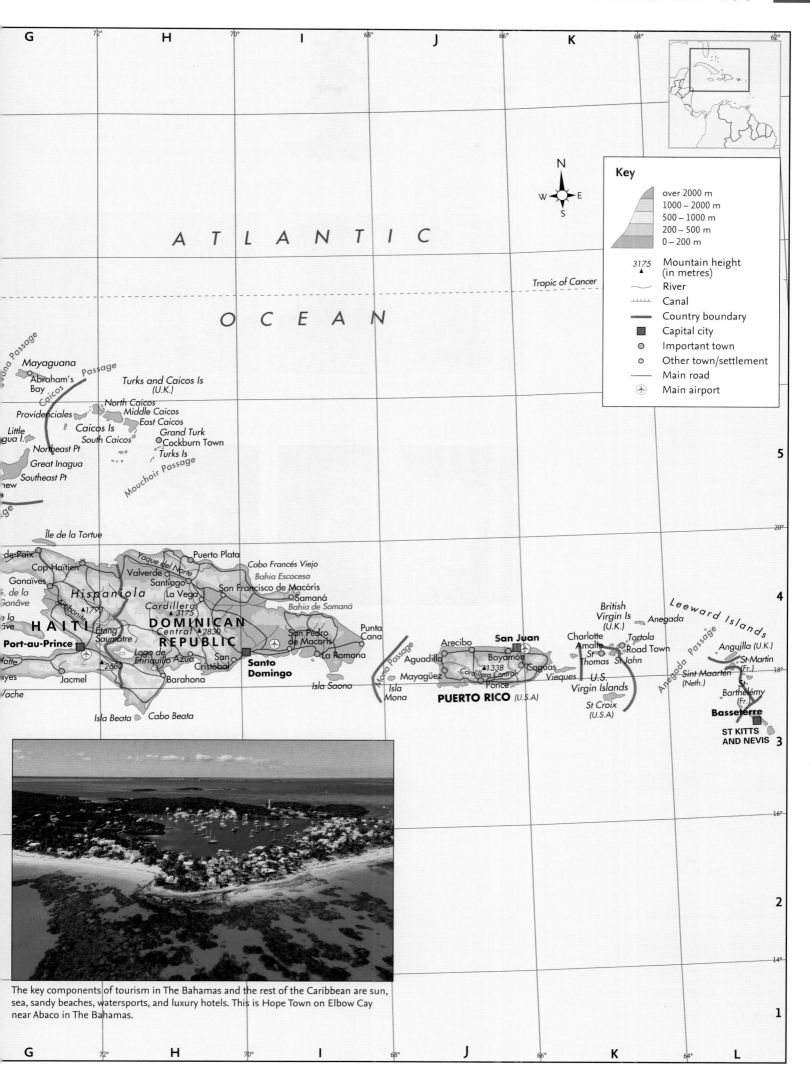

G H I J K L

## Key

- over 2000 m
- 1000 – 2000 m
- 500 – 1000 m
- 200 – 500 m
- 0 – 200 m

*3175* ▲ Mountain height (in metres)

～ River

⊥⊥⊥ Canal

━━ Country boundary

■ Capital city

◉ Important town

◦ Other town/settlement

── Main road

✈ Main airport

A T L A N T I C

O C E A N

Tropic of Cancer

N
W ◆ E
S

Isthmana Passage
Mayaguana
Abraham's Bay
Caicos Passage
Turks and Caicos Is (U.K.)
North Caicos
Providenciales
Middle Caicos
East Caicos
Little ~gua I.
Caicos Is
South Caicos
Grand Turk
Cockburn Town
Northeast Pt
Turks Is
Great Inagua
Southeast Pt
~ew
Mouchoir Passage

Île de la Tortue
~-de-Paix
Cap Haïtien
Puerto Plata
Cabo Francés Viejo
Yaque del Norte
Bahía Escocesa
Gonaïves
Valverde
Santiago
~ de la Gonâve
Hispaniola
La Vega
San Francisco de Macorís
Samaná
~ve
Cordillera
Bahía de Samaná
Artibonite ▲1793
DOMINICAN
▲2830
Central ▲3175
Punta Cana
HAITI
REPUBLIC
Étang Saumâtre
San Pedro de Macorís
British Virgin Is (U.K.)
Anegada
Leeward Islands
Port-au-Prince
Lago de Enriquillo
Azua
San Cristóbal
Santo Domingo
La Romana
Arecibo
San Juan
Charlotte Amalie
Tortola
Road Town
Anguilla (U.K.)
~otte
▲2680
Barahona
Mona Passage
Aguadilla
Bayamón
St Thomas
St John
St-Martin (Fr.)
~yes
Jacmel
Isla Saona
Mayagüez
Cordillera Central ▲1338
Caguas
Vieques
Anegada Passage
Sint Maarten (Neth.)
~ache
Ponce
U.S.
Virgin Islands
St-Barthélémy (Fr.)
Isla Beata
Cabo Beata
Isla Mona
PUERTO RICO (U.S.A)
St Croix (U.S.A.)
Basseterre
ST KITTS AND NEVIS

5
20°
4
18°
3
16°
14°
2
1

The key components of tourism in The Bahamas and the rest of the Caribbean are sun, sea, sandy beaches, watersports, and luxury hotels. This is Hope Town on Elbow Cay near Abaco in The Bahamas.

G H I J K L

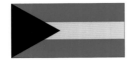

### Flag

The Flag of The Bahamas uses **black** to represent the strength of a united population, **aquamarine** to represent the sea and all its resources, and **gold** to represent the sun.

### Coat of arms

The coat of arms has wavy green **palm fronds** at the top, symbolising the natural vegetation of the islands. The pink **conch shell** below the palm fronds symbolises the islands' marine life. The rays of the **sun** represent the warm climate, and a bright future for the islands and their inhabitants. The **ship** is the *Santa Maria*, the flagship of Christopher Columbus who first sighted the islands in 1492. The shield is supported by the **flamingo** and the **blue marlin**. The national motto – **Forward, Upward, Onward Together** – is located at the bottom of the coat of arms.

### Anthem

#### March On Bahamaland

Lift up your head to the rising sun, Bahamaland;
March on to glory your bright banners waving high.
See how the world marks the manner of your bearing!
Pledge to excel through love and unity.

Pressing onward, march together to a common loftier goal;
Steady sunward, tho' the weather hide the wide and treacherous shoal.

Lift up your head to the rising sun, Bahamaland,
'Til the road you've trod lead unto your God,
March On, Bahamaland.

### Pledge

I Pledge my allegiance to the flag and to
the Commonwealth of The Bahamas
for which it stands,
one people united in love and service.

### Bird

The national bird of The Bahamas is the flamingo. Flamingos are found all over the islands. They get their bright pink or red colour from their diet of shellfish.

### Flower

The Yellow Elder is native to The Bahamas, blooms all year round, and is the national flower.

### Fish

The blue marlin is found in the waters around The Bahamas; it is the country's national fish.

### Tree

The national tree is the *Lignum Vitae*, which means 'Tree of Life' in Latin. Its wood is very hard and has several industrial uses. The bark can be used for medicinal purposes.

### Government structure

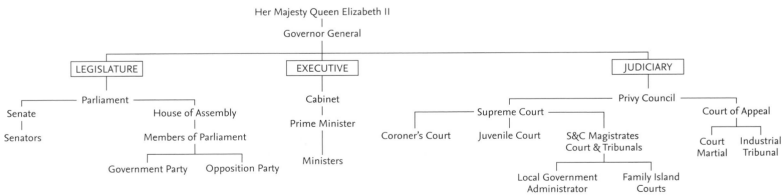

Her Majesty Queen Elizabeth II
Governor General

LEGISLATURE — EXECUTIVE — JUDICIARY

Parliament
Senate — House of Assembly
Senators — Members of Parliament
Government Party — Opposition Party

Cabinet
Prime Minister
Ministers

Privy Council
Supreme Court — Court of Appeal
Coroner's Court — Juvenile Court — S&C Magistrates Court & Tribunals
Local Government Administrator — Family Island Courts
Court Martial — Industrial Tribunal

### Governors General of The Bahamas

The Governor General is the representative of Queen Elizabeth II in The Bahamas. Queen Elizabeth II lives in London so the Governor General carries out the Queen's duties on her behalf, in The Bahamas. Governors General usually serve for five years. They are responsible for appointing the Prime Minister (after a General Election). The Governor General is usually addressed as *His Excellency* or *Her Excellency*.

| Name | Date | Name | Date |
|------|------|------|------|
| Dame Marguerite Pindling | 2014– | Sir Gerald Cash | 1979 – 1986 |
| Sir Arthur Foulkes | 2012–2014 | The Honourable Dr Dame Doris Louise Johnson | **22 January 1979** *(appointed Acting Governor General on the death of Sir Milo Butler, who died in office)* |
| A.D. Hanna | 2006–2012 | | |
| Paul Adderley | 2005–2006 | | |
| Dame Ivy Dumont | 2000–2005 | | |
| Sir Orville Turnquest | 1995–2000 | | |
| Sir Clifford Darling | 1992–1995 | | |
| Sir Henry Milton Taylor | 1986–1992 | Sir Milo Butler | 1978 – 22 January 1979 |

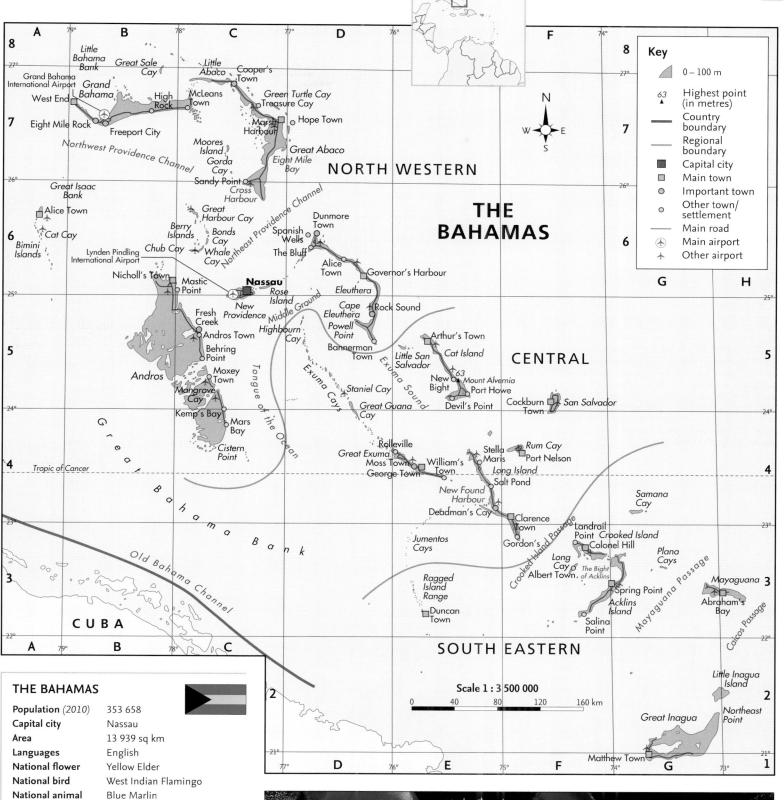

## Key

| | |
|---|---|
| | 0 – 100 m |
| 63 ▲ | Highest point (in metres) |
| ▬▬▬ | Country boundary |
| ─── | Regional boundary |
| ■ | Capital city |
| ◻ | Main town |
| ◦ | Important town |
| · | Other town/settlement |
| ─── | Main road |
| ✈ | Main airport |
| ✈ | Other airport |

**THE BAHAMAS**

| | |
|---|---|
| **Population** (2010) | 353 658 |
| **Capital city** | Nassau |
| **Area** | 13 939 sq km |
| **Languages** | English |
| **National flower** | Yellow Elder |
| **National bird** | West Indian Flamingo |
| **National animal** | Blue Marlin |

Columbus's first landfall in the New World was on San Salvador on 14 October **1492**

Columbus visited four islands in The Bahamas before travelling on

The prehistoric inhabitants were the Lucayans, a branch of the Taino people, but all were wiped out within 50 years of the country's first sighting

The first settlers were religious refugees from Bermuda who settled on Eleuthera in **1648**

The Bahamas became a British colony in **1718** and remained British until independence in **1973**

The Bahamas had a small cotton plantation economy with the arrival of the Loyalists, but also subsisted on shifting cultivation and fishing, and occasionally from wrecking, blockade running and other opportunistic enterprises

New Providence is the most densely populated island in the Caribbean region

The extent of the archipelago is the same as the distance from Antigua to Trinidad

The current economy is dependent on tourism and offshore finance

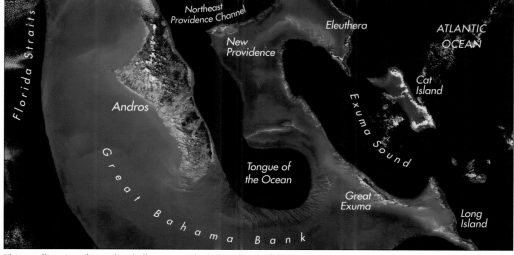

This satellite view shows the shallow waters (in lighter blue) of the Great Bahama Bank.

## Abaco

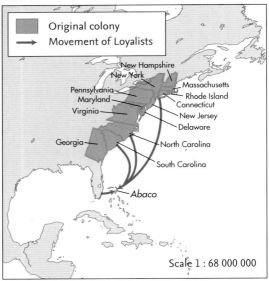

Legend:
- Original colony
- → Movement of Loyalists

New Hampshire
New York
Massachusetts
Pennsylvania
Rhode Island
Maryland
Connecticut
Virginia
New Jersey
Delaware
Georgia
North Carolina
South Carolina
Abaco

Scale 1 : 68 000 000

The first settlements on Abaco were established in 1783, after the American War of Independence (1775–1783). British citizens in America who were still loyal to the British crown found life difficult in the newly independent United States of America. About 1 000 of these British Loyalists left New York, the Carolinas and Florida, many taking their slaves with them. They fled to The Bahamas because it was the nearest British colony. The British government offered grants of land to many Loyalists and they established settlements in the Marsh Harbour area. Loyalists settled on other islands too, including New Providence.

## New Providence free settlements

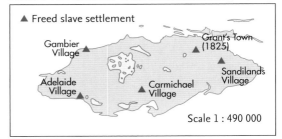

▲ Freed slave settlement

Gambier Village
Grant's Town (1825)
Adelaide Village
Carmichael Village
Sandilands Village

Scale 1 : 490 000

In 1807 Britain made it illegal to buy and sell slaves from Africa. The Royal Navy rescued thousands of Africans from slave ships and many of these slaves were resettled on New Providence, in settlements at Gambier Village and Adelaide Village. The largest of these – Grant's Town – was established in 1825. More people went to live in these settlements after the emancipation of all slaves throughout the British Empire in 1834.

Grand Bahama
Freeport City
Marsh Harbour
Abaco

Bimini Islands
Berry Islands
St Joh (176
Nassau (First city 18

Mastic Point (Sisal industry 20 000 acres 1890)
New Providen

Andros

## Andros

West Palm Beach
U.S.A.
Freeport City
Grand Bahama
Marsh Harbour
Fort Lauderdale
Great Abaco
FLORIDA
Miami
Bimini Is
THE BAHAMAS
Berry Islands
Nicoll's Town
New Providence
Red Bays
Nassau
North Andros
Fresh Creek
Florida Keys
Andros
Cay Sal Bank
South Andros
Mars Bay
Cistern Point
CUBA

Scale 1 : 5 550 000

The Seminoles are a Native American people originally from the area of America that became Florida. Some Seminoles allied with slaves in Florida and their descendants are called Black Seminoles. In 1821 the United States of America acquired the state of Florida from Spain. In that same year a number of Seminoles and slaves escaped by sailing to the west coast of Andros on the one-masted boat (called a 'sloop') *Steerwater*. In 1823 they were joined by hundreds of Black Seminoles and slaves who escaped from Florida in canoes and sloops. They established the settlement of Red Bays.

## New Providence

New Providence was settled by the British in the late seventeenth century. In the early years of the eighteenth century many of the settlers fled the island due to its popularity amongst pirates, and the island was left without a government. British pirates then took over the island and used it as a base from which to attack French and Spanish ships, looting them for gold and silver. Edward Teach (above) – known as 'Blackbeard' – was one of the many famous pirates in Nassau during this time.

## San Salvador

Christopher Columbus's very first sighting of the Caribbean was of the island of Guanahani, which he renamed San Salvador. He landed on the island on 12 October 1492. In this picture he is shown meeting Lucayan Tainos. His flagship, the *Santa Maria*, can be seen offshore.

## Key

➤ Columbus' first voyage, 1492
➤ Eleuthera Adventurers, 1648
◉ City
○ Settlement
🏛 Major plantation
✕ Rebellion
✝ First church
✉ First post office
🏨 First hotel
🏛 Parliament buildings

Scale 1:3 500 000

## Eleuthera

The mid seventeenth century was a time of religious and political turmoil in England and Europe, and the Puritans played an important role in redefining – and reducing – the power of the English king during this period. In 1648 a group of Puritans and religious independents on Bermuda refused to swear allegiance to the English king Charles I and were expelled from the island. These 'adventurers' were led by William Sayle to Eleuthera. They established a settlement – the first non-Lucayan settlement in The Bahamas – at Cupid's Cay. About one hundred years later – in 1746 – the first parliament of The Bahamas met at nearby Governor's Harbour.

Governor's
Harbour
(First parliament 1746)
ɔid's Cay
*Eleuthera*

*Cat
Island*
Colonel Andrew
Deveaux
Landfall of
Columbus 1492
*Rum
Cay*
Fortune Hill
(Mr Burton Williams)
*San
Salvador*
Sandy Point Estate
(George Watling)
*Exuma*
The Hermitage Estate
(Kelsall family)
*Long
Island*
*Crooked
Island*
Hope Great House
*Ragged
Island
Range*
*Long Cay*
Hard Hill
Plantation
*Acklins Island*
*Mayaguana*
Matthew
Town
*Inagua*
Inagua
Rebellion (1937)

## Acklins Island

The original inhabitants of the islands were the Lucayan Tainos, a peaceful tribe of Amerindians who migrated from South America, probably from what is now Venezuela, probably by the ninth century. The Lucayans lived throughout the islands until European contact, when the population was wiped out by disease and slavery within twenty-five years.

## The Bahamas timeline

1450
1500
1550
1600
1650
1700
1750
1800
1850
1900
1950
2000

**Before 1492** – The islands were inhabited by the Lucayan Tainos

**1492** – Columbus lands in San Salvador and claims the islands for Spain

**1520** – The Spanish leave, taking the last Lucayan Tainos to Hispaniol

**1640s** – Arrival of the Eleuthera Adventurers

**1717** – The Bahamas becomes a Crown Colony

**1746** – The first parliament is held at Governor's Harbour

**1783** – The end of the American War of Independence and the arrival of the Loyalists

**1820s** – Seminoles, Black Seminoles and slaves escape from Florida and settle in Andros; Free settlements are established in New Providence

**1834** – All slaves are emancipated

**1950** – Britain allows the USA to establish a missile tracking station in The Bahamas

**1955** – Free trade area established in the town of Freeport City

**1964** – The Bahamas granted internal self-government

**1968** – Lynden O. Pindling becomes Prime Minister and starts to negotiate a new constitution with Britain

**1969** – The islands become the Commonwealth of The Bahamas

**1973** – The islands gain full independence on 10 July

**2004** – Hurricane Frances causes widespread damage

## Climate zones

Scale 1 : 5 000 000

Winters in the north are the coolest in The Bahamas, as cold fronts from North America frequently reduce temperatures to between 10 and 15.5°C. It is also generally the wettest part of the country, and strong winds are common in winter. All of The Bahamas is hot and wet during the summer, including the north.

°C
30
20
10
0

mean summer temperature
mean winter temperature

115 Rain Days per year on average

NORTHERN

1200

°C
30
20
10
0

mean summer temperature
mean winter temperature

95 Rain Days per year on average

CENTRAL

### Average annual rainfall

| | |
|---|---|
| | over 1500 mm |
| | 1200–1500 mm |
| | 900–1200 mm |
| | under 900 mm |
| | Isohyet in mm |

The central area has year-round average temperatures above 21°C, making it drier and warmer than the north. Cold fronts happen less often, and are less cold, than they are in the north. In the summer, all of The Bahamas is hot and wet, and winter is the dry season.

Tropic of Cancer

900

The driest part of The Bahamas is the south. For example, Inagua gets less than 762 mm of rain a year. Cold fronts rarely affect this region, which keeps winter temperatures high, but they do cause some cloud coverage and high winds. As with the other regions, summer is wetter than winter, but the rainfall is more frequent at the start and end of the season.

°C
30
20
10
0

mean summer temperature
mean winter temperature

90 Rain Days per year on average

SOUTHERN

## Air masses and sea currents

Scale 1 : 30 000 000

| | |
|---|---|
| → | Warm sea current |
| → | Warm air mass |
| → | Cold air mass |

**Continental Air Mass**
(Winter only)

Cold Front

**Gulf Stream**

**Northeast Trade Winds**

**Maritime Air Mass**
(Winter)

**Maritime Air Mass**
(Summer)

Tropic of Cancer

**Antilles Current**

THE BAHAMAS

Caribbean Sea

**Tropical Air Mass**
(Winter only)

Equator

West Palm Beach
⑥ ⑤
⑦ Abaco
⑧ Grand Bahama
Marsh Harbour ③
U.S.A.
Freeport City
Miami
Bimini Is
Berry Islands
Dunmore Town
New Providence Eleuthera
Nicholl's Town
Nassau
THE BAHAMAS
Rock Sound
Arthur's Town
Andros
Cat Island
San Salvador
① ⑨ ② ⑪ Cockburn Town
George Town
Great Exuma
Long Island
Clarence Town
Crooked I.
Colonel Hill
Acklins I.
④ ⑫ Ragged Island Range
Duncan Town
⑬ Mayaguana
CUBA
Nuevitas
ATLANTIC OCEAN
Holguin
Matthew Town
Great Inagua ⑦
Bayamo
⑩
Guantanamo
Port-de-Paix

## Major hurricanes of the past century

Scale 1 : 7 000 000

| | | | |
|---|---|---|---|
| ① | Great Miami 1926 | | |
| ② | San Felipe 1928 | ⑧ | Ivan 2004 |
| ③ | Edna 1954 | ⑨ | Katrina 2005 |
| ④ | Donna 1960 | ⑩ | Ike 2008 |
| ⑤ | Floyd 1999 | ⑪ | Sandy 2012 |
| ⑥ | Frances 2004 | ⑫ | Matthew 2016 |
| ⑦ | Jeanne 2004 | ⑬ | Irma 2017 |

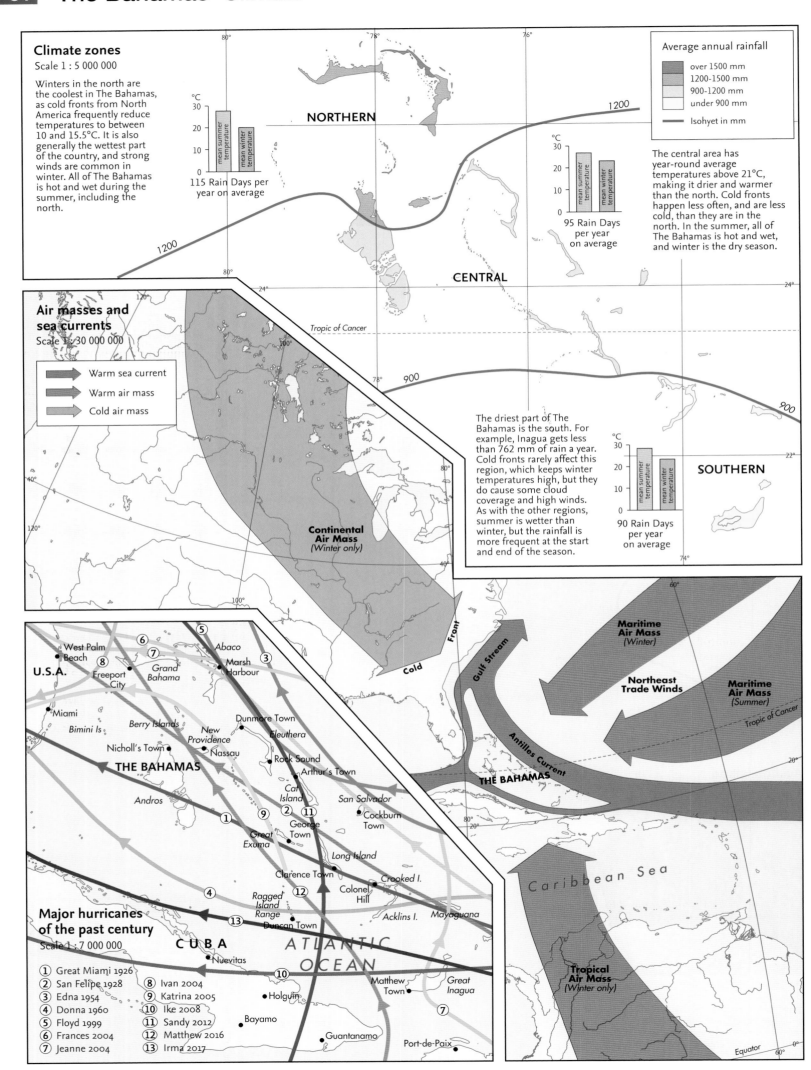

## Agriculture

**Crop production, 2016**

Thousand tonnes

grapefruit, fresh vegetables, bananas, meat, chicken, tropical fruit, tomatoes, oranges, coconuts, mangoes, guavas, lemons and limes, pumpkins, squash and gourds, sweet potatoes, cabbages and other brassicas, avocados, goat's milk, cassava

**Tropical fruit production, 1966–2016**

Thousand tonnes

**Citrus fruit production, 1966–2016**

Thousand tonnes

### Land cover

- Evergreen forest
- Deciduous forest
- Woody savanna
- Savanna
- Grassland
- Wetland
- Cropland
- Urban
- Sparsely vegetated
- Water

Scale 1 : 5 000 000

Grand Bahama, Little Abaco, Great Abaco, Bimini Islands, Berry Islands, Eleuthera, New Providence, Andros, Cat Island, San Salvador, Great Exuma, Rum Cay, Long Island, Crooked Island, Ragged Island Range, Acklins Island, Mayaguana

Citrus fruits are one of the main crops grown in The Bahamas, for domestic use, such as in this farmers' market, as well as for export.

### Capture fish production

Thousand tonnes

### Aquaculture fish production

Tonnes

Fishing boats in The Bahamas are of two types: the dingy and the mothership. This fisherman in Nassau has used a dingy to catch conch.

Launched in 2013, BAMSI (The Bahamas Agriculture and Marine Science Institute) is a key part of governmental plans to improve the agricultural and marine sectors, and create a more modern and prosperous nation. The centre of the organization is an 800-acre research and demonstration farm in North Andros, where crops are produced and livestock reared. The Institute is expanding, offering training and promoting community development, and now has offices in Eleuthera, Grand Bahama, Cat Island, Abaco, Crooked Island and Mayaguana.

## Fishing

- Fishing area
- Fishing area boundary

Scale 1 : 5 000 000

### Key facts

| | |
|---|---|
| Number of people employed in commercial fishing industry | 9300 |
| Major products | spiny lobster, conch, scale fish |
| Number of fishing vessels | 4000 |
| Export value | US$ 70 million |
| Annual production | 11.5 thousand tonnes |

Grand Bahama, Little Abaco, Cooper's Town, Eight Mile Rock, Freeport City, Marsh Harbour, Great Abaco, Alice Town, Bimini Islands, Berry Islands, Dunmore Town, Nicholl's Town, Nassau, Governor's Harbour, Fresh Creek, New Providence, Eleuthera, Rock Sound, Andros, Cat Island, San Salvador, Great Exuma, Moss Town, Rum Cay, Long Island, Deadman's Cay, Crooked Island, Ragged Island Range, Acklins Island, Mayaguana, Great Inagua, Matthew Town

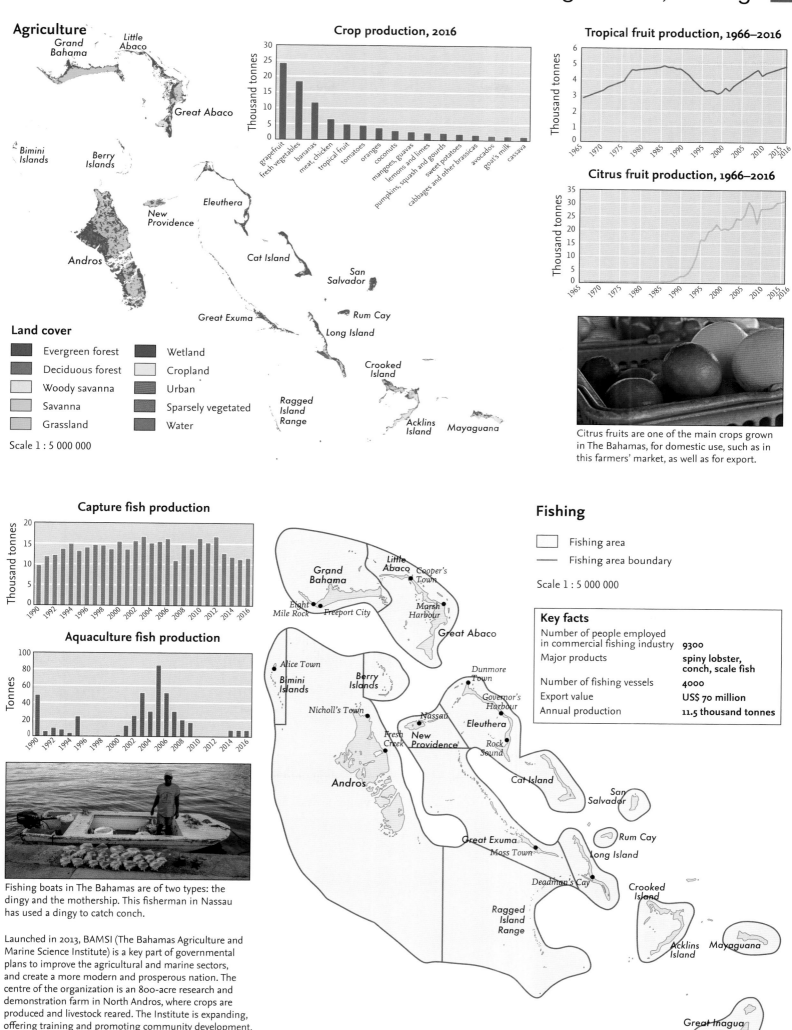

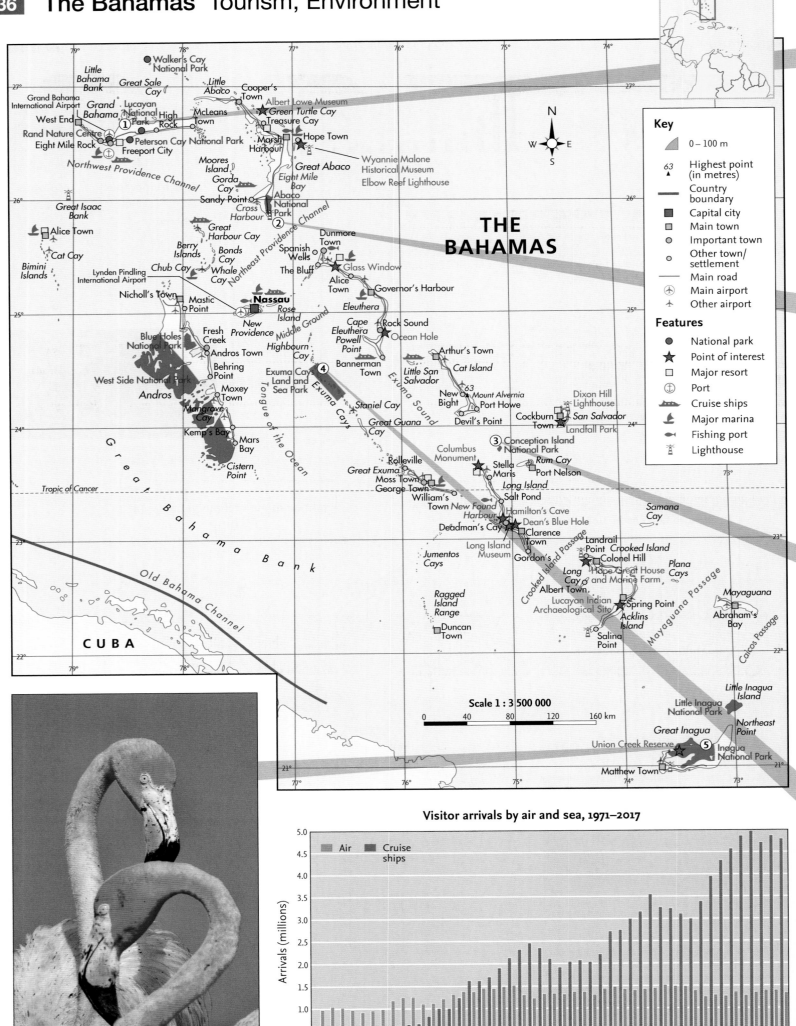

# THE BAHAMAS

**Key**

- 0 – 100 m
- 63 ▲ Highest point (in metres)
- Country boundary
- ■ Capital city
- □ Main town
- ● Important town
- ○ Other town/settlement
- Main road
- ⊕ Main airport
- ✈ Other airport

**Features**

- ● National park
- ★ Point of interest
- □ Major resort
- ⊕ Port
- ⛴ Cruise ships
- ⚓ Major marina
- 🐟 Fishing port
- Lighthouse

Scale 1 : 3 500 000

0    40    80    120    160 km

⑤ **Inagua National Park,** established in 1965, safeguards 60 000 West Indian flamingos, which makes up the world's largest breeding colony.

## Visitor arrivals by air and sea, 1971–2017

Air    Cruise ships

Arrivals (millions)

5.0
4.5
4.0
3.5
3.0
2.5
2.0
1.5
1.0
0.5
0

1971  1975  1980  1985  1990  1995  2000  2005  2010  2015  2017

① **Lucayan National Park,** established in 1977, includes 40 acres of palm and mangrove forests, and an extensive and spectacular underwater cave system.

② **Abaco National Park,** established in 1994, has 20 500 acres of pine forest, 5 000 acres of which are home to endangered Bahama Parrots, also known as Abaco Parrots.

③ **Conception Island National Park,** established in 1964, is a sanctuary and hatchery for green turtles, and is also home to migrant and nesting sea birds.

④ **Exuma Cays Land and Sea Park,** established in 1958, was the first land and sea park in the world and is an ecological preserve for marine and coastal wildlife, such as the Bahamian iguana.

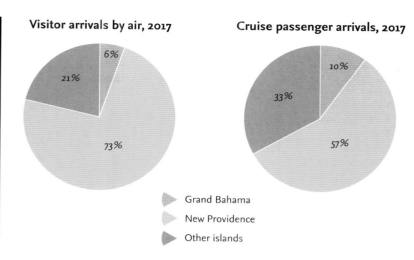

**Visitor arrivals by air, 2017**

6%
21%
73%

**Cruise passenger arrivals, 2017**

10%
33%
57%

Grand Bahama
New Providence
Other islands

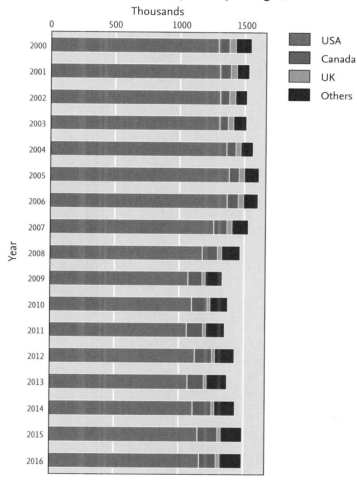

**Stop-over visitor arrivals by country of origin, 2000–2016**

USA
Canada
UK
Others

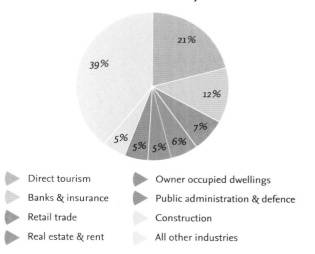

**Contribution of industry to GDP**

21%
39%
12%
7%
6%
5%
5%
5%

Direct tourism
Banks & insurance
Retail trade
Real estate & rent
Owner occupied dwellings
Public administration & defence
Construction
All other industries

## Population statistics

| | |
|---|---|
| Population (2010) | 351 461 |
| Population density (2010) | 25.2 per sq km |
| Average annual population growth rate (2010) | 1.6% |
| Male life expectancy (2016) | 73 years |
| Female life expectancy (2016) | 79 years |
| Birth rate (2016) | 14 per 1000 population |
| Death rate (2016) | 6 per 1000 population |
| Infant mortality (2017) | 6 per 1000 live births |

| Island | Population (2010) |
|---|---|
| New Providence | 246 329 |
| Grand Bahama | 51 368 |
| Abaco | 17 224 |
| Acklins Island | 565 |
| Andros | 7490 |
| Berry Islands | 807 |
| Bimini Islands | 1988 |
| Cat Island | 1522 |
| Crooked Island | 330 |
| Eleuthera | 8202 |
| Exuma and Cays | 6928 |
| Harbour Island | 1762 |
| Inagua | 913 |
| Long Island | 3094 |
| Mayaguana | 277 |
| Ragged Island | 72 |
| San Salvador | 940 |
| Rum Cay | 99 |
| Spanish Wells | 1551 |

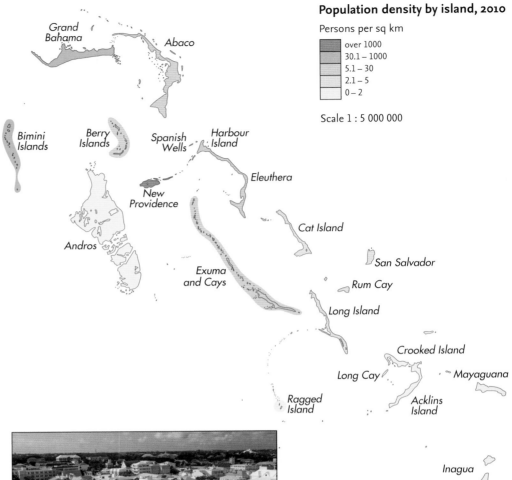

### Population density by island, 2010

Persons per sq km

- over 1000
- 30.1 – 1000
- 5.1 – 30
- 2.1 – 5
- 0 – 2

Scale 1 : 5 000 000

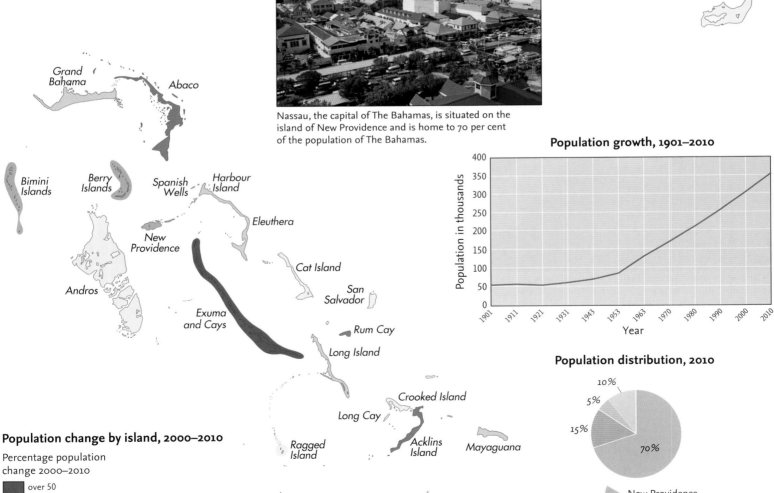

Nassau, the capital of The Bahamas, is situated on the island of New Providence and is home to 70 per cent of the population of The Bahamas.

### Population growth, 1901–2010

Population in thousands (y-axis: 0–400)

x-axis (Year): 1901, 1911, 1921, 1931, 1943, 1953, 1963, 1970, 1980, 1990, 2000, 2010

### Population distribution, 2010

- 10%
- 5%
- 15%
- 70%

- New Providence
- Grand Bahama
- Abaco
- Other islands

## Population change by island, 2000–2010

Percentage population change 2000–2010

- over 50
- 20 – 50
- 10 – 20
- 1 – 10
- -10 – 0

Scale 1 : 5 000 000

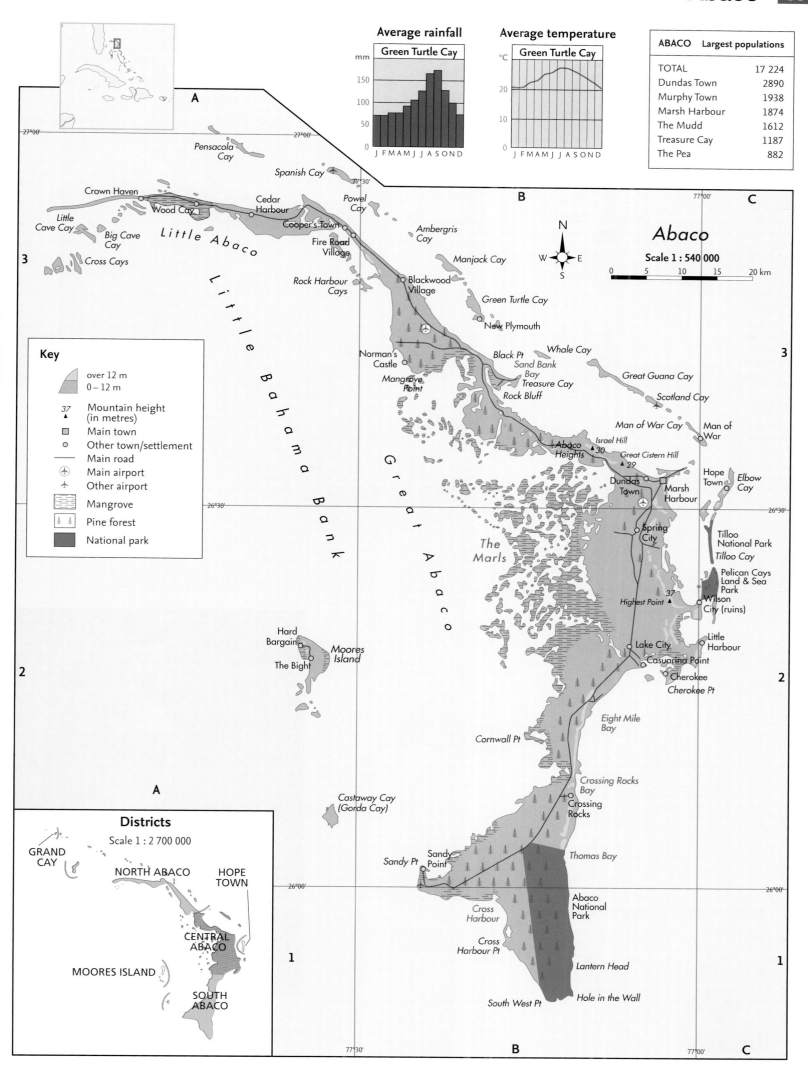

**Average rainfall**

Green Turtle Cay

mm
150
100
50
0
J F M A M J J A S O N D

**Average temperature**

Green Turtle Cay

°C
20
10
0
J F M A M J J A S O N D

| ABACO | Largest populations |
|---|---|
| TOTAL | 17 224 |
| Dundas Town | 2890 |
| Murphy Town | 1938 |
| Marsh Harbour | 1874 |
| The Mudd | 1612 |
| Treasure Cay | 1187 |
| The Pea | 882 |

## Abaco

**Scale 1 : 540 000**

0   5   10   15   20 km

### Key

- over 12 m
- 0 – 12 m
- 37 ▲ Mountain height (in metres)
- ▢ Main town
- ○ Other town/settlement
- — Main road
- ✈ Main airport
- ✈ Other airport
- Mangrove
- Pine forest
- National park

### Districts

**Scale 1 : 2 700 000**

GRAND CAY

NORTH ABACO        HOPE TOWN

CENTRAL ABACO

MOORES ISLAND

SOUTH ABACO

Pensacola Cay
Spanish Cay
Crown Haven
Little Cave Cay
Wood Cay
Cedar Harbour
Powel Cay
Cooper's Town
Fire Road Village
Big Cave Cay
Cross Cays
Rock Harbour Cays
Little Abaco
Ambergris Cay
Manjack Cay
Blackwood Village
Green Turtle Cay
New Plymouth
Whale Cay
Norman's Castle
Black Pt
Sand Bank Bay
Great Guana Cay
Mangrove Point
Treasure Cay
Scotland Cay
Rock Bluff
Little Bahama Bank
Man of War Cay
Man of War
Abaco Heights
Israel Hill ▲30
Great Cistern Hill ▲29
Dundas Town
Marsh Harbour
Hope Town
Elbow Cay
Great Abaco
The Marls
Spring City
Tilloo National Park
Tilloo Cay
Pelican Cays Land & Sea Park
Highest Point ▲37
Wilson City (ruins)
Hard Bargain
Moores Island
Lake City
Little Harbour
The Bight
Casuarina Point
Cherokee
Cherokee Pt
Eight Mile Bay
Cornwall Pt
Castaway Cay (Gorda Cay)
Crossing Rocks Bay
Crossing Rocks
Thomas Bay
Sandy Pt
Sandy Point
Abaco National Park
Cross Harbour
Cross Harbour Pt
Lantern Head
South West Pt
Hole in the Wall

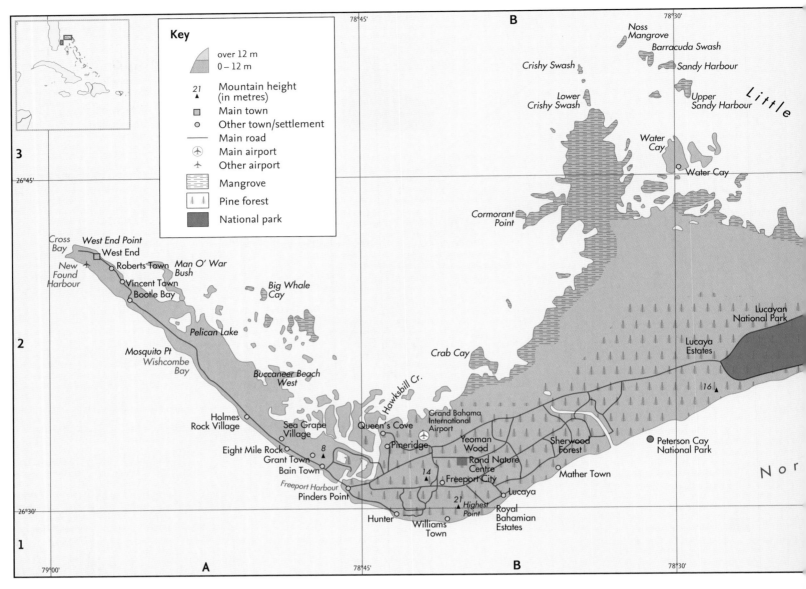

**Key**

| | |
|---|---|
| | over 12 m |
| | 0 – 12 m |
| 21 ▲ | Mountain height (in metres) |
| ◻ | Main town |
| ○ | Other town/settlement |
| — | Main road |
| ✈ | Main airport |
| ✈ | Other airport |
| | Mangrove |
| | Pine forest |
| | National park |

## Districts

Scale 1 : 1 070 000

WEST GRAND BAHAMA

EAST GRAND BAHAMA

CITY OF FREEPORT

## Average rainfall

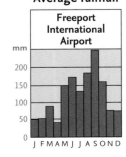

Freeport International Airport

mm
200
150
100
50
0
J F M A M J J A S O N D

## Average temperature

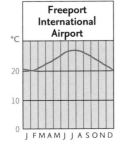

Freeport International Airport

°C
20
10
0
J F M A M J J A S O N D

| GRAND BAHAMA | Largest populations |
|---|---|
| TOTAL | 51 368 |
| Lucaya | 10 172 |
| High Rock | 10 127 |
| Eight Mile Rock | 9640 |
| Marco City | 8436 |
| Pineridge | 8419 |
| West End | 4574 |

The Garden of the Groves is a tranquil tourist destination in Freeport City, Grand Bahama. The Garden runs a wide range of educational programmes aimed at informing school children and the public about conservation and the animals and plants in the Garden's habitats.

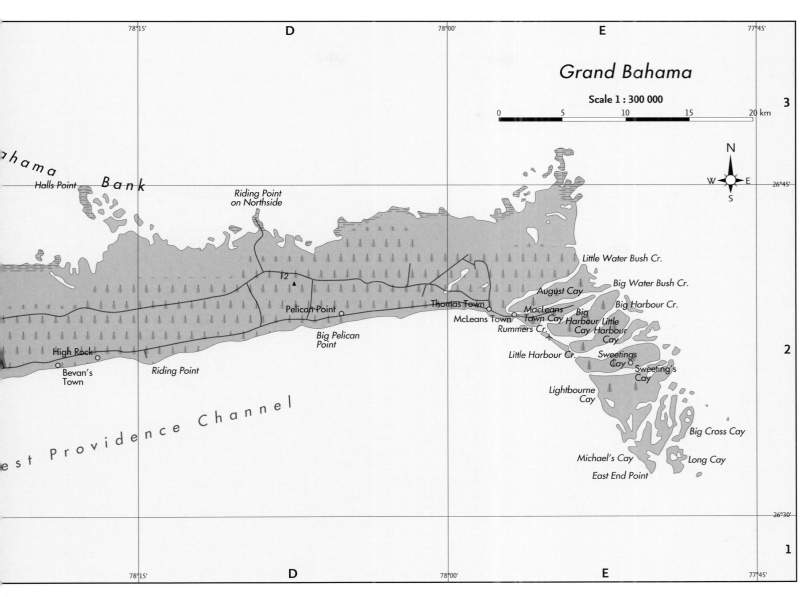

## Grand Bahama

**Scale 1 : 300 000**

0   5   10   15   20 km

Bahama Bank

Halls Point

West Providence Channel

Riding Point
on Northside

Riding Point

Pelican Point

Big Pelican
Point

High Rock

Bevan's
Town

Thomas Town

McLeans Town

MacLeans
Town Cay

Rummers Cr.

Little Water Bush Cr.

Big Water Bush Cr.

August Cay

Big Harbour Cr.

Big
Harbour
Cay

Little
Harbour
Cay

Little Harbour Cr.

Sweetings
Cay

Sweeting's
Cay

Lightbourne
Cay

Big Cross Cay

Michael's Cay

Long Cay

East End Point

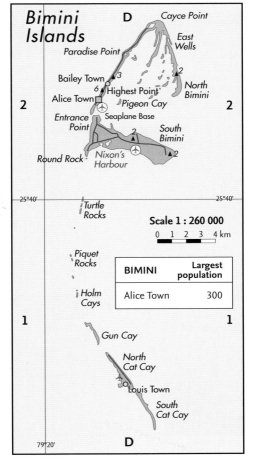

## Bimini Islands

**Scale 1 : 260 000**

0   1   2   3   4 km

Cayce Point

East
Wells

Paradise Point

Bailey Town

Highest Point

Alice Town

Entrance
Point

Round Rock

Pigeon Cay

Seaplane Base

Nixon's
Harbour

North
Bimini

South
Bimini

Turtle
Rocks

Piquet
Rocks

Holm
Cays

Gun Cay

North
Cat Cay

Louis Town

South
Cat Cay

| BIMINI | Largest population |
|---|---|
| Alice Town | 300 |

Bimini is well known for the Sharklab, a facility which researches sharks and conservation of the ocean's ecosystems.

Hotel resort near Paradise Point, north of Alice Town, North Bimini.

### Key

| | |
|---|---|
| | over 12 m |
| | 0 – 12 m |
| 38 ▲ | Mountain height (in metres) |
| | River |
| ■ | Capital city |
| ○ | Other town/ settlement |
| | Highway |
| | Main road |
| ✈ | Main airport |
| | Mangrove |
| | Pine forest |
| | National park |

N
W E
S

### New Providence

**Scale 1 : 78 000**

0  1  2  3  4  5 km

3

A    77°30'    B    77°2

25°05'

Delaport Point

Delaport B

Sandy Port

Rock Pt

Caves Pt

Orange Hill Beach

Lake View

29 ▲

Red Sound

Sky D

Love Beach

Northwest Pt

Love

Gambier Village

▲ 30 Orange Hill

Old Fort Pt

Old Fort Bay

Creek Pt

Lynden Pindling International Airport

Lake Killarney

2

Lightbourne Cr.

Lyford Cay

Simms Pt

Lyford Cay Beach

Pleasant Bay

Mount Pleasant

West Bay

Mount Pleasant ▲ 21

Goulding Cay

Blue Hole

Clifton Pt

Primeval Forest National Park

20 ▲

Blue Hole

Blue Hole

Blue Hole

Clifton

South Ocean Blue Hole

Adelaide Village

Corry Sound

Coral Heights

1

South West Bay

Millars Sound

Coral Harbour

Fleeming Pt

25°00'

A    77°30'    B    77°29

### Districts

Scale 1 : 275 000

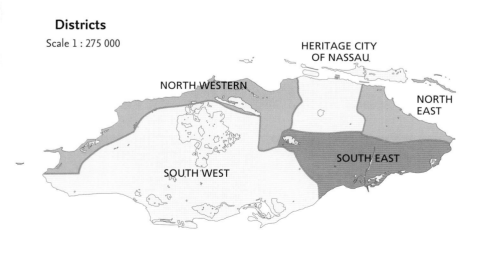

HERITAGE CITY OF NASSAU

NORTH WESTERN

NORTH EAST

SOUTH EAST

SOUTH WEST

| NEW PROVIDENCE | Largest populations |
|---|---|
| TOTAL | 246 329 |
| Golden Isles | 13 762 |
| Elizabeth | 13 233 |
| Blue Hills | 13 062 |
| Garden Hills | 11 257 |
| Englerston | 11 076 |
| Sea Breeze | 10 671 |

### Average rainfall

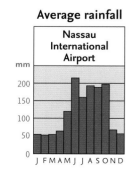

### Average temperature

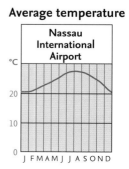

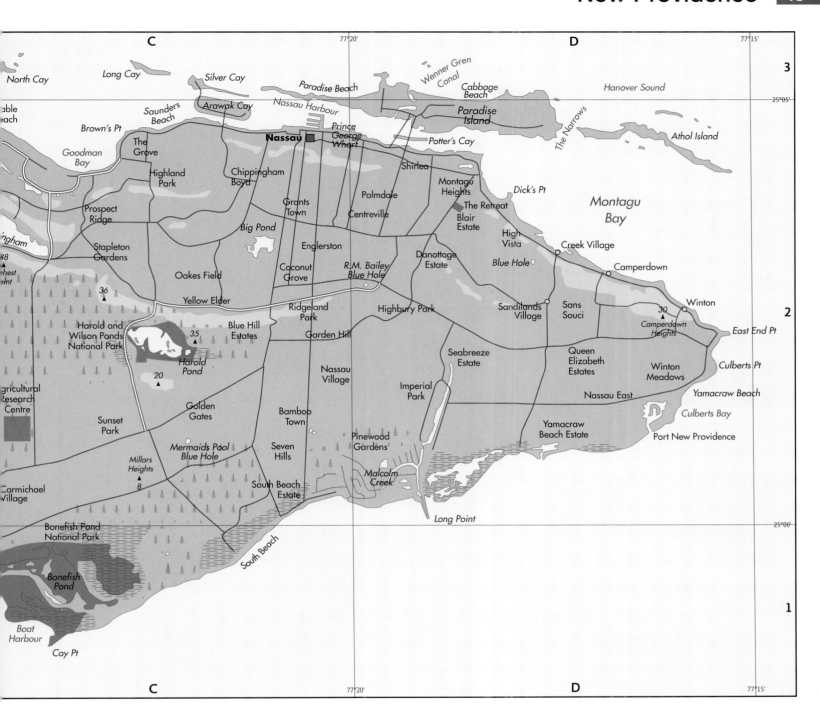

**C** · 77°20' · **D** · 77°15'

North Cay · Long Cay · Silver Cay · Paradise Beach · Wenner Gren Canal · Cabbage Beach · Hanover Sound

able each · Saunders Beach · Arawak Cay · Nassau Harbour · Paradise Island · The Narrows · Athol Island

Brown's Pt · **Nassau** · Prince George Wharf · Potter's Cay

Goodman Bay · The Grove · Highland Park · Chippingham Boyd · Shirlea · Montagu Heights · Dick's Pt · Montagu Bay

Prospect Ridge · Grants Town · Palmdale · Centreville · The Retreat · Blair Estate · High Vista · Creek Village

Stapleton Gardens · Big Pond · Englerston · Danottage Estate · Blue Hole · Camperdown

Oakes Field · Coconut Grove · R.M. Bailey Blue Hole · Winton

Yellow Elder · Sandilands Village · Sans Souci · Camperdown Heights

Harold and Wilson Ponds National Park · 36 · Blue Hill Estates · Ridgeland Park · Highbury Park · 30 · Winton

35 · Garden Hill · East End Pt

Harold Pond · Seabreeze Estate · Queen Elizabeth Estates · Winton Meadows · Culberts Pt

20 · Nassau Village · Imperial Park · Nassau East · Yamacraw Beach

Agricultural Research Centre · Golden Gates · Bamboo Town · Yamacraw Beach Estate · Culberts Bay

Sunset Park · Pinewood Gardens · Port New Providence

Mermaids Pool Blue Hole · Seven Hills · Malcolm Creek

Millars Heights · 8 · South Beach Estate

Carmichael Village · Long Point

Bonefish Pond National Park · South Beach

Bonefish Pond

Boat Harbour · Cay Pt

25°05' · 25°00'

3 · 2 · 1

Supreme Court, Nassau, New Providence. The three branches of the Government – the Executive (the Cabinet), the Legislative (Parliament) and the Judiciary (the law courts) – are all headquartered on New Providence.

Cruise ships docked in Nassau, the main port for tourist arrivals. The tourism industry is the biggest source of income in The Bahamas, with about half of the labour force working in tourism, supplying 70 per cent of tax revenue.

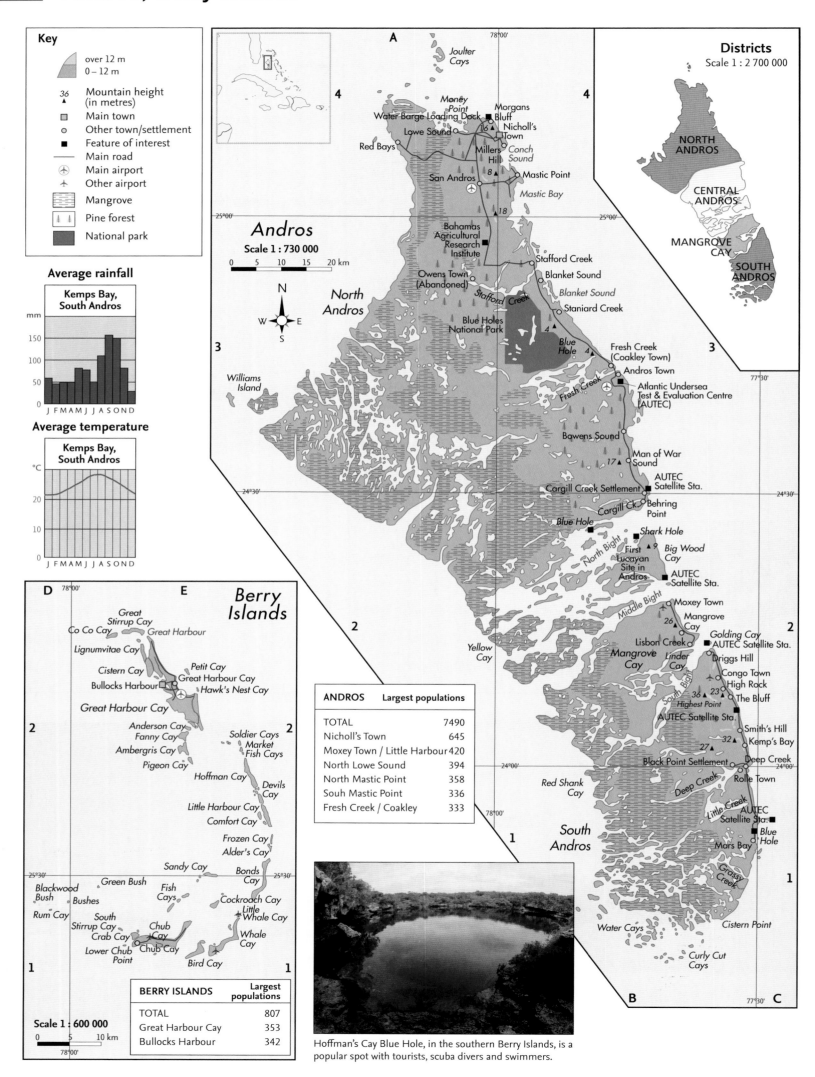

## Key

- over 12 m
- 0 – 12 m
- 36 ▲ Mountain height (in metres)
- ▢ Main town
- ○ Other town/settlement
- ■ Feature of interest
- — Main road
- ✈ Main airport
- ✈ Other airport
- Mangrove
- Pine forest
- National park

### Average rainfall

**Kemps Bay, South Andros**

mm
150
100
50
0
J F M A M J J A S O N D

### Average temperature

**Kemps Bay, South Andros**

°C
20
10
0
J F M A M J J A S O N D

## Andros
Scale 1 : 730 000

0 5 10 15 20 km

N
W — E
S

**North Andros**

Joulter Cays

Money Point
Water Barge Loading Dock
Lowe Sound
Red Bays
San Andros
Morgans Bluff
Nicholl's Town
Millers
Conch Sound
16 ▲
8 ▲
18 ▲
Mastic Point
Mastic Bay
Bahamas Agricultural Research Institute
Owens Town (Abandoned)
Stafford Creek
Blanket Sound
Blanket Sound
Staniard Creek
Stafford Creek
Blue Holes National Park
Blue Hole
4 ▲
4 ▲
Fresh Creek (Coakley Town)
Andros Town
Atlantic Undersea Test & Evaluation Centre (AUTEC)
Fresh Creek
Williams Island
Bowens Sound
17 ▲
Man of War Sound
AUTEC Satellite Sta.
Cargill Creek Settlement
Cargill Ck.
Behring Point
Blue Hole
Shark Hole
North Bight
First Lucayan Site in Andros
Big Wood Cay
AUTEC Satellite Sta.
Yellow Cay
Middle Bight
Moxey Town
Mangrove Cay
26 ▲
Golding Cay
Lisbon Creek
AUTEC Satellite Sta.
Mangrove Cay
Linder Cay
Driggs Hill
South Bight
Congo Town
High Rock
36 ▲ 23 ▲ The Bluff
Highest Point
AUTEC Satellite Sta.
Smith's Hill
32 ▲
Kemp's Bay
27 ▲
Black Point Settlement
Deep Creek
Deep Creek
Rolle Town
Red Shank Cay
Little Creek
AUTEC Satellite Sta.
Blue Hole
Mars Bay
South Andros
Grassy Creek
Water Cays
Cistern Point
Curly Cut Cays

## Districts
Scale 1 : 2 700 000

NORTH ANDROS
CENTRAL ANDROS
MANGROVE CAY
SOUTH ANDROS

## Berry Islands
Scale 1 : 600 000

0 5 10 km

Great Stirrup Cay
Co Co Cay
Great Harbour
Lignumvitae Cay
Cistern Cay
Petit Cay
Great Harbour Cay
Bullocks Harbour
Hawk's Nest Cay
Great Harbour Cay
Anderson Cay
Fanny Cay
Soldier Cays
Market Fish Cays
Ambergris Cay
Pigeon Cay
Hoffman Cay
Devils Cay
Little Harbour Cay
Comfort Cay
Frozen Cay
Alder's Cay
Sandy Cay
Bonds Cay
Green Bush
Fish Cays
Blackwood Bush
Bushes
Cockroach Cay
Rum Cay
South Stirrup Cay
Crab Cay
Chub Cay
Lower Chub Point
Chub Cay
Little Whale Cay
Whale Cay
Bird Cay

| ANDROS | Largest populations |
|---|---|
| TOTAL | 7490 |
| Nicholl's Town | 645 |
| Moxey Town / Little Harbour | 420 |
| North Lowe Sound | 394 |
| North Mastic Point | 358 |
| Souh Mastic Point | 336 |
| Fresh Creek / Coakley | 333 |

| BERRY ISLANDS | Largest populations |
|---|---|
| TOTAL | 807 |
| Great Harbour Cay | 353 |
| Bullocks Harbour | 342 |

Hoffman's Cay Blue Hole, in the southern Berry Islands, is a popular spot with tourists, scuba divers and swimmers.

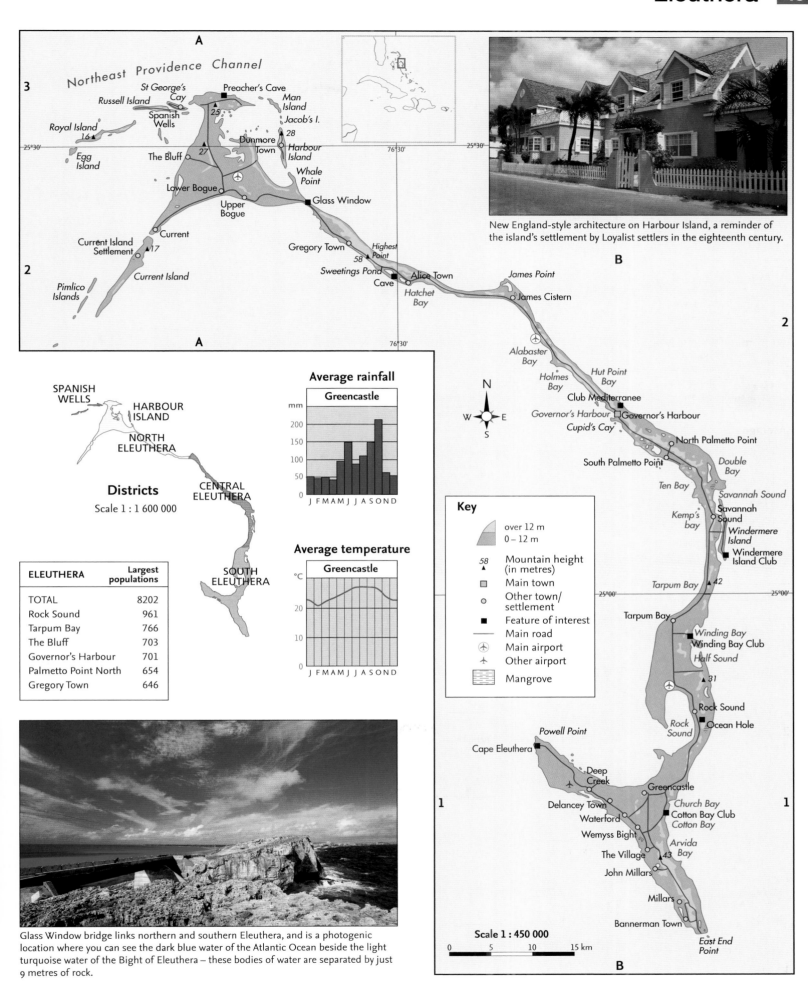

## A

**Northeast Providence Channel**

St George's Cay
Russell Island
Preacher's Cave
Man Island
Spanish Wells
Royal Island 16 ▲
The Bluff
Dunmore Town
Jacob's I. 28
Harbour Island
Egg Island
Lower Bogue
Upper Bogue
Whale Point
Glass Window
Current
Current Island Settlement ▲17
Gregory Town
Highest Point 58 ▲
Pimlico Islands
Current Island
Sweetings Pond Cave
Alice Town
Hatchet Bay
James Point
James Cistern
Alabaster Bay
Holmes Bay
Hut Point Bay
Club Mediterranee
Governor's Harbour
Cupid's Cay
Governor's Harbour
North Palmetto Point
South Palmetto Point
Double Bay
Ten Bay
Savannah Sound
Kemp's bay
Savannah Sound
Windermere Island
Windermere Island Club
Tarpum Bay ▲42
Tarpum Bay
Powell Point
Winding Bay
Winding Bay Club
Half Sound
▲31
Rock Sound
Rock Sound
Ocean Hole
Cape Eleuthera
Deep Creek
Greencastle
Delancey Town
Church Bay
Cotton Bay Club
Cotton Bay
Waterford
Wemyss Bight
Arvida Bay
The Village
▲43
John Millars
Millars
Bannerman Town
East End Point

New England-style architecture on Harbour Island, a reminder of the island's settlement by Loyalist settlers in the eighteenth century.

### Districts
Scale 1 : 1 600 000

SPANISH WELLS
HARBOUR ISLAND
NORTH ELEUTHERA
CENTRAL ELEUTHERA
SOUTH ELEUTHERA

| ELEUTHERA | Largest populations |
|---|---|
| TOTAL | 8202 |
| Rock Sound | 961 |
| Tarpum Bay | 766 |
| The Bluff | 703 |
| Governor's Harbour | 701 |
| Palmetto Point North | 654 |
| Gregory Town | 646 |

### Average rainfall
**Greencastle**

mm
200
150
100
50
0
J F M A M J J A S O N D

### Average temperature
**Greencastle**

°C
20
10
0
J F M A M J J A S O N D

### Key

| | |
|---|---|
| | over 12 m |
| | 0 – 12 m |
| 58 ▲ | Mountain height (in metres) |
| ▪ | Main town |
| ○ | Other town/ settlement |
| ■ | Feature of interest |
| — | Main road |
| ✈ | Main airport |
| ✈ | Other airport |
| | Mangrove |

Scale 1 : 450 000
0   5   10   15 km

Glass Window bridge links northern and southern Eleuthera, and is a photogenic location where you can see the dark blue water of the Atlantic Ocean beside the light turquoise water of the Bight of Eleuthera – these bodies of water are separated by just 9 metres of rock.

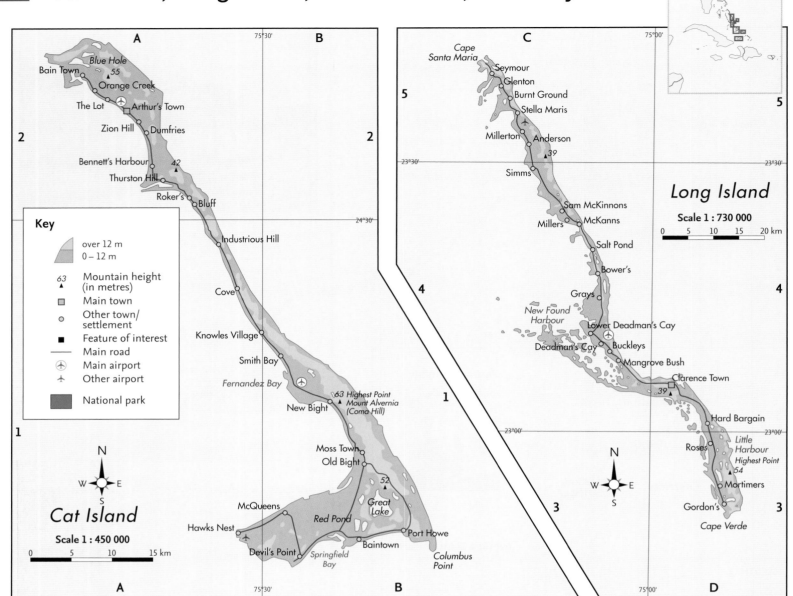

## Cat Island
Scale 1 : 450 000

0 5 10 15 km

Bain Town
Blue Hole
55
Orange Creek
The Lot
Arthur's Town
Zion Hill
Dumfries
Bennett's Harbour
Thurston Hill
42
Roker's
Bluff
Industrious Hill
Cove
Knowles Village
Smith Bay
Fernandez Bay
New Bight
63 Highest Point
Mount Alvernia
(Coma Hill)
Moss Town
Old Bight
52
McQueens
Great Lake
Red Pond
Hawks Nest
Port Howe
Devil's Point
Baintown
Springfield Bay
Columbus Point

### Key
| | |
|---|---|
| | over 12 m |
| | 0 – 12 m |
| 63 ▲ | Mountain height (in metres) |
| ▪ | Main town |
| ○ | Other town/settlement |
| ■ | Feature of interest |
| —— | Main road |
| ✈ | Main airport |
| ✈ | Other airport |
| | National park |

## Long Island
Scale 1 : 730 000

0 5 10 15 20 km

Cape Santa Maria
Seymour
Glenton
Burnt Ground
Stella Maris
Millerton
Anderson
39
Simms
Sam McKinnons
Millers
McKanns
Salt Pond
Bower's
Grays
New Found Harbour
Lower Deadman's Cay
Deadman's Cay
Buckleys
Mangrove Bush
Clarence Town
39
Hard Bargain
Roses
Little Harbour
Highest Point
54
Mortimers
Gordon's
Cape Verde

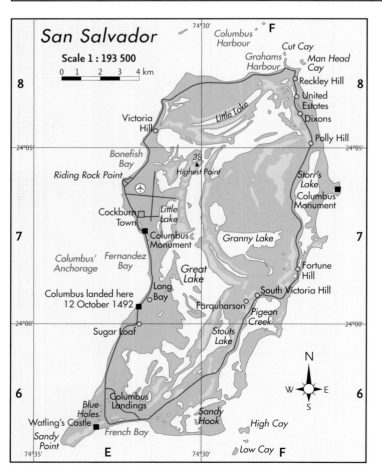

## San Salvador
Scale 1 : 193 500

0 1 2 3 4 km

Columbus Harbour
Cut Cay
Grahams Harbour
Man Head Cay
Reckley Hill
United Estates
Dixons
Victoria Hill
Little Lake
Polly Hill
Bonefish Bay
38
Highest Point
Riding Rock Point
Storr's Lake
Columbus Monument
Cockburn Town
Little Lake
Granny Lake
Columbus' Anchorage
Fernandez Bay
Great Lake
Fortune Hill
Long Bay
South Victoria Hill
Columbus landed here 12 October 1492
Farquharson
Pigeon Creek
Sugar Loaf
Stouts Lake
Blue Holes
Columbus Landings
Sandy Hook
High Cay
Watling's Castle
French Bay
Sandy Point
Low Cay

| CAT ISLAND | Largest populations |
|---|---|
| TOTAL | 1522 |
| Old Bight | 200 |
| Authur's Town | 143 |
| New Bight | 117 |

| SAN SALVADOR | Largest populations |
|---|---|
| TOTAL | 940 |
| Cockburn Town | 271 |
| United Estates | 262 |
| Sugar Loaf | 127 |
| North Victoria Hill | 113 |

| LONG ISLAND | Largest populations |
|---|---|
| TOTAL | 3094 |
| Lower Deadman's Cay | 272 |
| Hamilton | 196 |
| Mangrove Bush | 142 |
| Deadman's Cay | 110 |
| Cartwrights | 109 |

| RUM CAY | Largest populations |
|---|---|
| TOTAL | 99 |

Scale 1 : 730 000

0 5 10 km

Sandy Point
Port Nelson

## Rum Cay

The Hermitage, Cat Island, is a small monastery which was hand carved out of rock on Mount Alvernia, the highest point in The Bahamas.

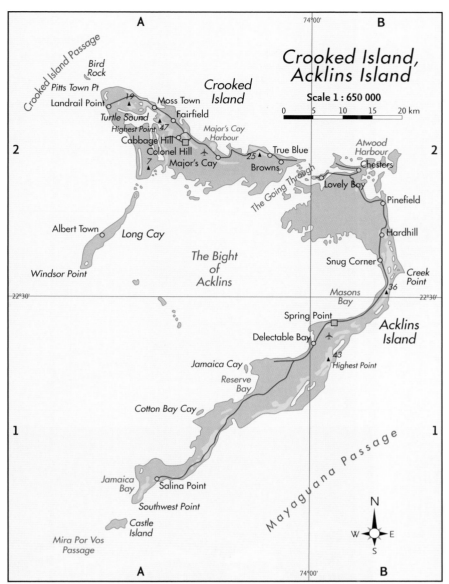

## Crooked Island, Acklins Island

Scale 1 : 650 000

0   5   10   15   20 km

Crooked Island Passage
Bird Rock
Pitts Town Pt
Landrail Point
Moss Town
Turtle Sound  Fairfield
Highest Point  19  47
Cabbage Hill
Colonel Hill
Major's Cay
7
Major's Cay Harbour
True Blue
25
Browns
Crooked Island
Atwood Harbour
Chesters
Lovely Bay
The Going Through
Pinefield
Albert Town
Long Cay
The Bight of Acklins
Hardhill
Snug Corner
Creek Point
36
Windsor Point
Masons Bay
Spring Point
Delectable Bay
Jamaica Cay
43
Highest Point
Acklins Island
Reserve Bay
Cotton Bay Cay
Jamaica Bay
Salina Point
Southwest Point
Castle Island
Mira Por Vos Passage
Mayaguana Passage
N W E S

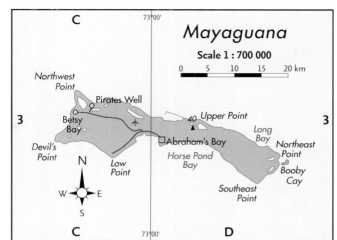

## Mayaguana

Scale 1 : 700 000

0   5   10   15   20 km

Northwest Point
Pirates Well
Betsy Bay
Upper Point
40
Long Bay
Devil's Point
Abraham's Bay
Horse Pond Bay
Northeast Point
Low Point
Southeast Point
Booby Cay
N W E S

| CROOKED ISLAND | Largest populations |
|---|---|
| TOTAL | 330 |
| Landrial Point | 107 |

| MAYAGUANA | Largest populations |
|---|---|
| TOTAL | 277 |
| Abraham's Bay | 143 |

| ACKLINS ISLAND | Largest populations |
|---|---|
| TOTAL | 565 |
| Salina Point | 190 |
| Lovely Bay | 106 |

| INAGUA | Largest populations |
|---|---|
| TOTAL | 913 |

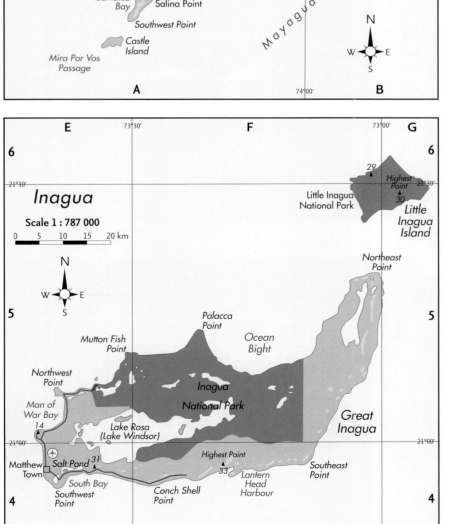

## Inagua

Scale 1 : 787 000

0   5   10   15   20 km

N W E S

Little Inagua National Park
29
Highest Point
30
Little Inagua Island
Northeast Point
Palacca Point
Mutton Fish Point
Ocean Bight
Northwest Point
Inagua National Park
Man of War Bay
14
Lake Rosa (Lake Windsor)
Great Inagua
Matthew Town
Salt Pond
31
Highest Point
33
Southeast Point
South Bay
Southwest Point
Conch Shell Point
Lantern Head Harbour

Travellers use Crooked Island's small airport, Colonel Hill Airport.

The police station in Matthew Town, the capital of Great Inagua, the third-largest island in The Bahamas.

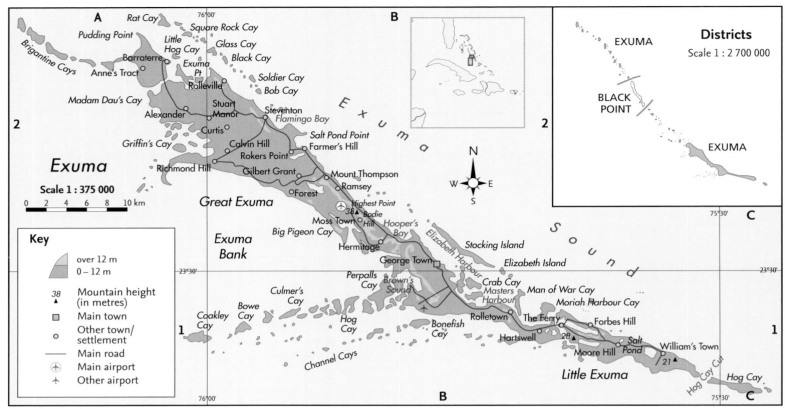

## Key

| | |
|---|---|
| | over 12 m |
| | 0 – 12 m |
| 38 ▲ | Mountain height (in metres) |
| ◻ | Main town |
| ◦ | Other town/ settlement |
| — | Main road |
| ✈ | Main airport |
| ✈ | Other airport |

**Exuma**
Scale 1 : 375 000
0  2  4  6  8  10 km

**Districts**
Scale 1 : 2 700 000

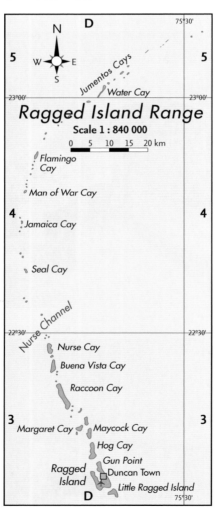

**Ragged Island Range**
Scale 1 : 840 000
0  5  10  15  20 km

| EXUMA AND CAYS | Largest populations |
|---|---|
| TOTAL | 6928 |
| George Town | 1437 |
| Mount Thompson | 557 |
| Hooper's Bay | 514 |
| Farmer's Hill | 456 |
| Bahama Sound | 445 |
| Forest | 419 |

### Average rainfall

**George Town, Exuma**

### Average temperature

**George Town, Exuma**

| RAGGED ISLAND | Largest population |
|---|---|
| TOTAL | 72 |

Staniel Cay in the outer Exuma Islands has been a popular destination with visitors since the foundation of the Staniel Cay Yacht Club in 1956.

Administration Building and Post Office, George Town, Great Exuma. The architecture is said to be inspired by Government House in Nassau.

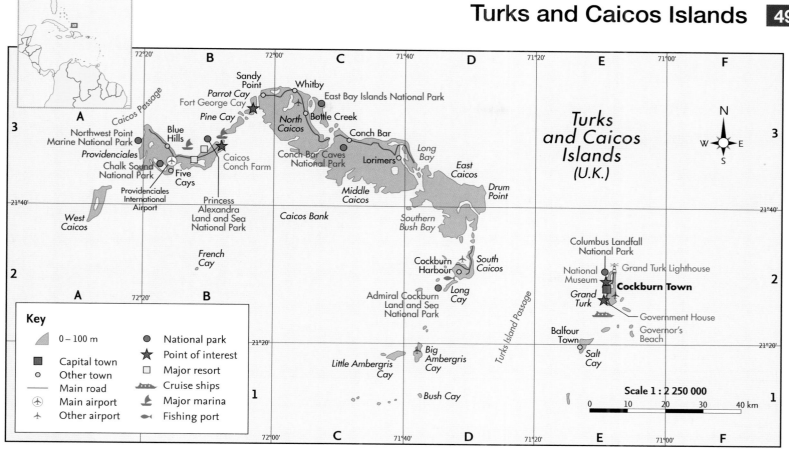

## Key

| | | | |
|---|---|---|---|
| 0 – 100 m | | National park | |
| Capital town | | Point of interest | |
| Other town | | Major resort | |
| Main road | | Cruise ships | |
| Main airport | | Major marina | |
| Other airport | | Fishing port | |

| TURKS & CAICOS island data | Area (sq km) | Population (2012) | Pop. density (per sq km) |
|---|---|---|---|
| TOTAL | 616 | 31 458 | 51 |
| Grand Turk | 17 | 4831 | 284 |
| Middle Caicos | 144 | 168 | 1 |
| North Caicos | 116 | 1312 | 11 |
| Parrot Cay | 6 | 131 | 22 |
| Providenciales | 122 | 23 769 | 195 |
| Salt Cay | 7 | 108 | 15 |
| South Caicos | 21 | 1139 | 54 |

### Average rainfall

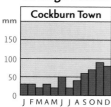

### Turks and Caicos population distribution, 2012

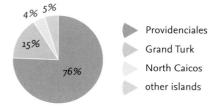

- Providenciales
- Grand Turk
- North Caicos
- other islands

Cockburn Town, on Grand Turk Island, was founded on the sea salt industry. Cockburn Town is the capital city of the Turks and Caicos Islands, and Duke Street (above) is a historic street in the city lined with British colonial architecture.

## TURKS AND CAICOS ISLANDS

*British Overseas Territory*

| | |
|---|---|
| **Population** (2012) | 31 458 |
| **Capital town** | Cockburn Town |
| **Area** | 616 sq km |
| **Languages** | English |
| **National flower** | Turk's Head Cactus |
| **National bird** | Brown Pelican |
| **National animal** | Rock Iguana |

The prehistoric inhabitants were the Taino

First sighted by Ponce de León in **1512**

Settled by Bermudans collecting salt after **1680**

Occupied by the French **1765–1799**

Became part of the British Bahamas in **1799**

Governed variously by Jamaica and The Bahamas until **1973** when it became a British Overseas Territory

Grace Bay, Providenciales, Turks and Caicos Islands is one of the most pristine beaches in the world.

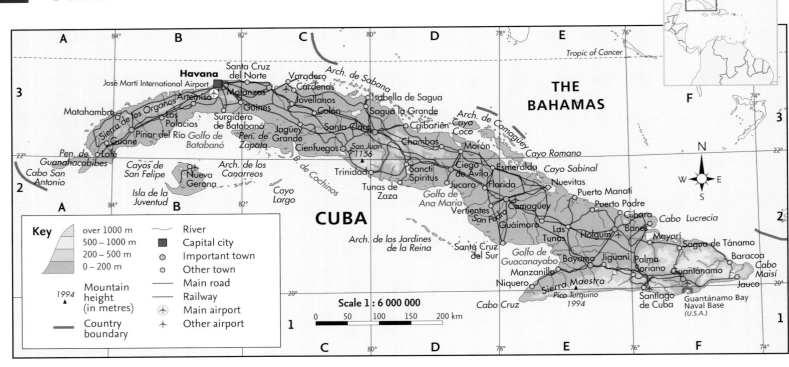

**Map labels:**

THE BAHAMAS

CUBA

Tropic of Cancer

Havana, José Martí International Airport, Santa Cruz del Norte, Matanzas, Artemisa, Guines, Surgidero de Batabanó, Matahambre, Los Palacios, Pinar del Río, Golfo de Batabanó, Sierra de los Organos, Pen. de Guane, Pen. de Zapata, Jagüey Grande, Cienfuegos, San Juan 1156, Trinidad, Varadero, Cárdenas, Jovellanos, Colón, Santa Clara, Sagua la Grande, Isabella de Sagua, Caibarién, Chambas, Sancti Spíritus, Ciego de Ávila, Morón, Tunas de Zaza, Jucaro, Florida, Esmeralda, Cayo Coco, Cayo Romano, Cayo Sabinal, Nuevitas, Puerto Manatí, Puerto Padre, Gibara, Banes, Holguín, Mayarí, Sagua de Tánamo, Baracoa, Cabo Maisí, Jauco, Santiago de Cuba, Guantánamo Bay Naval Base (U.S.A.), Guantánamo, Palma Soriano, Jiguaní, Bayamo, Niquero, Manzanillo, Sierra Maestra, Pico Turquino 1994, Cabo Cruz, Golfo de Guacanayabo, Santa Cruz del Sur, Las Tunas, Camagüey, Guáimaro, Vertientes, San Pedro, Golfo de Ana María, Arch. de los Jardines de la Reina, Cayo Largo, Cayo Sabinal, Arch. de Sabana, Arch. de Camagüey, Cabo Lucrecia, Cabo San Antonio, Pen. de Guanahacabibes, Cayos de San Felipe, Nueva Gerona, Isla de la Juventud, Arch. de los Canarreos, B. de Cochinos, Guaneel

Pico Turquino 1994

**Key**
- over 1000 m
- 500 – 1000 m
- 200 – 500 m
- 0 – 200 m
- 1994 Mountain height (in metres)
- Country boundary
- River
- Capital city
- Important town
- Other town
- Main road
- Railway
- Main airport
- Other airport

Scale 1 : 6 000 000
0  50  100  150  200 km

## Features

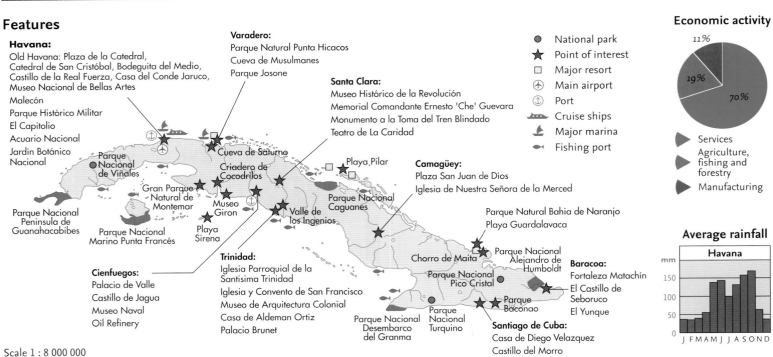

Scale 1 : 8 000 000

**Havana:**
Old Havana: Plaza de la Catedral, Catedral de San Cristóbal, Bodeguita del Medio, Castillo de la Real Fuerza, Casa del Conde Jaruco, Museo Nacional de Bellas Artes
Malecón
Parque Histórico Militar
El Capitolio
Acuario Nacional
Jardín Botánico Nacional

Parque Nacional Península de Guanahacabibes

**Cienfuegos:**
Palacio de Valle
Castillo de Jagua
Museo Naval
Oil Refinery

**Varadero:**
Parque Natural Punta Hicacos
Cueva de Musulmanes
Parque Josone

**Santa Clara:**
Museo Histórico de la Revolución
Memorial Comandante Ernesto 'Che' Guevara
Monumento a la Toma del Tren Blindado
Teatro de La Caridad

**Trinidad:**
Iglesia Parroquial de la Santisima Trinidad
Iglesia y Convento de San Francisco
Museo de Arquitectura Colonial
Casa de Aldeman Ortiz
Palacio Brunet

**Camagüey:**
Plaza San Juan de Díos
Iglesia de Nuestra Señora de la Merced

**Baracoa:**
Fortaleza Matachín
El Castillo de Seboruco
El Yunque

**Santiago de Cuba:**
Casa de Diego Velazquez
Castillo del Morro

Feature map labels: Parque Nacional de Viñales, Gran Parque Natural de Montemar, Museo Giron, Playa Sirena, Parque Nacional Marino Punta Francés, Criadero de Cocodrilos, Cueva de Saturno, Valle de los Ingenios, Playa Pilar, Parque Nacional Caguanes, Chorro de Maita, Parque Nacional Alejandro de Humboldt, Parque Nacional Pico Cristal, Parque Nacional Desembarco del Granma, Parque Nacional Turquino, Parque Baconao, Parque Natural Bahia de Naranjo, Playa Guardalavaca

Legend:
- National park
- Point of interest
- Major resort
- Main airport
- Port
- Cruise ships
- Major marina
- Fishing port

### Economic activity

- 70% Services
- 19% Agriculture, fishing and forestry
- 11% Manufacturing

### Average rainfall

**Havana**
mm
150
100
50
0
J F M A M J J A S O N D

Fulgencio Batista was president of Cuba from 1940 to 1944. He came back to power in 1952 through a military coup and remained dictator of Cuba until deposed by the Cuban Revolution in 1959. He died in exile in Spain in 1973.

Fidel Castro was the ruler of Cuba from 1959 until 2008. He gained power through the Cuban Revolution, which he led with Che Guevara and his brother Raúl Castro. Due to failing health he passed the presidency to his brother in 2008, and died in 2016.

## CUBA

| | |
|---|---|
| **Population** (2012) | 11 167 325 |
| **Capital city** | Havana |
| **Area** | 110 860 sq km |
| **Languages** | Spanish |
| **National flower** | White Mariposa |
| **National bird** | Tocororo |
| **National animal** | Cuban Trogon |

First sighted by Columbus on his first voyage in 1492. Columbus thought he had reached Japan (Cipangu)

Original inhabitants were the Taino and Ciboney. Both groups had died out, mainly from disease, by 1600

Cuba was a Spanish colony from its sighting by Columbus until 1898

The Spanish-American war of 1898 led to the independence of Cuba, but until 1902 it was governed by the USA

In 1959 the Cuban Revolution took over the government and founded a socialist state, and by 1965 a communist state

In 1961 a US supported invasion at the Bay of Pigs was repelled by the Cubans

A US embargo on trade and travel to Cuba was begun in 1960, but was partly reduced in 2015

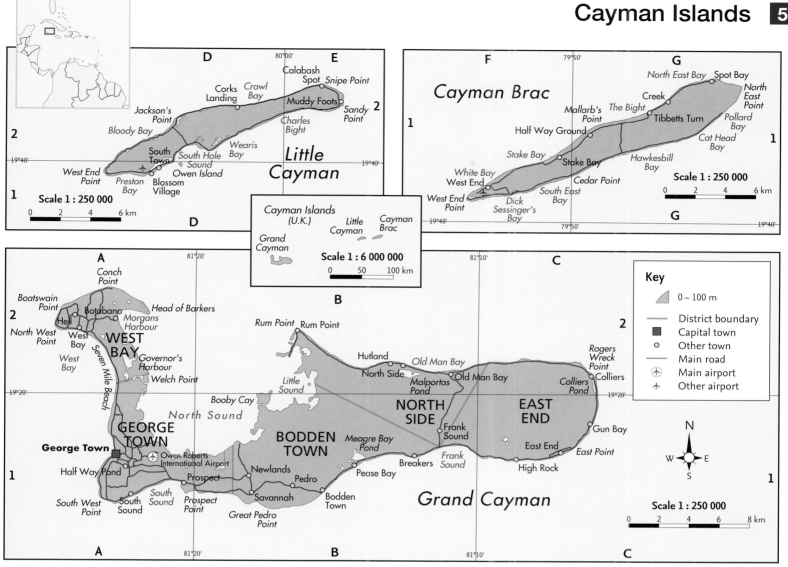

## Little Cayman (map inset D–E)

Scale 1 : 250 000
0  2  4  6 km

Corks Landing, Calabash, Spot, Snipe Point, Crawl Bay, Jackson's Point, Muddy Foots, Sandy Point, Bloody Bay, Charles Bight, Wearis Bay, South Town, South Hole Sound, Owen Island, West End Point, Preston Bay, Blossom Village, **Little Cayman**

## Cayman Brac (map inset F–G)

Scale 1 : 250 000
0  2  4  6 km

North East Bay, Spot Bay, Creek, North East Point, Mallarb's Point, The Bight, Tibbetts Turn, Pollard Bay, Half Way Ground, Cat Head Bay, Stake Bay, Hawkesbill Bay, White Bay, West End, Stake Bay, Cedar Point, South East Bay, West End Point, Dick Sessinger's Bay

## Cayman Islands (U.K.) inset

Scale 1 : 6 000 000
0  50  100 km
Grand Cayman, Little Cayman, Cayman Brac

## Grand Cayman (main map A–C)

Scale 1 : 250 000
0  2  4  6  8 km

Conch Point, Boatswain Point, Head of Barkers, Botabano, Morgans Harbour, Hell, North West Point, West Bay, WEST BAY, Governor's Harbour, West Bay, Welch Point, Seven Mile Beach, Rum Point, Rum Point, Hutland, Old Man Bay, North Side, Old Man Bay, Rogers Wreck Point, Colliers, Colliers Pond, Little Sound, Malportas Pond, NORTH SIDE, EAST END, GEORGE TOWN, **George Town**, North Sound, Booby Cay, BODDEN TOWN, Meagre Bay Pond, Frank Sound, Gun Bay, Owen Roberts International Airport, Half Way Pond, Newlands, Pedro, Pease Bay, Breakers, Frank Sound, East End, East Point, High Rock, Prospect, Savannah, Bodden Town, **Grand Cayman**, South West Point, South Sound, Prospect Point, Great Pedro Point

**Key**
- 0 – 100 m
- District boundary
- Capital town
- Other town
- Main road
- Main airport
- Other airport

---

## CAYMAN ISLANDS

*British Overseas Territory*

| | |
|---|---|
| **Population** (2010) | 55 036 |
| **Capital town** | George Town |
| **Area** | 264 sq km |
| **Languages** | English |
| **National flower** | Wild Banana Orchid |
| **National bird** | Cayman Parrot |

No prehistoric settlement is known

Little Cayman and Cayman Brac were first sighted by Columbus in **1503**

Occasional European settlements were attempted on Grand Cayman in the **17th** century

The Cayman Islands formally became British in **1670**, and permanent settlement was established after **1730**

The Caymans were governed as a British colony with Jamaica until **1962**, when it became a separate crown colony, and subsequently a British Overseas Territory

It has since become a tax haven and a major tourist destination in the modern era

The Blue Iguana is found only on Grand Cayman. It can reach 1.5 metres in length and live for over 60 years. It is an endangered species and only 750 are believed to exist.

## Features

- National park
- Point of interest
- Major resort
- Main airport
- Port
- Cruise ships
- Major marina
- Fishing port

Hell Rock Formations, Barker's National Park, Cayman Turtle Farm, Stingray City, Cemetery Beach and Reef, Kittiwake Shipwreck and Artificial Reef, Government House, Seven Mile Beach, Devil's Grotto, Davinoff's Concrete Sculpture Garden, Mastic Trail, Blue Iguana Nature Reserve, Queen Elizabeth II Botanic Park, East End Lighthouse Park, Pedro St James National Historic Site

**George Town:**
Fort George
Government Buildings
National Museum
National Gallery

Scale 1 : 400 000

|  | Area (sq km) | Population (2010) | Population density (per sq km) |
|---|---|---|---|
| Grand Cayman | 197 | 52 740 | 268 |
| Cayman Brac | 39 | 2098 | 54 |
| Little Cayman | 28 | 198 | 7 |

### Tourist arrivals, 2000–2014

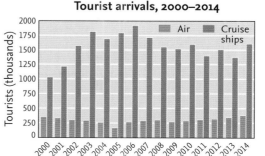

Air, Cruise ships
Tourists (thousands)
2000 2001 2002 2003 2004 2005 2006 2007 2008 2009 2010 2011 2012 2013 2014

### Average rainfall

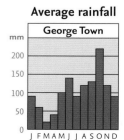

George Town
mm
J F M A M J J A S O N D

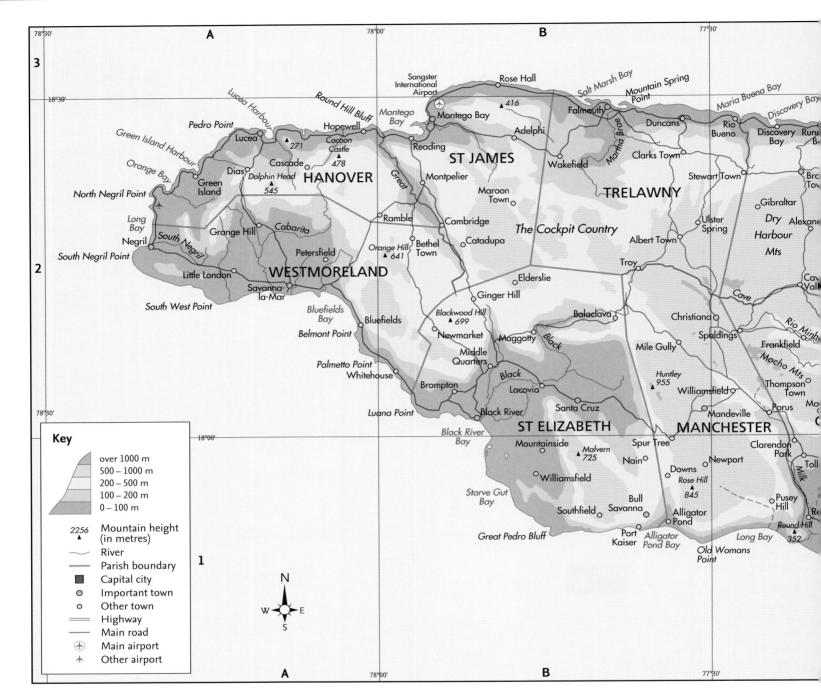

## Key

| | |
|---|---|
| | over 1000 m |
| | 500 – 1000 m |
| | 200 – 500 m |
| | 100 – 200 m |
| | 0 – 100 m |
| ▲ 2256 | Mountain height (in metres) |
| | River |
| | Parish boundary |
| ■ | Capital city |
| ● | Important town |
| ○ | Other town |
| | Highway |
| | Main road |
| ✈ | Main airport |
| ✈ | Other airport |

## JAMAICA

| | | | |
|---|---|---|---|
| **Population** (2011) | 2 697 983 | **National flower** | Lignum Vitae |
| **Capital city** | Kingston | **National fruit** | Ackee |
| **Area** | 10 991 sq km | **National tree** | Blue Mahoe |
| **Languages** | English, creole | **National bird** | Red-billed Streamertail (Doctor Bird) |

## Counties and parishes

— County boundary
— Parish boundary
○ Parish capital

Scale 1 : 2 000 000

Salt fish and ackee is the traditional dish of Jamaica. The ackee (top) is the national fruit, originally from West Africa, while the salt fish is dried and salted cod from Canada, and originally imported as a food for the population during slavery.

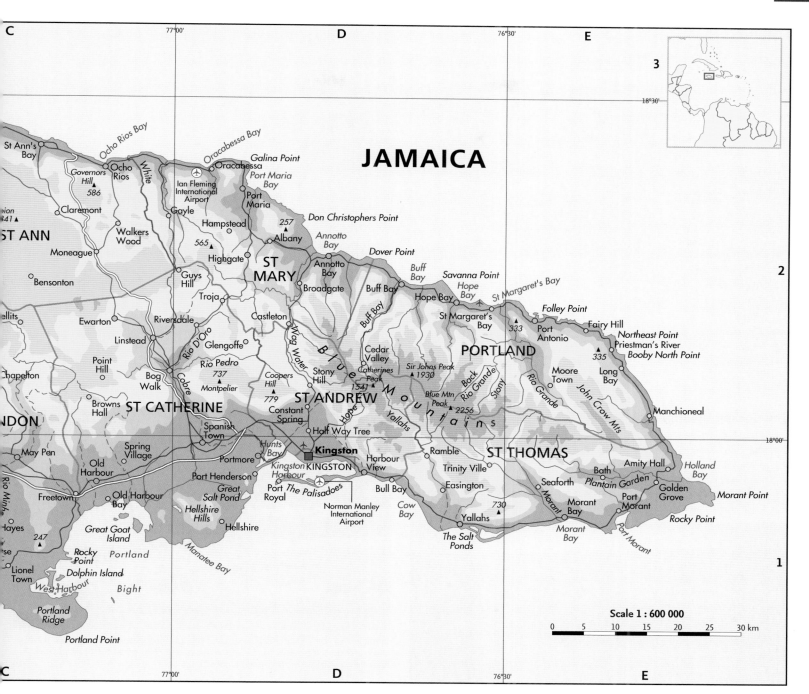

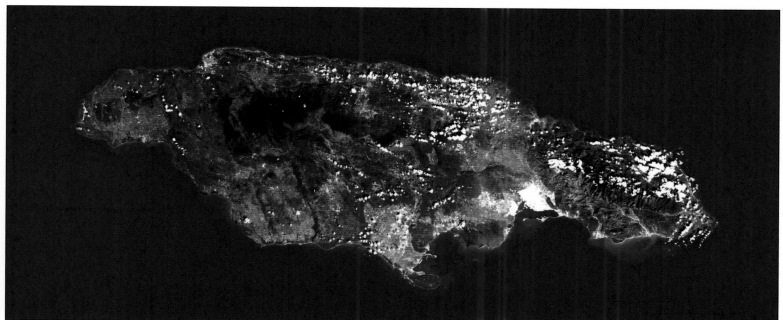

This satellite image shows Kingston and nearby Spanish Town as bright white areas, while the red patches are the bauxite workings in the interior. To the far east the rugged Blue Mountains can be seen, and in the west the very dark green represents the forests of the Cockpit Country. Note the clouds along the north coast, the wetter side of Jamaica as opposed to the drier south coast.

## Features

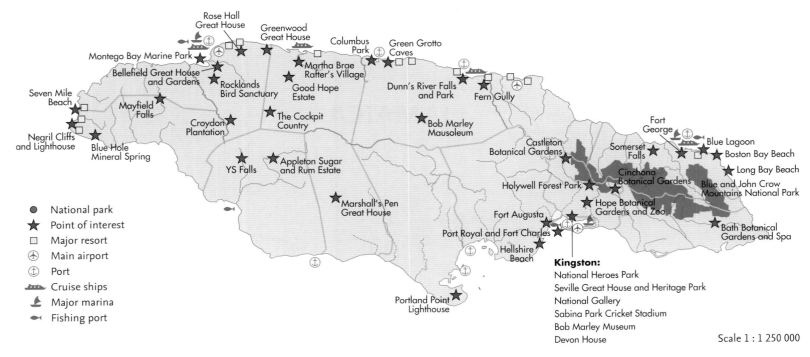

Rose Hall
Great House
Greenwood
Great House
Columbus
Park
Green Grotto
Caves
Montego Bay Marine Park
Martha Brae
Rafter's Village
Bellefield Great House
and Gardens
Rocklands
Bird Sanctuary
Good Hope
Estate
Dunn's River Falls
and Park
Fern Gully
Seven Mile
Beach
Mayfield
Falls
Croydon
Plantation
The Cockpit
Country
Bob Marley
Mausoleum
Fort
George
Negril Cliffs
and Lighthouse
Blue Hole
Mineral Spring
Castleton
Botanical Gardens
Somerset
Falls
Blue Lagoon
Boston Bay Beach
Appleton Sugar
and Rum Estate
Cinchona
Botanical Gardens
Long Bay Beach
YS Falls
Holywell Forest Park
Blue and John Crow
Mountains National Park
Marshall's Pen
Great House
Hope Botanical
Gardens and Zoo
Fort Augusta
Bath Botanical
Gardens and Spa
Port Royal and Fort Charles
Hellshire
Beach
Portland Point
Lighthouse

**Kingston:**
National Heroes Park
Seville Great House and Heritage Park
National Gallery
Sabina Park Cricket Stadium
Bob Marley Museum
Devon House

- **National park** (symbol)
- **Point of interest** (★)
- **Major resort** (□)
- **Main airport** (✈)
- **Port** (⚓)
- **Cruise ships**
- **Major marina**
- **Fishing port**

Scale 1 : 1 250 000

## The Cockpit Country

- Severely eroded limestone district in northwest Jamaica
- The area is a wilderness of conical hills and deep hollows
- It contains the largest area of rainforest in Jamaica
- It is a proposed National Park and World Heritage site
- It was a hideout for escaped slaves (known as the maroons) in the 18th century
- It is still largely inaccessible today

The Cockpit Country is an area of heavily weathered limestone. It is a network of conical hills separated by deep sinkholes. It has been described as 'one of the world's most dramatic examples of karst topography'. Due to its difficult access it is still heavily forested.

In the last 50 years, Ocho Rios has grown from a fishing village to a major resort city and cruise port. It benefits from its attractive coastal setting and the nearby Dunn's River Falls, Jamaica's most visited tourist site.

### Average rainfall
**Kingston**
mm
200
150
100
50
0
J F M A M J J A S O N D

### Average rainfall
**Montego Bay**
mm
200
150
100
50
0
J F M A M J J A S O N D

### Average rainfall
**Port Antonio**
mm
350
300
250
200
150
100
50
0
J F M A M J J A S O N D

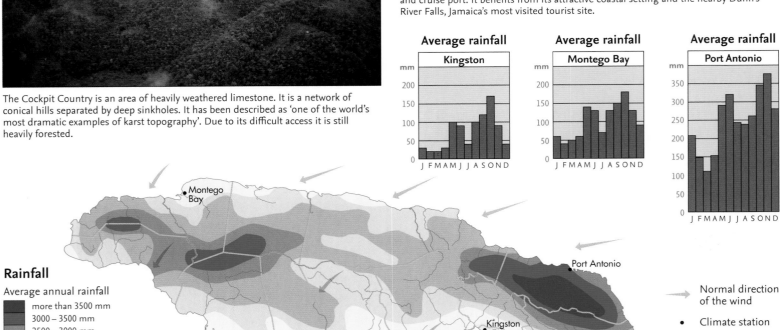

Montego
Bay

Port Antonio

Kingston

## Rainfall
Average annual rainfall
- more than 3500 mm
- 3000 – 3500 mm
- 2500 – 3000 mm
- 2000 – 2500 mm
- 1500 – 2000 mm
- 1000 – 1500 mm
- less than 1000 mm

→ Normal direction
of the wind

• Climate station

Scale 1 : 1 500 000

## Population density, 2011

Persons per sq km

- over 500
- 250 – 500
- 200 – 250
- 150 – 200
- under 150

• Parish capital

Scale 1 : 2 500 000

1. KINGSTON
2. ST ANDREW

## Population change, 2001–2011

Percentage population
change 2001–2011

- over 6.0
- 4.0 – 5.9
- 3.0 – 3.9
- 2.0 – 2.9
- 0.1 – 1.9
- no change
- under -7.0

Scale 1 : 2 500 000

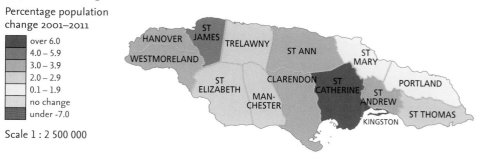

## Population structure

### 1955

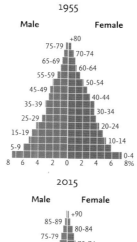

### 2015

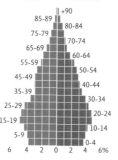

Each full square represents 1% of the total population

## Population increase, 1960–2011

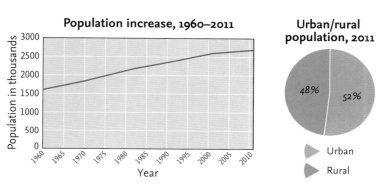

## Urban/rural population, 2011

48% Urban
52% Rural

▶ Urban
▶ Rural

A busy street scene in Downtown, Kingston.

## Kingston-Spanish Town conurbation

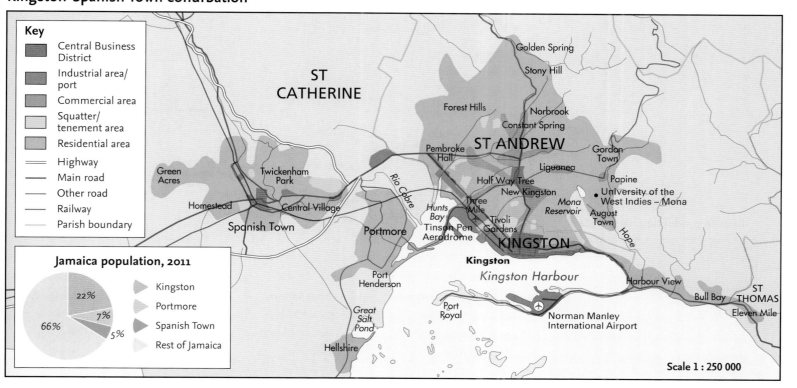

### Key

- Central Business District
- Industrial area/port
- Commercial area
- Squatter/tenement area
- Residential area
- Highway
- Main road
- Other road
- Railway
- Parish boundary

### Jamaica population, 2011

- 22% Kingston
- 7% Portmore
- 5% Spanish Town
- 66% Rest of Jamaica

Scale 1 : 250 000

## Agriculture

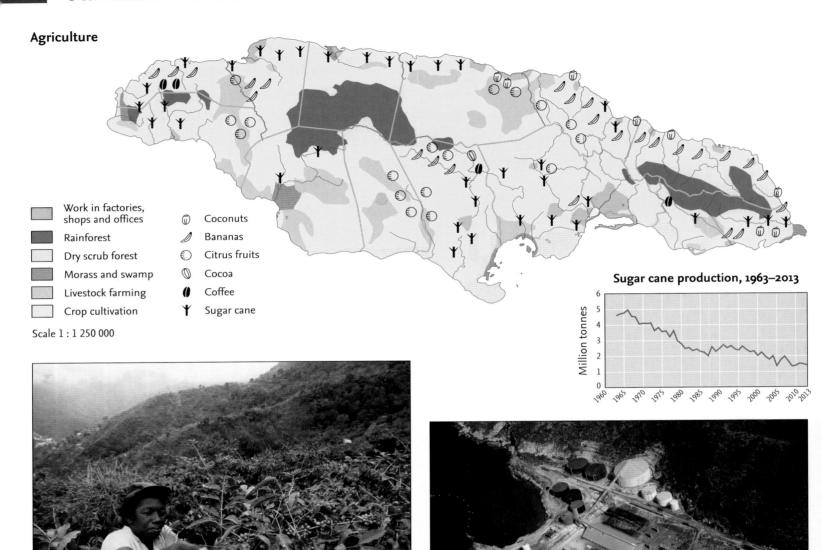

| | |
|---|---|
| Work in factories, shops and offices | Coconuts |
| Rainforest | Bananas |
| Dry scrub forest | Citrus fruits |
| Morass and swamp | Cocoa |
| Livestock farming | Coffee |
| Crop cultivation | Sugar cane |

Scale 1 : 1 250 000

### Sugar cane production, 1963–2013

*Million tonnes* — graph showing values from 6 down over years 1960 to 2013.

The cool humid atmosphere of the Blue Mountains ensures that the finest coffee can grow here. Blue Mountain Coffee has a limited production, but it is considered one of the world's finest (and most expensive) coffees.

Port Kaiser is the export point for bauxite and alumina being shipped from Alpart's mines at Nain. The port was closed until 2015 when the mines were re-opened, and the first exports went to the Ukraine.

## Industry

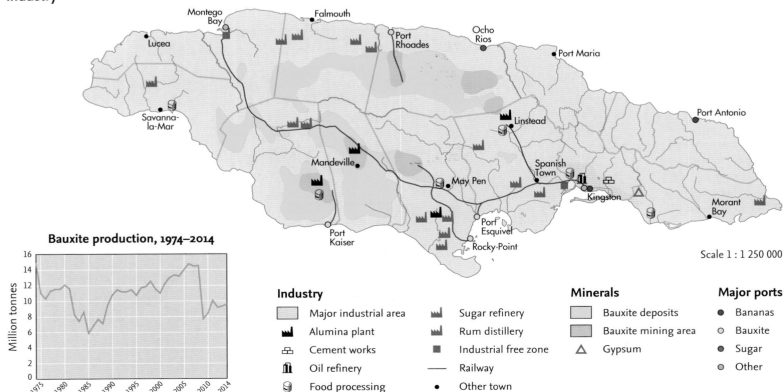

### Bauxite production, 1974–2014

*Million tonnes* — graph showing values from 16 over years 1975 to 2014.

**Industry**
- Major industrial area
- Alumina plant
- Cement works
- Oil refinery
- Food processing
- Sugar refinery
- Rum distillery
- Industrial free zone
- Railway
- Other town

**Minerals**
- Bauxite deposits
- Bauxite mining area
- Gypsum

**Major ports**
- Bananas
- Bauxite
- Sugar
- Other

Scale 1 : 1 250 000

## History

- Between **4000** and **1000** BC Arawak and Taino peoples from South America migrated northwards. Some of these migrants settled in Jamaica
- Christopher Columbus arrived in **1494** and claimed Jamaica for Spain. The first Spanish settlement was established in **1509**. Spanish Town was settled by the Spanish in **1534**
- In **1655** the British captured Jamaica from the Spanish and ruled the island until **1962**
- Under British rule Jamaica became one of the world's main producers and exporters of sugar using a plantation economy and African slave labour
- With the full abolition of slavery in **1838** the British did not have a large enough work force for their plantations and so hired Indian and Chinese contract labourers
- Since **1952** bauxite has replaced sugar and other agricultural products as Jamaica's main export
- Jamaica gained full independence in **1962**

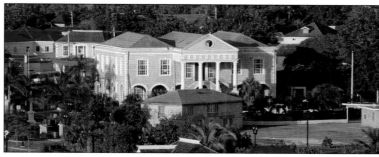

The Falmouth Courthouse is a fine example of Jamaica's widespread restoration projects. The Courthouse was built in 1815, but eventually deteriorated and was gutted by fire in 1926. Between 2007 and 2011 the windows and portico were rebuilt, and today the building presents a fine prospect for vessels entering the harbour.

## Culture

### Music

- Jamaica has had a big impact on the development of popular music worldwide. Musical styles such as ska, reggae and dancehall all originated in Jamaica and these in turn influenced the development of punk rock and American rap and hip hop music
- Many internationally known musicians were born in Jamaica, one of the most famous being the reggae artist Bob Marley who died in 1981. There is a museum dedicated to his life in Kingston

Musical innovation and musicians are not only a Jamaican characteristic, but they are also a valuable export, attracting many thousands to the country. Chronixx specialises in reggae, but is a young and versatile artist.

### Literature

- The author of the James Bond novels, Ian Fleming, lived in Jamaica and set some of his stories on the island
- Marlon James, a Jamaican-born writer, won the 2015 Man Booker Prize for his novel *A Brief History of Seven Killings*

### Sport

- Sport is an important part of life for Jamaicans. The most popular sports include athletics, cricket, soccer and basketball
- Jamaica is one of the top nations in sprinting. The current World and Olympic record holder in the 100 m and 200 m is the Jamaican-born Usain Bolt
- Veronica Campbell-Brown won the Olympic gold for the 200 m in both 2004 and 2008, becoming the first Caribbean woman to win this event and also to retain the title. In 2008 Shelly-Ann Fraser-Pryce matched this feat and became the first Caribbean woman to win the 100 m sprint
- Some of the world's most famous cricketers have come from Jamaica including Michael Holding, Courtney Walsh and Chris Gayle. Jamaica provides players for the West Indies cricket team and the Test venue is at Sabina Park in Kingston

Shelly-Ann Fraser-Pryce won the women's Olympic 100 m in 2008 and repeated the achievement in 2012, only the third woman ever to have done this. In 2012 she also won the Olympic silver medal for the 200 m and 4 x 100 m races. She is seen here anchoring a 4 x 100 m relay race in Philadelphia, USA.

## Tourism

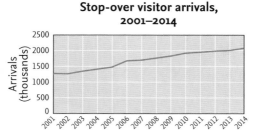

**Stop-over visitor arrivals, 2001–2014**

**Stop-over visitor arrivals by country of origin, 2014**

- USA — 62%
- Canada — 20%
- UK — 9%
- Caribbean — 3%
- Rest of the world — 6%

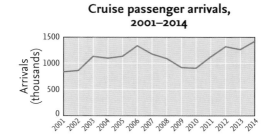

**Cruise passenger arrivals, 2001–2014**

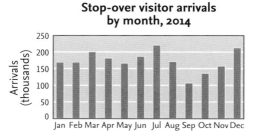

**Stop-over visitor arrivals by month, 2014**

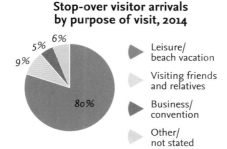

**Stop-over visitor arrivals by purpose of visit, 2014**

- Leisure/ beach vacation — 80%
- Visiting friends and relatives — 9%
- Business/ convention — 5%
- Other/ not stated — 6%

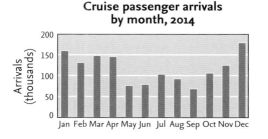

**Cruise passenger arrivals by month, 2014**

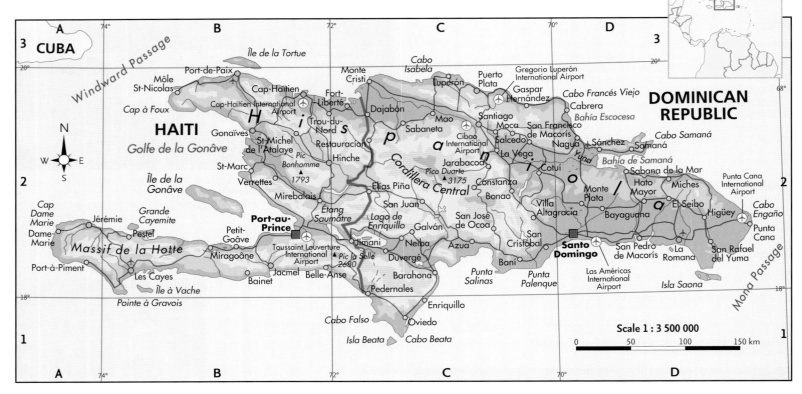

## Features

**Palais Sans-Souci**
**Citadelle Laferrière**
**Fortifié des Ramiers**

**Cathédrale Notre Dame de Cap-Haïtien**

**Parque Nacional Monte Cristi**

**Puerta Plata:**
Museo del Ambar
Pico Isabel de Torres
Fortaleza San Felipe

**Santiago:**
Centro León
Museo Folklórico
Museo del Tabaco
Monumento a los Héroes de la Restauración

**Port-au-Prince:**
Musee du Pantheon National Haïtien (MUPANAH)
Palais National
Musée d'Art Haïtien
Marche de Fer

Musée de Guahaba

Damajagua Cascades

Parque Nacional Armando Bermúdez

El Sendero del Cacao

Playa Bonita
Salto El Limón

Parque Nacional Los Haitises

Playa Baváro

Musée Ogier-Fombrun

Salto de Jimenoa

Cueva de las Maravillas

Parc National Pic Macaya

Kokoye Plage

Fort Jacques

Parque Nacional Valle Nuevo

Grotte Marie-Jeanne

Bassin-Bleu

Parc National La Visite

Parque Nacional Jaragua

Parque Nacional Sierra de Bahoruco

Parque Nacional José del Carmen Ramírez

Altos de Chavón

Parque Nacional del Este

**Santo Domingo:**
Zona Colonial
Faro a Colón (Columbus Lighthouse)
Jardin Botánico Nacional
Parque Zoológico Nacional

⬤ National park
★ Point of interest
◻ Major resort
✈ Main airport
⚓ Port
🚢 Cruise ships
⚓ Major marina
🐟 Fishing port

Scale 1 : 6 000 000

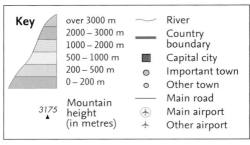

| Key | | |
|---|---|---|
| | over 3000 m | ⌒ River |
| | 2000 – 3000 m | Country boundary |
| | 1000 – 2000 m | |
| | 500 – 1000 m | ◼ Capital city |
| | 200 – 500 m | ◉ Important town |
| | 0 – 200 m | ○ Other town |
| | | Main road |
| 3175 ▲ | Mountain height (in metres) | ✈ Main airport |
| | | ✈ Other airport |

### Average rainfall

**Port-au-Prince**

### Average rainfall

**Santo Domingo**

## HAITI

**Population** *(2013 est.)* 10 320 000
**Capital city** Port-au-Prince
**Area** 27 750 sq km
**Languages** French, creole
**National flower** Hibiscus
**National bird** Hispaniolan Trogon

First sighted by Columbus, who thought he had reached India, on his first voyage in **1492**

The original inhabitants were the Taino who died out mainly from disease in the next 100 years

Initially part of the larger Spanish colony of Hispaniola, the whole island was ceded to France in **1625**. In **1697** Hispaniola became a French colony called Saint-Domingue

The French created a sugar plantation economy for their new colony

In **1804** the Haitian Revolution (began **1791**) created the Republic of Haiti, the first independent country in the Caribbean

From **1915** until **1934** the country was occupied by the United States

On 12 January **2010** a major earthquake destroyed much of the capital Port-au-Prince and killed an estimated 100 000 people

## DOMINICAN REPUBLIC

**Population** *(2010)* 9 445 281
**Capital city** Santo Domingo
**Area** 48 442 sq km
**Languages** Spanish, creole
**National flower** Bayahibe Rose
**National bird** Palm Chat

First sighted by Columbus on his first voyage in **1492**

The original inhabitants were the Taino who died out mainly from disease in the next 100 years

The colony of Hispaniola remained Spanish until the French took over in **1625**

French rule continued after the Haitian revolution until **1809** when the present Dominican Republic's boundaries were established

The Dominican Republic, part of Saint-Domingue, again became Spanish, until **1821**, when it was occupied by Haiti, and the whole island became Haitian until **1844**

The modern Dominican Republic was created as an independent country on 27 February **1844** (independence from Haiti), but was commonly called Santo Domingo

From **1861** until 16 August **1865** the Dominican Republic was again a Spanish colony, so there are two independence days (independence from Spain)

Street sellers are often the main sellers of food in Haiti.

Spanish historic remains in Santo Domingo.

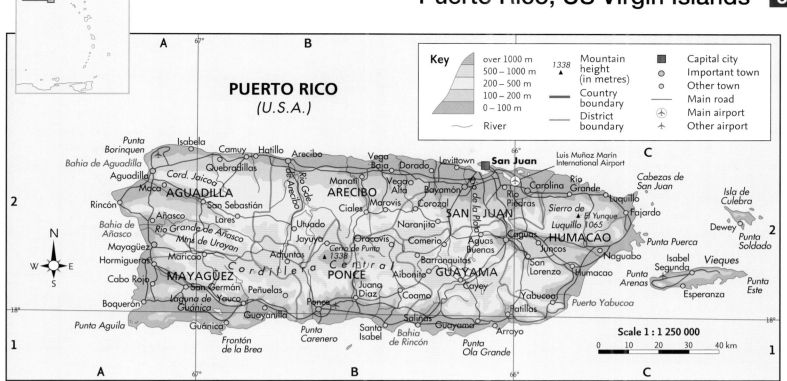

## PUERTO RICO (U.S.A.)

**Key**

| | |
|---|---|
| over 1000 m | |
| 500 – 1000 m | |
| 200 – 500 m | |
| 100 – 200 m | |
| 0 – 100 m | |

*1338* ▲ Mountain height (in metres)
— Country boundary
— District boundary
~ River

■ Capital city
◉ Important town
○ Other town
— Main road
⊕ Main airport
✈ Other airport

Scale 1 : 1 250 000

0　10　20　30　40 km

*(map labels:)* Punta Borinquen, Isabela, Camuy, Hatillo, Arecibo, Vega Baja, Dorado, Levittown, **San Juan**, Luis Muñoz Marín International Airport, Cabezas de San Juan, Bahia de Aguadilla, Aguadilla, Quebradillas, Cord. Jaicoa, Manati, Vega Alta, Bayamón, Corozal, Carolina, Río Grande, Luquillo, Isla de Culebra, Moca, AGUADILLA, San Sebastián, ARECIBO, Marovis, SAN JUAN, Río Piedras, Sierro de, El Yunque, Luquillo 1065, Fajardo, Dewey, Rincón, Añasco, Lares, Ciales, Naranjito, Comerio, Aguas Buenas, Caguas, HUMACAO, Naguabo, Isabel Segunda, Vieques, Punta Soldado, Bahia de Añasco, Rio Grande de Añasco, Mtns de Uroyan, Utuado, Jayuya, Oracovis, Cerro de Punta ▲ 1338, Cordillera Central, San Lorenzo, Juncos, Humacao, Punta Puerca, Mayagüez, Maricao, Adjuntas, PONCE, Barranquitas, Aibonite, GUAYAMA, Cayey, Punta Arenas, Esperanza, Punta Este, Hormigueras, MAYAGÜEZ, San Germán, Peñuelas, Juana Diaz, Coamo, Yabucoa, Puerto Yabucoa, Cabo Rojo, Laguna de Guánica, Yauco, Ponce, Salinas, Guayama, Arroyo, Boquerón, Guayanilla, Guánica, Punta Carenero, Santa Isabel, Bahia de Rincón, Patillas, Punta Aguila, Frontón de la Brea, Guánica, Punta Ola Grande

C　Scale 1 : 1 250 000

## Features

● National park
★ Point of interest
□ Major resort
⊕ Main airport
⊕ Port
⚓ Cruise ships
⚓ Major marina

Faro de Punta Higuero, Bosque Estatal de Guajataca, Arecibo Radio Telescope Observatory, Arecibo Lighthouse and Historical Park, Cueva del Indio, Museo del Café, Jardín Botánico y Cultural de Caguas, Reserva Natural de las Cabezas de San Juan, Culebra National Wildlife Refuge, Parque de las Cavernas del Río Camuy, Zoologico, Centro Ceremonial Indígena de Tibes, Reserve Natural de Humacao, El Yunque National Forest, Vieques National Wildlife Refuge, Reserve Natural Laguna de Joyuda, Hacienda Buena Vista, Fortín Conde de Mirasol, Bosque Estatal de Guánica

Scale 1 : 2 500 000

**San Juan:**
San Juan National Historic Site:
La Fortaleza; Castillo San Cristóbal; Castillo San Felipe del Morro
Catedral San Juan Bautista
Museo de Arte de Puerto Rico
Museo de Las Americas

**Ponce:** Museo de Arte de Ponce;
Parque de Bombas; Museo de la Historia de Ponce;
Museo de la Música Puertorriqueña

## PUERTO RICO

*United States Commonwealth*

| | |
|---|---|
| **Population** (2010) | 3 725 789 |
| **Capital city** | San Juan |
| **Area** | 9104 sq km |
| **Languages** | Spanish, English |
| **National flower** | Flor de Maga |
| **National bird** | Stripe-headed Tanager |
| **National animal** | Coqui Frog |

First sighted by Columbus on his second voyage in **1493**

The original inhabitants were the Taino who died out mainly from disease in the next 100 years

Puerto Rico remained a Spanish colony until **1898**

In **1898** Puerto Rico was invaded by the USA and became a US possession

In **1952** the island became self-governing under its own constitution, but remains an unincorporated US territory

### Average rainfall

**San Juan**

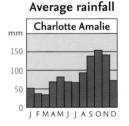

mm
150
100
50
0
J F M A M J J A S O N D

### Average rainfall

**Charlotte Amalie**

mm
150
100
50
0
J F M A M J J A S O N D

### Features

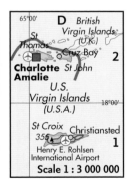

D British Virgin Islands (U.K.), St Thomas, Cruz Bay, **Charlotte Amalie**, St John, U.S. Virgin Islands (U.S.A.), St Croix, Christiansted, Henry E. Rohlsen International Airport

Scale 1 : 3 000 000

E 65°00', St Thomas, **Charlotte Amalie**, British Virgin Islands (U.K.), 18°20', Cyril E. King International Airport, Cruz Bay, St John, U.S. Virgin Islands (U.S.A.), 18°20'

Scale 1 : 700 000

0　5　10 km

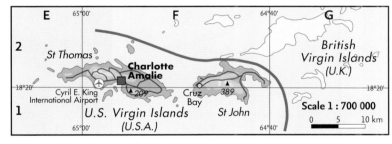

Coral World Ocean Park
St Peter Greathouse and Botanical Gardens
Trunk Bay Beach
Virgin Islands National Park
**Charlotte Amalie:**
Blackbeard's Castle
Fort Christian
St Thomas Synagogue
Frederick Lutheran Church
Buck Island National Wildlife Refuge
Salt River Bay National Historic Park and Ecological Preserve
Buck Island Reef National Monument
Frederiksted Historic District: Fort Frederik
Christiansted National Historic Site: Fort Christiansvaern
Steeple Building
Danish Custom House
Sandy Point National Wildlife Refuge
Cruzan Rum Distillery

Scale 1 : 2 000 000

## U.S. VIRGIN ISLANDS

*United States Unincorporated Territory*

| | |
|---|---|
| **Population** (2010) | 106 405 |
| **Capital city** | Charlotte Amalie |
| **Area** | 347 sq km |
| **Languages** | English, Spanish |
| **National flower** | Yellow Cedar |
| **National bird** | Bananaquit |

First sighted and named by Columbus on his second voyage in **1493**

The Taino (Arawaks and Caribs) were the original inhabitants

Spain and France at times colonized the islands, but permanent settlement only came when the Danish settled in St Thomas in **1672**, followed by St John in **1694**. Denmark also bought St Croix from the French in **1733**. From **1754** the islands were officially Royal Danish colonies with sugar plantations

Denmark sold the islands to the United States which took possession on 31 March **1917**, now known as Transfer Day, a public holiday

The busy harbour of San Juan with the skyline of the city across the bay.

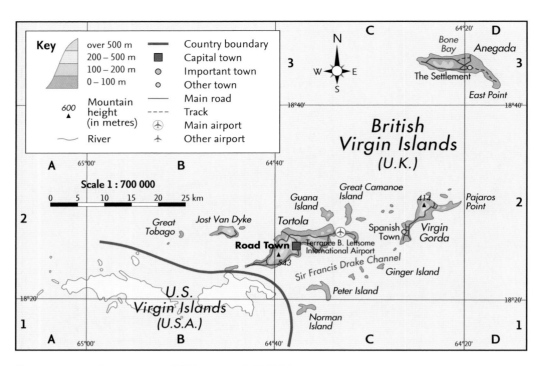

**Key**

- over 500 m
- 200 – 500 m
- 100 – 200 m
- 0 – 100 m

▲ 600 Mountain height (in metres)

～ River

━ Country boundary
■ Capital town
◉ Important town
○ Other town
— Main road
--- Track
✈ Main airport
✈ Other airport

**British Virgin Islands (U.K.)**

Bone Bay
Anegada
The Settlement
East Point

Scale 1 : 700 000
0 5 10 15 20 25 km

Great Camanoe Island
Guana Island
Jost Van Dyke
Great Tobago
Tortola
Spanish Town
Virgin Gorda
Pajaros Point
414▲
Road Town
Terrance B. Lettsome International Airport
543▲
Sir Francis Drake Channel
Ginger Island

**U.S. Virgin Islands (U.S.A.)**

Peter Island
Norman Island

**Features**

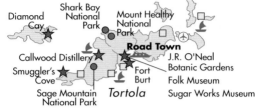

- ● National park
- ★ Point of interest
- □ Major resort
- ⊕ Main airport
- ⊕ Port
- 🚢 Cruise ships
- ⚓ Major marina

Scale 1 : 500 000

Diamond Cay
Shark Bay National Park
Mount Healthy National Park
Road Town
Callwood Distillery
J.R. O'Neal Botanic Gardens
Smuggler's Cove
Fort Burt
Folk Museum
Sage Mountain National Park
**Tortola**
Sugar Works Museum

Shoal Bay-Island Harbour Marine Park
Shoal Bay East
Heritage Collection Museum
Little Bay Marine Park
The Valley
Wallblake Historic House
**Anguilla**
Meads Bay
Rendezvous Bay

National Nature Reserve
St-Martin
Baie Orientale
**Marigot**
Fort Louis
Loterie Farm
St-Martin's Museum
St Maarten Zoo and Botanical Park
Mullet Beach
Fort Amsterdam
**Philipsburg**
**Sint Maarten**
St Maarten Museum
The Courthouse

**Anguilla (U.K.)**

Scale 1 : 300 000
0 2 4 6 8 10 km

Scrub Island
Windward Point
Island Harbour
Shoal Bay
Savannah Bay
Flat Cap Point
North Side 59▲
Stoney Ground
East End
The Valley
Crocus Bay
North Hill
Sandy Hill Bay
Road Bay
Sandy Ground
The Quarter
Clayton J. Lloyd International Airport
Long Bay
South Hill 49▲
West End
Blowing Point
Rendezvous Bay

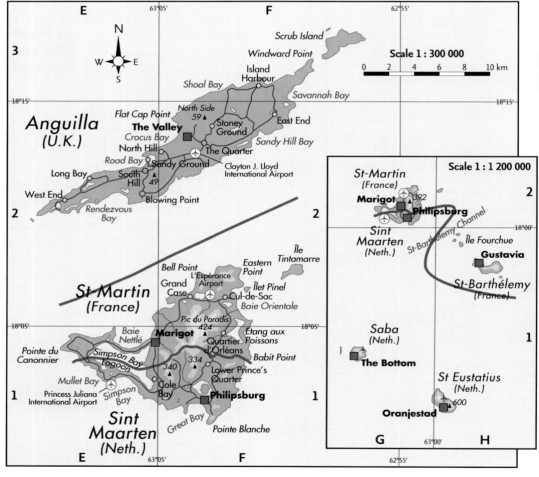

**St-Martin (France)**

Île Tintamarre
Bell Point
Eastern Point
L'Espérance Airport
Grand Case
Îlet Pinel
Cul-de-Sac
Baie Orientale
Pic du Paradis 424▲
**Marigot**
Quartier d'Orléans
Étang aux Poissons
Babit Point
Baie Nettlé
334▲
Pointe du Canonnier
Simpson Bay Lagoon
340▲
Lower Prince's Quarter
Mullet Bay
Cole Bay
Princess Juliana International Airport
Simpson Bay
**Philipsburg**
**Sint Maarten (Neth.)**
Great Bay
Pointe Blanche

Scale 1 : 1 200 000

**St-Martin (France)**
**Marigot**
392▲
**Philipsburg**
**Sint Maarten (Neth.)**
St-Barthélemy Channel
Île Fourchue
**Gustavia**
**St-Barthélemy (France)**
Saba (Neth.)
**The Bottom**
St Eustatius (Neth.)
600▲
**Oranjestad**

Saba can be seen from Fort Oranje on St Eustatius. Both islands have a volcanic origin.

| |  **BRITISH VIRGIN ISLANDS** |  **ANGUILLA** |  **ST-MARTIN** |  **SINT MAARTEN** |  **SABA** |  **ST EUSTATIUS** | **ST-BARTHÉLEMY** |
|---|---|---|---|---|---|---|---|
| | British Overseas Territory | British Overseas Territory | French Overseas Collectivity | Self-governing Netherlands Territory | Netherlands Special Municipality | Netherlands Special Municipality | French Overseas Collectivity |
| **Population** | 28 054 (2010) | 13 037 (2011) | 36 286 (2011) | 33 609 (2011) | 1971 (2014 est.) | 3791 (2014 est.) | 9072 (2010) |
| **Capital town** | Road Town | The Valley | Marigot | Philipsburg | The Bottom | Oranjestad | Gustavia |
| **Area** | 153 sq km | 91 sq km | 54 sq km | 34 sq km | 13 sq km | 21 sq km | 21 sq km |
| **Languages** | English | English | French | Dutch, English | Dutch, English | Dutch, English | French |
| **National flower** | White Cedar Flower | White Cedar | Hibiscus | Orange-yellow Sage | Black-eyed Susan | Morning Glory | Lily |
| **National bird** | Zenaida Dove | Zenaida Dove | Brown Pelican | Brown Pelican | Audubon's Shearwater | Nahamaya | - |

## Economic activity

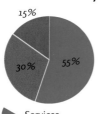

15%
30%
55%

▶ Services
▶ Agriculture, fishing and forestry
▶ Manufacturing

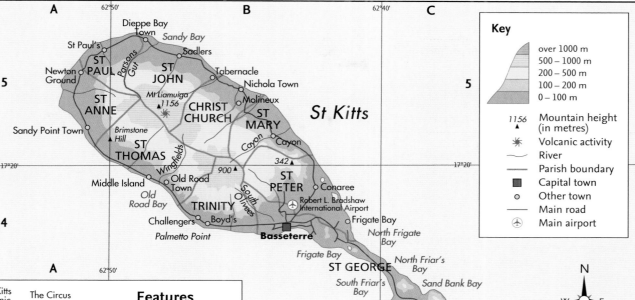

### St Kitts

A — 62°50'
B — 62°40'
C

Dieppe Bay Town
St Paul's
Sandy Bay
Sadlers
Newton Ground
ST PAUL
ST JOHN
Tabernacle
Nichola Town
ST ANNE
Mt Liamuiga ▲1156
Molineux
ST MARY
Sandy Point Town
Brimstone Hill ▲
CHRIST CHURCH
Cayon
Cayon
Middle Island
Wingfields
ST THOMAS
Old Road Town
900 ▲
342 ▲
ST PETER
Conaree
Old Road Bay
TRINITY
South Olives
Robert L. Bradshaw International Airport
Frigate Bay
Challengers
Boyd's
North Frigate Bay
Palmetto Point
**Basseterre**
ST GEORGE
Frigate Bay
North Friar's Bay
South Friar's Bay
Sand Bank Bay
319 ▲
Great Salt Pond
Scotch Bonnet
Major's Bay
Nag's Head
The Narrows

**Key**

over 1000 m
500 – 1000 m
200 – 500 m
100 – 200 m
0 – 100 m

1156 ▲ Mountain height (in metres)
✳ Volcanic activity
〜 River
— Parish boundary
■ Capital town
○ Other town
— Main road
✈ Main airport

### ST KITTS AND NEVIS

**Scale 1 : 250 000**
0 2 4 6 8 km

### Nevis

Vance W. Amory International Airport
Newcastle
ST JAMES
Brick Kiln
Cotton Ground
Fountain Ghut
Butlers
Pinneys Beach
ST THOMAS
Nevis Peak ▲985
Charlestown
ST PAUL
ST GEORGE
Gingerland
Fig Tree
Saddle Hill ▲381
Red Cliff
ST JOHN
Grande Ghut

---

### Features

St Kitts Scenic Railway
St Kitts Eco-Park
Mount Liamuiga
Fort Charles
Romney Manor
The Circus
National Museum / Old Treasury Building
Palms Court Gardens
Sugar Factory Museum
Brimstone Hill Fortress National Park
Clay Villa Plantation House and Gardens
Fairview Great House and Botanical Gardens
Cockleshell Beach
**Basseterre**

● National park
★ Point of interest
□ Major resort
✈ Main airport
⚓ Port
🚢 Cruise ships
⚓ Major marina
🐟 Fishing port

Scale 1 : 500 000

**Charlestown:**
Museum of Nevis History / Alexander Hamilton House
Horatio Nelson Museum
Government House

Pinneys Beach
Botanical Gardens of Nevis
Bath Hotel and Spring House
Montpelier House

---

## ST KITTS AND NEVIS

**Population** (2014 est.) 54 940
**Capital town** Basseterre
**Area** (St Kitts) 168 sq km
**Area** (Nevis) 93 sq km
**Languages** English, creole
**National flower** Flamboyant
**National bird** Brown Pelican

First sighted by Columbus **1493**

Occupied by Arawaks and later Caribs

Jointly settled by English in **1623** and French in **1625**

Alternately occupied by English and French until became British in **1783**

A sugar colony into the **20th** century. Sugar cultivation ended in **2005**

## Average rainfall

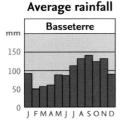

**Basseterre**
mm
150
100
50
0
J F M A M J J A S O N D

---

## MONTSERRAT

*British Overseas Territory*

**Population** (2011) 4922
**Capital town** Brades
**Area** 102 sq km
**Languages** English
**National flower** Heliconia
**National bird** Montserrat Oriole

First sighted by Columbus **1493**

Occupied by Irish settlers **1632**

Sugar, and later lime, plantations were established, but none exist today

In **1995** the Soufrière Hills volcano erupted. Ultimately the town of Plymouth was buried and two thirds of the island was abandoned

The island remains a British Overseas Territory

### Features

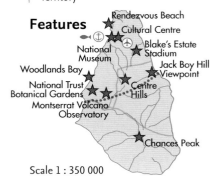

Rendezvous Beach
Cultural Centre
National Museum
Blake's Estate Stadium
Woodlands Bay
Jack Boy Hill Viewpoint
National Trust Botanical Gardens
Centre Hills
Montserrat Volcano Observatory
Chances Peak

Scale 1 : 350 000

---

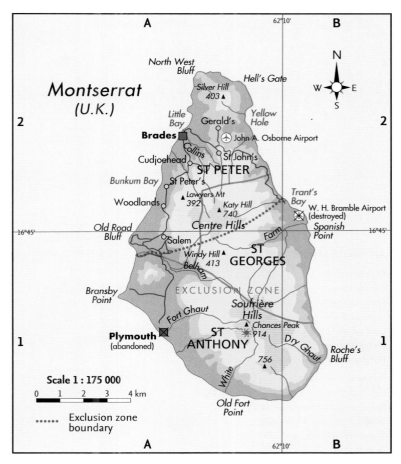

### Montserrat (U.K.)

A — 62°10'
B

North West Bluff
Hell's Gate
Silver Hill ▲403
Little Bay
Gerald's
Yellow Hole
**Brades** ■
John A. Osborne Airport
Collins
St John's
Cudjoehead
ST PETER
Bunkum Bay
St Peter's
Trant's Bay
W. H. Bramble Airport (destroyed) ✈
Woodlands
Lawyers Mt ▲392
Katy Hill ▲740
Spanish Point
Old Road Bluff
Centre Hills
Farm
Salem
Windy Hill ▲413
ST GEORGES
Belham
Bransby Point
EXCLUSION ZONE
Soufrière Hills
Fort Ghaut
Chances Peak ▲914
Dry Ghaut
**Plymouth** (abandoned) ✈
ST ANTHONY
Roche's Bluff
756 ▲
White
Old Fort Point

**Scale 1 : 175 000**
0 1 2 3 4 km

······ Exclusion zone boundary

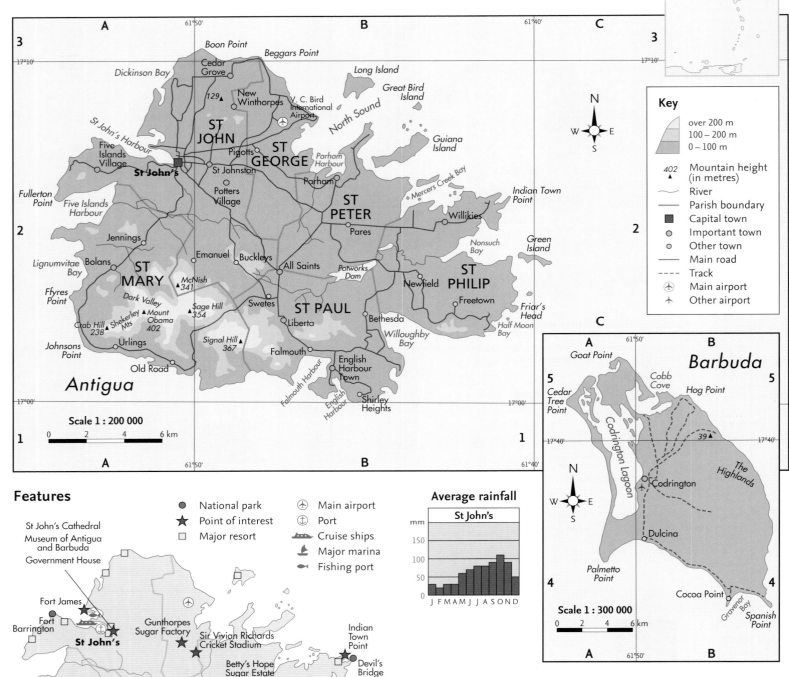

## Antigua

**Scale 1 : 200 000**

0   2   4   6 km

**Key**

over 200 m
100 – 200 m
0 – 100 m

402 ▲ Mountain height (in metres)
— River
— Parish boundary
■ Capital town
◉ Important town
○ Other town
— Main road
--- Track
✈ Main airport
✈ Other airport

### Barbuda

**Scale 1 : 300 000**

0   2   4   6 km

## Features

● National park
★ Point of interest
□ Major resort
✈ Main airport
⚓ Port
🚢 Cruise ships
⛵ Major marina
🐟 Fishing port

Scale 1 : 275 000

### Average rainfall

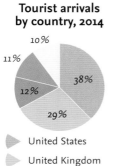

St John's

mm
150
100
50
0
J F M A M J J A S O N D

### ANTIGUA AND BARBUDA

| | |
|---|---|
| **Population** (2011) | 81 799 |
| **Capital town** | St John's |
| **Area** (Antigua) | 281 sq km |
| **Area** (Barbuda) | 161 sq km |
| **Languages** | English, creole |
| **National flower** | Dagger Log |
| **National bird** | Magnificent Frigatebird |

Prehistoric inhabitants: Arawaks then Caribs
First sighted and named by Columbus **1493**
British sugar colony **1632–1981**
British naval base **1725–1889**
Sugar cultivation ceased **1971**
Independent 1 November **1981**

### Tourist arrivals by country, 2014

10 %
11 %
12 %
38 %
29 %

▸ United States
▸ United Kingdom
▸ Caribbean
▸ Canada
▸ Other

Nelson's Dockyard was the Royal Navy's naval base in the Caribbean for over 100 years. It is now a national park and includes a dockyard museum and an active yacht club and marina.

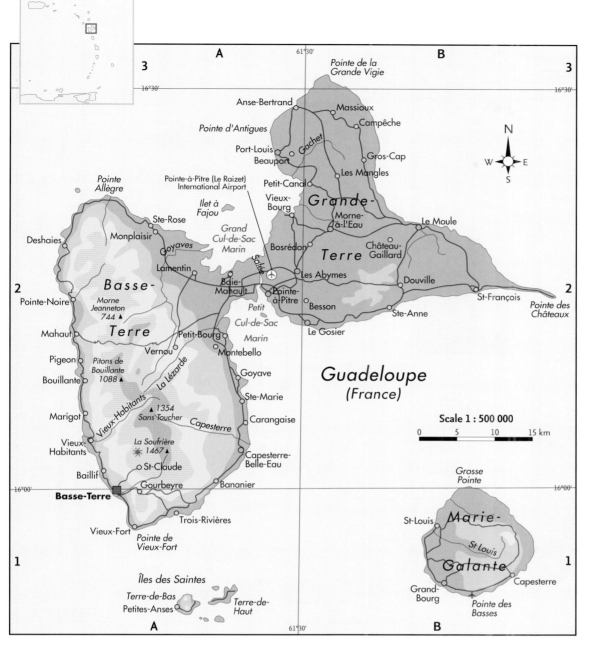

**Scale 1 : 500 000**

0   5   10   15 km

**GUADELOUPE**

*Department of France*

| | |
|---|---|
| **Population** (2014 est.) | 403 750 |
| **Capital town** | Basse-Terre |
| **Area** | 1780 sq km |
| **Languages** | French, creole |
| **National flower** | Lily |
| **National bird** | Gallic Rooster |

Original inhabitants: Caribs

First sighted and named by Columbus **1493**

Occupied by the French **1635**

Annexed by France **1674**

Became a major French sugar colony, but occupied by the British at times in the **17th** century

In **1946** became a department (an integral part) of France, and therefore is part of the European Union

Sugar is still exported, along with bananas

## Key

| | |
|---|---|
| | over 1000 m |
| | 500 – 1000 m |
| | 200 – 500 m |
| | 100 – 200 m |
| | 0 – 100 m |
| 1467 ▲ | Mountain height (in metres) |
| ✳ | Volcanic activity |
| ∿ | River |
| ■ | Capital town |
| ⊙ | Important town |
| ○ | Other town |
| — | Main road |
| ✈ | Main airport |
| ✈ | Other airport |

## Features

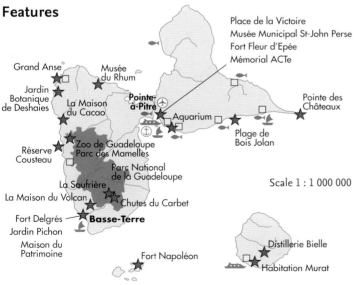

Place de la Victoire
Musée Municipal St-John Perse
Fort Fleur d'Epée
Mémorial ACTe

Scale 1 : 1 000 000

| | |
|---|---|
| ⬤ | National park |
| ★ | Point of interest |
| □ | Major resort |
| ✈ | Main airport |
| ⊕ | Port |
| ⚓ | Cruise ships |
| ⛵ | Major marina |
| 🐟 | Fishing port |

### Average rainfall

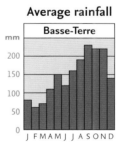

Basse-Terre

mm — 200, 150, 100, 50, 0 — J F M A M J J A S O N D

### Economic activity

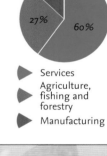

13%
27%
60%

▶ Services
▶ Agriculture, fishing and forestry
▶ Manufacturing

Although Basse-Terre is the capital of Guadeloupe, Pointe-à-Pitre is the largest city, commercial capital, and the main port. Its population is over 132 000, compared with less than 40 000 for Basse-Terre.

### Traditional dishes

- *Matete* – a hot crab curry
- *Colombo* – a curry made with chicken or cabri (goat)
- *Callaloo* – a soup made with bacon and leafy greens
- *Bébélé* – a tripe soup with dumplings and green bananas
- *Blaff* – seafood cooked in a seasoned soup
- *Accras* – cod or vegetable fritters
- *Ouassou* – large freshwater shrimp

Chicken Colombo, one of the traditional dishes of Guadeloupe.

## DOMINICA

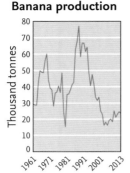

| | |
|---|---|
| **Population** (2011) | 71 293 |
| **Capital town** | Roseau |
| **Area** | 750 sq km |
| **Languages** | English, creole |
| **National flower** | Carib Wood |
| **National bird** | Imperial Parrot (Sisserou) |

Prehistoric inhabitants: Arawaks followed by Caribs

First sighted and named by Columbus **1493**

Some minor Spanish attempts at settlement resisted by the Caribs in **16th** and **17th** centuries

Colonised by the French as a sugar colony **1690–1763**

British colony **1763–1978**

Occupied by the French **1778–1783**

The sugar plantations were replaced by bananas in the **1960s**

Became independent 3 November **1978** and declared itself a Republic with a President

### Banana production

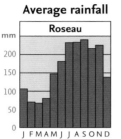

### Average rainfall

Roseau

### Features

- 🔴 National park
- ⭐ Point of interest
- ◻ Major resort
- ✈ Main airport
- ⚓ Port
- 🚢 Cruise ships
- ⚓ Major marina
- 🐟 Fishing port
- 🔵 Carib Territory

Cabrits National Park
Fort Shirley
Batibou Beach
Morne Diablotins National Park
Kalinago Barana Autê (Culture Village)
Coconut Products Factory
Morne Trois Pitons National Park
Middleham Falls
Trafalgar Falls
**Roseau**
Museum of Rum
Boiling Lake
Victoria Falls
Botanical Gardens
Morne Bruce
Champagne Beach and Reef
Dominica Museum
Bois Cotlette Estate
Government House

Scale 1 : 600 000

### Key

| | |
|---|---|
| | over 1000 m |
| | 500 – 1000 m |
| | 200 – 500 m |
| | 100 – 200 m |
| | 0 – 100 m |
| ▲ 1447 | Mountain height (in metres) |
| ✳ | Volcanic activity |
| ∿ | River |
| ↯ | Waterfall |
| | Parish boundary |
| ◼ | Capital town |
| ⊙ | Important town |
| ○ | Other town |
| | Main road |
| ✈ | Main airport |

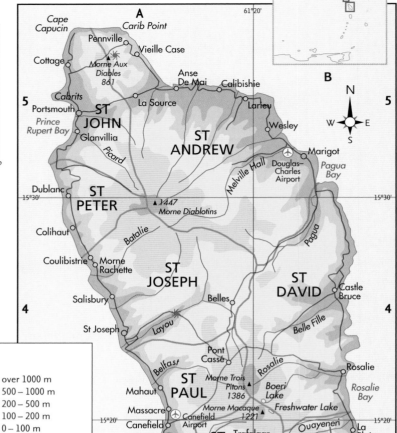

**DOMINICA**

Scale 1 : 300 000
0  2  4  6 km

## MARTINIQUE

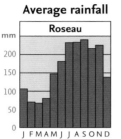

*Department of France*

| | |
|---|---|
| **Population** (2014 est.) | 381 326 |
| **Capital town** | Fort-de-France |
| **Area** | 1079 sq km |
| **Languages** | French, creole |
| **National flower** | Lily |
| **National bird** | Gallic Rooster |

Prehistoric inhabitants: Arawaks followed by Caribs

First sighted and named by Columbus **1493**, visited and named by him in **1502** ('Martinica')

Settled by the French from St Kitts **1635**

The French conquered the Caribs and the survivors fled to Dominica

Mainly occupied by the British **1794–1815**

In **1946** became a department of France

Montagne Pelée
Distillerie J M
Les Gorges de la Falaise
La Maison Regionale des Volcans
Le Figuier
Musée Gauguin
Musée Volcanologique
Jardin de Balata
Presqu'île de la Caravelle
Fort St-Louis
**Fort-de-France**
Habitation Clement
La Savane
Cathédrale St-Louis
Bibliothèque Schoelcher
Musée de la Pagerie
Musée Regional d'Histoire et d'Ethnographie
Le Diamant
Les Salines

Scale 1 : 1 000 000

### Montagne Pelée

- This active volcano exploded on 2 May 1902
- About 30 000 persons were killed
- The town of St-Pierre, capital of Martinique, was destroyed
- The capital was later moved to Fort-de-France, far from the volcano
- The nature of the explosion was an incandescent gas cloud known as a Nuée Ardente, which incinerated everything in its path
- Only two persons survived, one in a dungeon and one on a ship

St-Pierre, at the foot of Montagne Pelée.

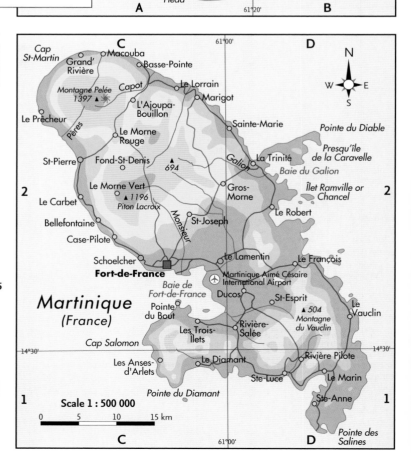

*Martinique*
*(France)*

Scale 1 : 500 000
0  5  10  15 km

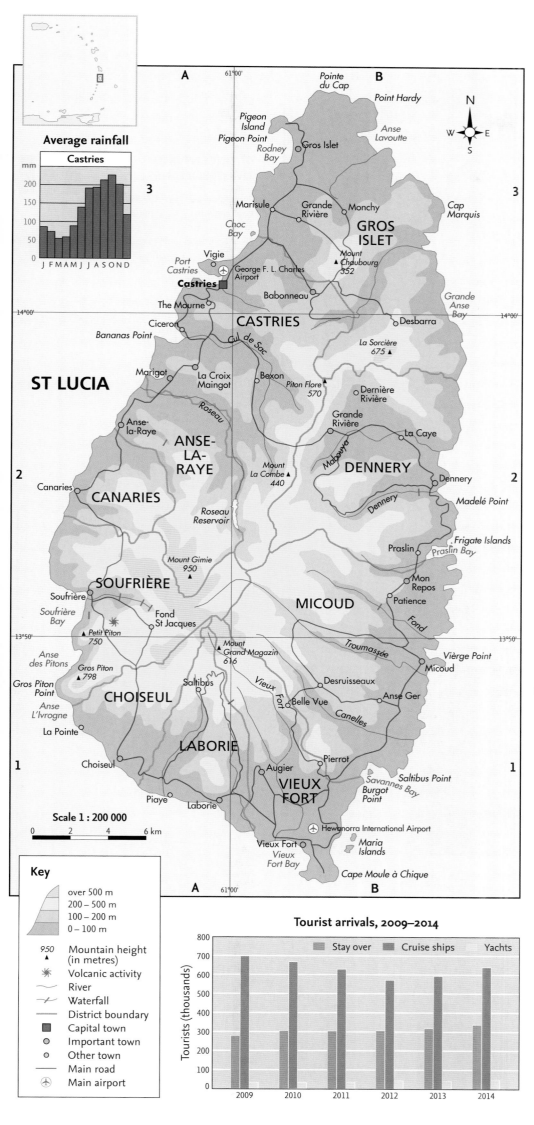

## Average rainfall

**Castries**

mm
200
150
100
50
0
J F M A M J J A S O N D

**ST LUCIA**

A  B

*Pointe du Cap*
*Point Hardy*
*Pigeon Island*
*Pigeon Point*
*Anse Lavoutte*
*Rodney Bay*
Gros Islet
3
N
W        E
S
Marisule
Grande Rivière
Monchy
*Cap Marquis*
*Choc Bay*
Vigie
**GROS ISLET**
▲ Mount Chaubourg 352
*Port Castries*
George F. L. Charles Airport
**Castries** ■
Babonneau
*Grande Anse Bay*
The Mourne
**CASTRIES**
Desbarra
Ciceron
*Bananas Point*
*La Sorcière 675* ▲
Marigot
La Croix Maingot
Bexon
Piton Flore 570 ▲
Dernière Rivière
*Roseau*
Grande Rivière
Anse-la-Raye
**ANSE-LA-RAYE**
La Caye
*Mabouya*
Canaries
**CANARIES**
Mount La Combe ▲ 440
**DENNERY**
Dennery
*Madelé Point*
*Roseau Reservoir*
*Dennery*
Mount Gimie 950 ▲
*Frigate Islands*
Praslin
*Praslin Bay*
**SOUFRIÈRE**
Soufrière
Fond St Jacques
**MICOUD**
Mon Repos
Patience
*Soufrière Bay*
▲ Petit Piton 750
Mount Grand Magazin 616
*Fond*
*Anse des Pitons*
Gros Piton 798 ▲
Saltibus
*Troumassée*
Vièrge Point
*Gros Piton Point*
Desruisseaux
Micoud
*Anse L'Ivrogne*
**CHOISEUL**
*Vieux Fort*
Belle Vue
Anse Ger
La Pointe
*Canelles*
**LABORIE**
Pierrot
Choiseul
Augier
*Savannes Bay*
*Saltibus Point*
*Burgot Point*
Piaye
Laborie
**VIEUX FORT**
Hewanorra International Airport
Vieux Fort
*Vieux Fort Bay*
*Maria Islands*
*Cape Moule à Chique*

Scale 1 : 200 000
0    2    4    6 km

14°00'
13°50'
61°00'

## Key

over 500 m
200 – 500 m
100 – 200 m
0 – 100 m

950 ▲ Mountain height (in metres)
✳ Volcanic activity
〜 River
⊶ Waterfall
— District boundary
■ Capital town
● Important town
○ Other town
— Main road
✈ Main airport

---

## ST LUCIA

**Population** (2009)    173 765
**Capital town**    Castries
**Area**    617 sq km
**Languages**    English, creole
**National flower**    Rose
**National bird**    St Lucian Parrot

Prehistoric inhabitants: Arawaks followed by Caribs

First sighted and named by Columbus **1493**

Many failed attempts at settling the island were made by French, Dutch and British colonists from **1550** until **1640**

Colonised by the French as a sugar colony **1643–1803**. This period included several British occupations

British colony **1803–1979**

The sugar plantations were replaced by bananas in the **1960s**

Independent 22 February **1979**

Two St Lucians have won Nobel Prizes. The Nobel Prize for Economics was won by Sir Arthur Lewis in **1979**, and the Nobel Prize for Literature by Derek Walcott in **1992**

## Features

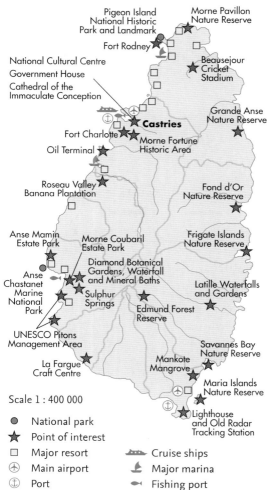

Pigeon Island National Historic Park and Landmark
Fort Rodney
Morne Pavillon Nature Reserve
National Cultural Centre
Government House
Cathedral of the Immaculate Conception
Beausejour Cricket Stadium
**Castries**
Grande Anse Nature Reserve
Fort Charlotte
Morne Fortune Historic Area
Oil Terminal
Roseau Valley Banana Plantation
Fond d'Or Nature Reserve
Anse Mamin Estate Park
Morne Coubaril Estate Park
Diamond Botanical Gardens, Waterfall and Mineral Baths
Frigate Islands Nature Reserve
Anse Chastanet Marine National Park
Latille Waterfalls and Gardens
Sulphur Springs
Edmund Forest Reserve
UNESCO Pitons Management Area
Savannes Bay Nature Reserve
La Fargue Craft Centre
Mankote Mangrove
Maria Islands Nature Reserve
Lighthouse and Old Radar Tracking Station

Scale 1 : 400 000

● National park
★ Point of interest
□ Major resort
✈ Main airport
⚓ Port
🚢 Cruise ships
⚓ Major marina
🐟 Fishing port

---

## Tourist arrivals, 2009–2014

Tourists (thousands)

■ Stay over   ■ Cruise ships   ■ Yachts

800
700
600
500
400
300
200
100
0
2009   2010   2011   2012   2013   2014

---

The *Carnival Valor* in Castries. This cruise ship can carry 3000 passengers and has a crew of over 1100.

## Key

over 1000 m
500 – 1000 m
200 – 500 m
100 – 200 m
0 – 100 m

1234 ▲ Mountain height (in metres)
☀ Volcanic activity
River
Waterfall
Parish boundary
■ Capital town
◉ Important town
○ Other town
Main road
✈ Main airport
✈ Other airport

## ST VINCENT AND THE GRENADINES

**Population** (2011)    109 991
**Capital town**    Kingstown
**Area** (St Vincent)    344 sq km
**Area** (Grenadines)    45 sq km (15 islands)
**Languages**    English, creole
**National flower**    Soufrière Tree
**National bird**    St Vincent Parrot

Prehistoric inhabitants: Caribs
First sighted and named by Columbus **1498**
Colonised by the French as a plantation colony **1719–1783**
British colony **1793–1979**
Sugar cane cultivation was replaced by bananas in the **1950s**
Soufrière volcano erupted in **1902** causing 1680 deaths
Independent 27 October **1979**

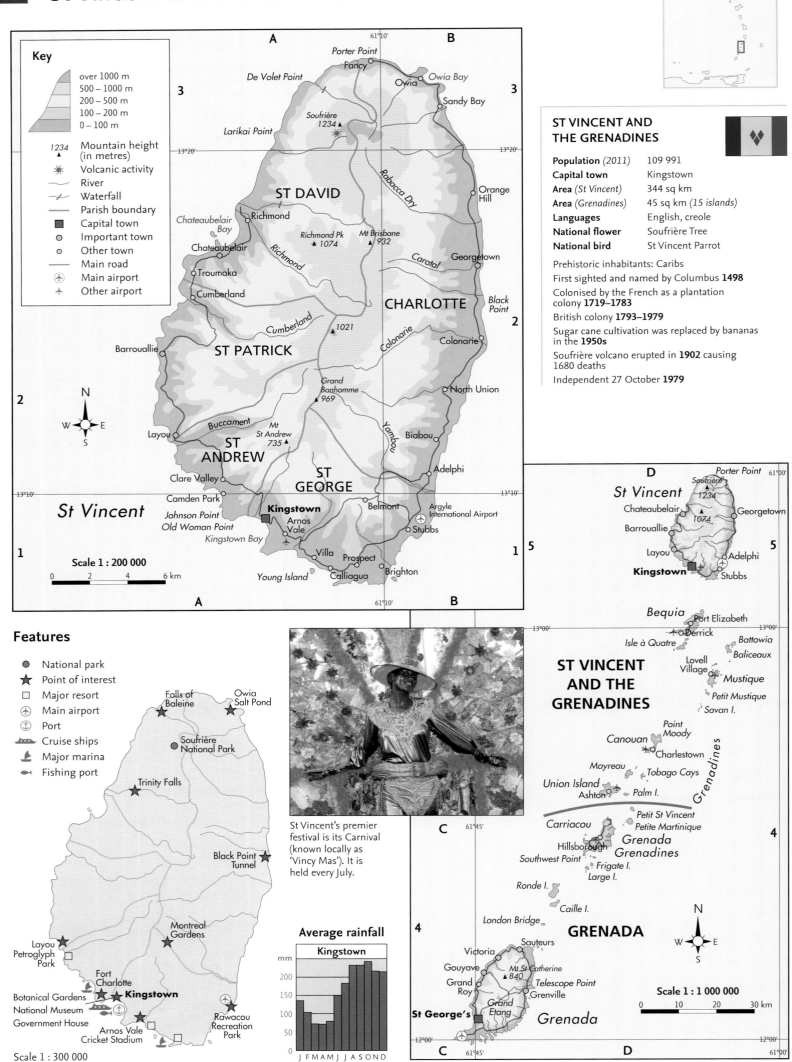

St Vincent's premier festival is its Carnival (known locally as 'Vincy Mas'). It is held every July.

## Features

◉ National park
★ Point of interest
□ Major resort
✈ Main airport
⚓ Port
🚢 Cruise ships
⚓ Major marina
🐟 Fishing port

## Average rainfall

**Kingstown**

mm
200
150
100
50
0
J F M A M J J A S O N D

Scale 1 : 200 000
0   2   4   6 km

Scale 1 : 300 000

Scale 1 : 1 000 000
0   10   20   30 km

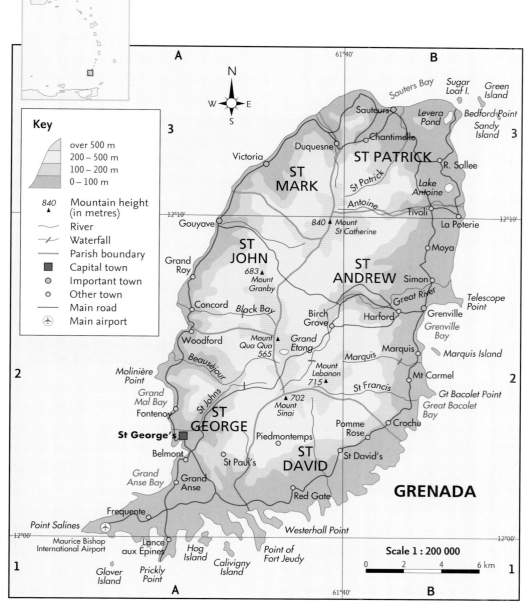

## Key

- over 500 m
- 200 – 500 m
- 100 – 200 m
- 0 – 100 m

- ▲ 840   Mountain height (in metres)
- ~~~ River
- Waterfall
- Parish boundary
- ■ Capital town
- ⦿ Important town
- ○ Other town
- Main road
- ✈ Main airport

**St Mark**, **St Patrick**, **St John**, **St Andrew**, **St George**, **St David**

Sauters Bay, Sugar Loaf I., Green Island, Sauteurs, Levera Pond, Bedford Point, Sandy Island, Chantimelle, R. Sallee, Victoria, Duquesne, St Patrick, Lake Antoine, Antoine, Gouyave, 840 ▲ Mount St Catherine, Tivoli, La Poterie, Moya, Grand Roy, 683 ▲ Mount Granby, Simon, Concord, Black Bay, Birch Grove, Harford, Great River, Grenville, Telescope Point, Woodford, Mount Qua Qua 565 ▲, Grand Etang, Grenville Bay, Beauséjour, Marquis, Marquis Island, Molinière Point, Mount Lebanon 715 ▲, St Francis, Mt Carmel, Grand Mal Bay, ▲ 702 Mount Sinai, Gt Bacolet Point, Great Bacolet Bay, St Johns, Fontenoy, Piedmontemps, Pomme Rose, Crochu, St George's, Belmont, St Paul's, St David's, Grand Anse Bay, Grand Anse, Red Gate, Westerhall Point, Frequente, Point Salines, Maurice Bishop International Airport, Lance aux Épines, Hog Island, Calivigny Island, Point of Fort Jeudy, Glover Island, Prickly Point

**GRENADA**

Scale 1 : 200 000
0   2   4   6 km

61°40', 12°10', 12°00'

### GRENADA

| | |
|---|---|
| **Population** (2011) | 103 328 |
| **Capital town** | St George's |
| **Total area** | 348 sq km |
| **Area** (Grenada) | 313 sq km |
| **Area** (Carriacou) | 33 sq km |
| **Area** (Petite Martinique) | 2 sq km |
| **Languages** | English, creole |
| **National flower** | Bougainvillea |
| **National bird** | Grenada Dove |

Prehistoric inhabitants: Caribs

First sighted and named by Columbus **1498**

Colonised by the French as a sugar colony **1649–1763**

British colony **1793–1974**

Sugar soon gave way to cocoa production and later bananas

Independent 7 February **1974**

Invaded by USA in **1983**

World renowned producer of nutmeg and other spices. Sugar cane cultivation has largely ceased and bananas are a minor crop

### Economic activity

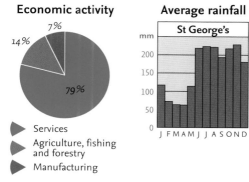

- 7%
- 14%
- 79%

▶ Services
▶ Agriculture, fishing and forestry
▶ Manufacturing

### Average rainfall

St George's

mm 200, 150, 100, 50, 0
J F M A M J J A S O N D

## Features

- ⦿ National park
- ★ Point of interest
- ☐ Major resort
- ✈ Main airport
- ⚓ Port
- 🚢 Cruise ships
- ⚓ Major marina
- 🐟 Fishing port

Caribs' Leap, Sandy Island, Levera National Park, Bathway Beach, Lake Antoine National Landmark, Belmont Estate Chocolate Factory, Rum Distillery, Gouyave Nutmeg Processing Station, Black Bay Beach, Concord Falls, Grand Etang National Park, Fort Frederick, Fort George, Fort Matthew, Government Buildings, National Cricket Stadium, Tropical Gardens, National Museum, Underwater Sculpture Park, Annandale Falls, Mt Carmel Falls (Marquis Falls), St George's, Great Anse Beach, Grooms Beach, Westerhall Estate, La Sagesse Nature Centre, Old Whaling Station

Scale 1 : 300 000

## Grenada is known as the Spice Island

- *Nutmeg and Mace* – second largest producer after Indonesia (also called 'Spice Islands'). Mace is a coating on the outside of the nutmeg
- *Cinnamon* – production has increased in recent years
- *Cloves* – production has increased in recent years
- *Ginger* – versatile root widely grown
- *Cocoa* – used locally to make cocoa tea and exported as organic dark chocolate
- *Pimento* – also known as allspice, an easily grown tree
- *Turmeric* – produced from a root, also known as saffron. Used in curries and popular for its medicinal value

Tramping through cocoa beans at the Belmont Estate to ensure they dry evenly.

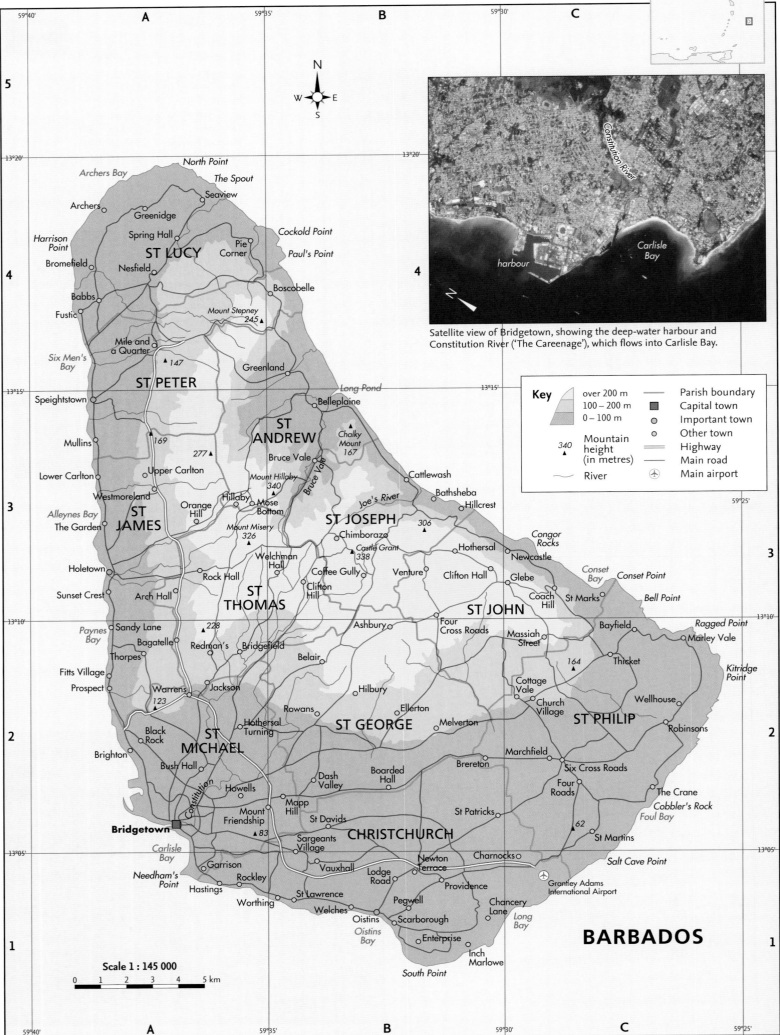

Satellite view of Bridgetown, showing the deep-water harbour and Constitution River ('The Careenage'), which flows into Carlisle Bay.

**Key**

| | |
|---|---|
| over 200 m | |
| 100 – 200 m | |
| 0 – 100 m | |
| 340 ▲ | Mountain height (in metres) |

| | |
|---|---|
| | Parish boundary |
| ■ | Capital town |
| ◉ | Important town |
| ○ | Other town |
| ═══ | Highway |
| ── | Main road |
| ✈ | Main airport |
| ∿ | River |

Scale 1 : 145 000

0  1  2  3  4  5 km

**BARBADOS**

*Parishes and places:*

ST LUCY, ST PETER, ST ANDREW, ST JAMES, ST THOMAS, ST JOSEPH, ST JOHN, ST MICHAEL, ST GEORGE, ST PHILIP, CHRISTCHURCH

Archers Bay, North Point, The Spout, Archers, Greenidge, Seaview, Spring Hall, Pie Corner, Cockold Point, Paul's Point, Harrison Point, Bromefield, Nesfield, Boscobelle, Babbs, Fustic, Mount Stepney 245 ▲, Mile and a Quarter, ▲ 147, Greenland, Six Men's Bay, Speightstown, Long Pond, Belleplaine, Mullins, 169, Chalky Mount 167 ▲, Bruce Vale, Lower Carlton, Upper Carlton, 277 ▲, Cattlewash, Mount Hillaby 340, Bathsheba, Westmoreland, Hillaby, Mose Bottom, Joe's River, Hillcrest, Alleynes Bay, Orange Hill, 306 ▲, Congor Rocks, The Garden, Mount Misery 326 ▲, Chimborazo, Hothersal, Newcastle, Holetown, Welchman Hall, Castle Grant 338 ▲, Venture, Clifton Hall, Glebe, Conset Bay, Conset Point, Sunset Crest, Rock Hall, Coffee Gully, Coach Hill, St Marks, Bell Point, Arch Hall, Clifton Hill, Four Cross Roads, Sandy Lane, 228 ▲, Ashbury, Bayfield, Ragged Point, Paynes Bay, Bagatelle, Redman's, Bridgefield, Massiah Street, Marley Vale, Thorpes, Belair, 164 ▲, Thicket, Kitridge Point, Fitts Village, Warrens, Jackson, Cottage Vale, Wellhouse, Prospect, 123 ▲, Rowans, Hilbury, Ellerton, Church Village, Black Rock, Hothersal Turning, Melverton, Robinsons, Brighton, Bush Hall, Marchfield, Howells, Dash Valley, Boarded Hall, Brereton, Six Cross Roads, Mapp Hill, St Davids, Four Roads, The Crane, Mount Friendship, 83 ▲, St Patricks, Cobbler's Rock, Foul Bay, Bridgetown, Sargeants Village, CHRISTCHURCH, Charnocks, 62 ▲, St Martins, Salt Cave Point, Carlisle Bay, Garrison, Vauxhall, Newton Terrace, Providence, Needham's Point, Rockley, Lodge Road, Grantley Adams International Airport, Hastings, Pegwell, Chancery Lane, Worthing, St Lawrence, Welches, Oistins, Scarborough, Long Bay, Oistins Bay, Enterprise, Inch Marlowe, South Point

## BARBADOS

| | |
|---|---|
| **Population** *(2010)* | 277 821 |
| **Capital town** | Bridgetown |
| **Area** | 430 sq km |
| **Languages** | English, creole |
| **National flower** | Pride of Barbados |
| **National animal** | Dolphin (the fish, also known as Mahi-mahi) |

The original inhabitants were various Amerindians (Arawaks and Caribs), the last tribe being the Kalingo (Caribs). Barbados was uninhabited when it was settled

Unlike most Caribbean islands Barbados was not first sighted by Columbus – rather, it was by unknown Spanish mariners. The first recorded visit was by the Portuguese in **1536**

From **1625** English settlers arrived and the country became, and remained, a British colony until **1966**

Initially the colony grew tobacco and cotton and other non-plantation crops

In **1640** the economy changed to one of sugar plantations

Internal self-government was granted from **1961** until independence on 30 November **1966**

The economy diversified by the **1980s** to include tourism, and sugar is no longer the main source of income

### Economic activity

6% 3%
91%

▶ Services
▶ Manufacturing
▶ Agriculture, fishing and forestry

### Average rainfall

**Bridgetown**

mm
150
100
50
0
J F M A M J J A S O N D

### Fishing industry

- Flying fish account for over half the total catch
- Flying fish and dolphin (the fish) are major restaurant dishes for the tourist industry
- Kingfish (wahoo) and shark are also popular
- Oistins and Bridgetown have the two largest fish markets
- About 6000 people are employed in the fisheries industry
- The white sea egg is a local delicacy with a fishing season limited to September through December

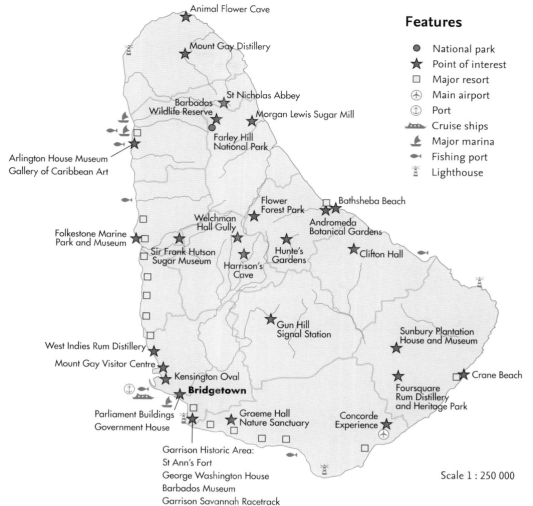

**Features**

- ● National park
- ★ Point of interest
- ☐ Major resort
- ⊕ Main airport
- ⚓ Port
- Cruise ships
- ⚓ Major marina
- Fishing port
- Lighthouse

Animal Flower Cave
Mount Gay Distillery
St Nicholas Abbey
Barbados Wildlife Reserve
Morgan Lewis Sugar Mill
Farley Hill National Park
Arlington House Museum Gallery of Caribbean Art
Flower Forest Park
Bathsheba Beach
Welchman Hall Gully
Andromeda Botanical Gardens
Folkestone Marine Park and Museum
Sir Frank Hutson Sugar Museum
Hunte's Gardens
Clifton Hall
Harrison's Cave
Gun Hill Signal Station
Sunbury Plantation House and Museum
West Indies Rum Distillery
Mount Gay Visitor Centre
Kensington Oval
**Bridgetown**
Crane Beach
Foursquare Rum Distillery and Heritage Park
Parliament Buildings Government House
Graeme Hall Nature Sanctuary
Concorde Experience
Garrison Historic Area:
St Ann's Fort
George Washington House
Barbados Museum
Garrison Savannah Racetrack

Scale 1 : 250 000

### Sugar and rum

- Barbados is noted for its sugar and rum. Over the years the sugar industry has declined, but rum has been very successful
- In the 19th century there were 12 **sugar** factories that crushed the cane, but as sugar sales declined these were closed one by one
- By 2000 there were only two factories still working, Andrew's and Portvale
- In 2014 the Andrew's Factory closed and is being dismantled. A new factory to produce multiple sugar products will eventually be built
- The Portvale Factory is now the only working factory in Barbados. There is a Sugar Museum in the grounds of the factory and both are open to visitors
- Foursquare Factory closed in the 1980s and is now a museum and park, with a modern rum distillery built on the site
- There are 3 **rum** distilleries in Barbados
- Mount Gay in the north in St Lucy has had great success in exporting its rum worldwide. It is now owned by the French Rémy Cointreau liquor company
- The West Indies Distillery is located in Brighton and is used by several rum companies to produce Cockspur and other rums
- Foursquare is the newest distillery, built on the site of the old sugar factory in St Philip, and produces a variety of popular and quality rums. It is open for tours

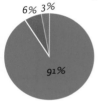

Berinda Cox Fish Market, Oistins.

Crop Over in Barbados is a harvest festival which first began in the 17th century, celebrating the end of the sugar cane season. It is now the island's biggest event running from June until the first Monday in August, ending with the Grand Kadooment Day Parade.

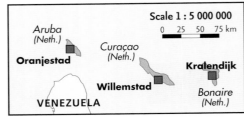

Scale 1 : 5 000 000
0   25   50   75 km

*Aruba (Neth.)*
**Oranjestad**
*Curaçao (Neth.)*
**Willemstad**
*Bonaire (Neth.)*
**Kralendijk**
VENEZUELA

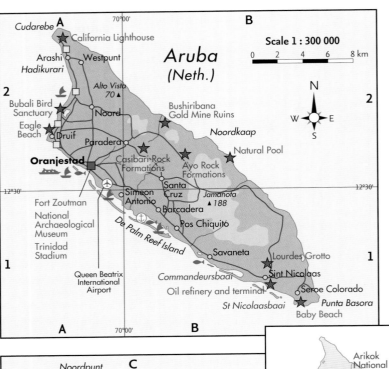

## Aruba (Neth.)

Scale 1 : 300 000
0   2   4   6   8 km

*Cudarebe*
California Lighthouse
*Arashi*
Westpunt
*Hadikurari*
*Alto Vista 70 ▲*
Bubali Bird Sanctuary
Noord
*Bushiribana Gold Mine Ruins*
Eagle Beach
Druif
Paradera
*Noordkaap*
**Oranjestad**
Casibari Rock Formations
Santa Cruz
Ayo Rock Formations
Natural Pool
Fort Zoutman
Simeon Antonio
Balcadera
*Jamanota ▲ 188*
National Archaeological Museum
Pos Chiquito
Trinidad Stadium
*De Palm Reef Island*
Savaneta
Queen Beatrix International Airport
Lourdes Grotto
Sint Nicolaas
*Commandeursbaai*
Oil refinery and terminal
Seroe Colorado
*St Nicolaasbaai*
Punta Basora
Baby Beach

## Bonaire (Neth.)

Scale 1 : 300 000
0   2   4   6   8 km

*Malmok*
Playa Funchi
*Brandaris ▲ 240*
*Boca Slagbaai*
*Boca Olivia*
Goto Meer
Rincón
*Punt'l Wecúa*
Oil terminal
Fort Oranje
Bonaire Museum
Pasangrahan (Parliament House)
Hato
Noord Salina
*Boven Bolivia*
*Boka Chikitu*
*Lagun*
Antriol
**Kralendijk**
Sabana
*Klein Bonaire*
Nikiboko
Tera Kora
Punt Vierkant
Donkey Sanctuary
*Lac Bay*
Mangrove Information and Kayaking Centre
Flamingo (Bonaire) International Airport
*Salt Works*
*Pekelmeer*
Flamingo Sanctuary
*Lacre Punt*

Shete Boka National Park
Arikok National Park
Washington Slagbaai National Park
Christoffel National Park
Bonaire National Marine Park

● National park
Scale 1 : 1 000 000

## Curaçao (Neth.)

*Noordpunt*
Boca Tabla Caves
*Westpunt*
Sabana Westpunt
*St Christoffelberg ▲ 372*
*Boca Tabla*
Lagun
*Boca Santa Cruz*
Barber
*Boca Ascención*
Soto
Ascensión
*Santa Martabaai*
*San Juanbaai*
*Punta Halvedag*
Playa Cas Abou
Tera Kora
*Bocht Van Hato*
St Willibrordus
Salina Santa Marie
Grote Berg
Curaçao International Airport
*Kaap Santa Marie*
*Bullenbaai*
Juliandorp
Hato Caves
Boca Sami
St Michiel
Rio Canario
Santa Catarina
Emmastad
*Piscaderabaai*
Isla Oil Refinery
Zoo Parke Tropikal
Ostrich Farm
*St Jorisbaai*
Schottegat
Santa Rosa
Otrobanda
Punda
Bottelier
Maritime Museum
Curaçao Underwater Marine Park
**Willemstad:**
Fort Amsterdam
Rif Fort
Handelskade
Kura Hulanda Museum
Jewish Cultural Historical Museum
Dolphin Academy
Sea Aquarium
Jan Thiel
*Lagun Jan Thiel*
*Spaanse Water*
Santa Barbara
New Port
*Oostpunt*

Scale 1 : 300 000
0   2   4   6   8   10 km

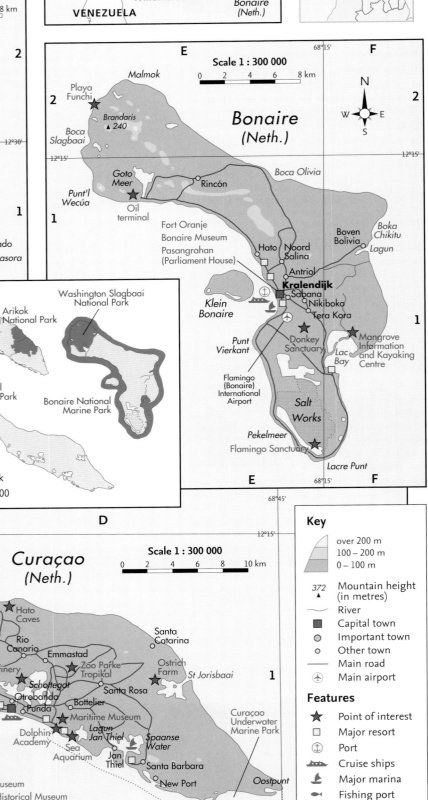

A diver examines a wreck on the Front Porch dive site, Bonaire.

### Key

over 200 m
100 – 200 m
0 – 100 m

*372 ▲* Mountain height (in metres)
River
Capital town
Important town
Other town
Main road
Main airport

### Features

★ Point of interest
□ Major resort
Port
Cruise ships
Major marina
Fishing port

## Oil refineries

- The large Isla refinery was built on Curaçao in 1918
- It was the largest refinery in the world for many years
- It is still operating and contributes 90% of the export earnings to the economy
- Copying Curaçao, two large refineries were built on Aruba in 1929 and 1930
- They refined oil from Venezuela, and later Brazil
- The Eagle refinery closed in 1950
- The Lago refinery was attacked by a U-Boat in 1942
- The Lago refinery, once one of the world's largest, closed in 2009
- Due to the loss of jobs from the closed refineries, Aruba started its modern tourist industry

Aruba and Curaçao are Self-governing Netherlands Territories. Bonaire is a Netherlands Special Municipality

| | **ARUBA** | **CURAÇAO** | **BONAIRE** |
|---|---|---|---|
| **Population** | 101 484 (2010) | 150 563 (2011) | 16 541 (2014 est.) |
| **Capital town** | Oranjestad | Willemstad | Kralendijk |
| **Area** | 193 sq km | 444 sq km | 288 sq km |
| **National flower** | Wanglo Flower | Kibrahacha | Divi-divi |
| **National bird** | Burrowing Owl | Majestic Oriole | Greater Flamingo |
| **Languages** | Dutch, Papiamento, English | | |

Scale 1 : 8 000 000

Tobago

Trinidad

**Port of Spain**

VENEZUELA

## TRINIDAD AND TOBAGO

| | |
|---|---|
| **Population** *(2011)* | 1 328 019 |
| **Capital city** | Port of Spain |
| **Area** | 5128 sq km |
| **Languages** | English, creole, Hindi |
| **National flower** | Wild Poinsettia |
| **National bird** *(Trinidad)* | Scarlet Ibis |
| **National bird** *(Tobago)* | Rufous-vented Chachalaca |

| Island | Area (sq km) | Population (2011) | Pop. density (per sq km) |
|---|---|---|---|
| Trinidad | 4828 | 1 267 145 | 262 |
| Tobago | 300 | 60 874 | 203 |

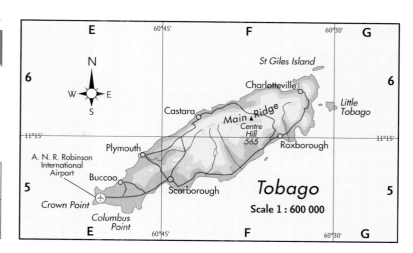

St Giles Island

Charlotteville

Castara　Little Tobago

Main Ridge　Centre Hill 565　Roxborough

Plymouth

A. N. R. Robinson International Airport

Buccoo

Crown Point　Scarborough

Columbus Point

*Tobago*
Scale 1 : 600 000

### Key

over 500 m
200 – 500 m
100 – 200 m
0 – 100 m

*940* ▲ Mountain height (in metres)

River

━━ Country boundary
── County boundary
■ Capital city
◉ Important town
○ Other town
═══ Highway
── Main road
✈ Main airport

VENEZUELA

*Gulf*

*of*

*Paria*

*Trinidad*

Maracas Bay

Chupara Point

La Vache Point

Corozal Point

Huevos

Chaguaramas
Monos
Gaspar Grande
Chacachacare

Diego Martin
545 ▲
Carenage
Maraval

El Tucuche 936 ▲
Cantaro
727 ▲
La Veronica

Las Cuevas

Blanchisseuse

Matelot

Sans Souci　Toco

Galera Point

**ST DAVID**

Redhead

*Northern*　848 ▲　Mount Aripo 940 ▲
*Range*　859 ▲
534 ▲

Oropuche Range

Matura　Salybia

Balandra Bay

Saline Bay

**ST GEORGE**

San Juan
St Joseph
Tunapuna
Tacarigua
Arouca

Hollis Reservoir

Matura

Matura Bay

**Port of Spain**

Caroni

Caroni Swamp

Piarco International Airport

Guayamare

Cunupia

Arima

Valencia

**ST ANDREW**
Cuare

Cumuto

San Rafael

Sangre Grande

Cunaripa

Manzanilla Point

Chaguanas

Waterloo

**CARONI**
*Arena*

Caparo

Couva　Couva

Point Lisas

Claxton Bay

Pointe-à-Pierre

San Fernando

Gran Couva

Talparo

Caroni Arena Reservoir

Four Roads

Mount Tamana 308 ▲

Brasso

Tabaquite

Mayo

Busy Corner

Princes Town

New Grant

*Central*　*Range*

Charuma

Biche

Navet Killdeer

Poole

Poole

Rio Claro

Upper Manzanilla

Coryal

Manzanilla Bay

Cocas Bay

**NARIVA**
*Nariva Swamp*

Guatuaro Point

Ecclesville

St Joseph

Pierreville

Pitch Lake

La Brea

Guapo Bay

St Mary's

Point Fortin

Fyzabad

Cap de Ville

Oropuche Lagoon

Debe

Barrackpore

Oropuche

Preau

**VICTORIA**

Cipero Ste Croix

Guatuaro (Ortoire)

**MAYARO**

Mayaro Bay

Siparia
Penal

Erin

Palo Seco

**ST PATRICK**

Cedros Bay

Fullerton

Bonasse

Islote Bay

Buenos Ayres

Erin Bay

San Francique

Palmiste Point

La Lune

Inniss

Basse Terre

Curamata

Moruga

*Southern Range*

Moruga

*Trinity Hills*

Guayaguayare

Galeota Point

Icacos Point　Icacos

VENEZUELA

Scale 1 : 600 000

0　10　20　30 km

## Features

★ Point of interest
□ Major resort
⊕ Main airport
⚓ Port
🚢 Cruise ships
⚓ Major marina
🐟 Fishing port

Scale 1 : 800 000

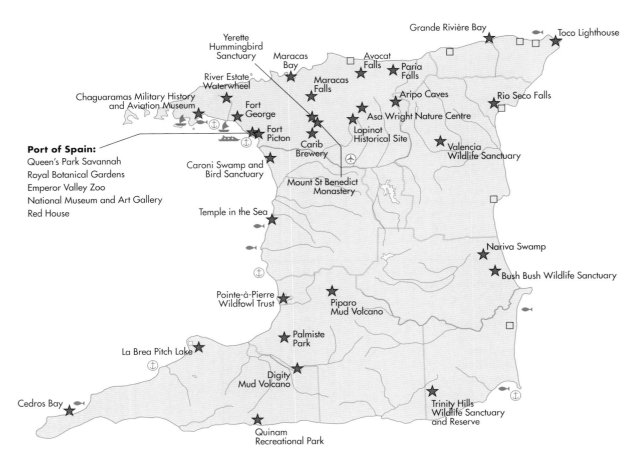

Yerette Hummingbird Sanctuary
Grande Rivière Bay
Toco Lighthouse
Maracas Bay
Avocat Falls
Paria Falls
River Estate Waterwheel
Maracas Falls
Aripo Caves
Rio Seco Falls
Chaguaramas Military History and Aviation Museum
Fort George
Asa Wright Nature Centre
Fort Picton
Lopinot Historical Site
Carib Brewery
Valencia Wildlife Sanctuary

**Port of Spain:**
Queen's Park Savannah
Royal Botanical Gardens
Emperor Valley Zoo
National Museum and Art Gallery
Red House

Caroni Swamp and Bird Sanctuary
Mount St Benedict Monastery
Temple in the Sea
Nariva Swamp
Bush Bush Wildlife Sanctuary
Pointe-à-Pierre Wildfowl Trust
Piparo Mud Volcano
Palmiste Park
La Brea Pitch Lake
Digity Mud Volcano
Trinity Hills Wildlife Sanctuary and Reserve
Cedros Bay
Quinam Recreational Park

## Local Government

▨ City
▨ Borough
▨ Regional Corporation

Scale 1 : 2 000 000

SAN JUAN-LAVENTILLE
DIEGO MARTIN
TUNAPUNA-PIARCO
PORT OF SPAIN
SANGRE GRANDE
ARIMA
CHAGUANAS
COUVA-TABAQUITE-TALPARO
MAYARO-RIO CLARO
SAN FERNANDO
POINT FORTIN
PRINCES TOWN
PENAL-DEBE
SIPARIA

As its name suggests, Port of Spain became the entry point into the country under Spanish rule, and is still the main port for general cargo today.

### Pitch Lake at La Brea (aka *Trinidad Lake Asphalt*)

- The Pitch Lake is the world's largest natural deposit of asphalt covering about 410 000 sq m with an estimated depth of 76 m at the centre
- Mining of asphalt started in 1867 and an estimated 10 million tonnes has been extracted since
- The asphalt was used for road surfacing in Europe and the USA but was eventually replaced by bitumen from oil refineries
- Production peaked at about 200 000 tonnes in the 1960s but then declined considerably
- Exports have been quite variable over the years
- Currently the asphalt is processed to make automobile under-coating and similar weather-proof coatings
- Today the Pitch Lake is a major tourist attraction with up to 20 000 visitors a year

The extraordinary Pitch Lake at La Brea was mined for asphalt for many years. Today it is a major tourist attraction.

Maracas Bay is a popular weekend beach resort for residents of Port of Spain. It is also a fishing village and features the classic pirogue boats, usually fitted with an outboard motor.

## Rainfall

Average annual rainfall

- more than 3000 mm
- 2500 – 3000 mm
- 2000 – 2500 mm
- 1500 – 2000 mm
- 1000 – 1500 mm
- less than 1000 mm

→ Normal direction of the wind

• Climate station

Scale 1 : 1 500 000

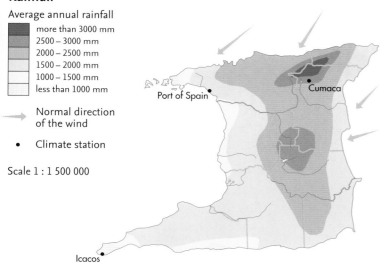

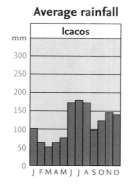

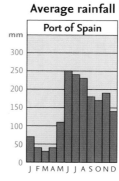

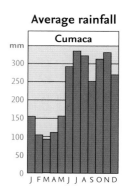

## Mud volcanoes

- Mud volcanoes are a mixture of gas, mud and hot water
- The gas most associated with Trinidad's mud volcanoes is methane
- They are mainly found in the southern half of Trinidad near oil reserves
- There is no eruption of lava but the volcanoes bubble most of the time and generally form a cone of mud and clay
- The volcano near Piparo, in south-central Trinidad, erupted in 1997, covering the village in a layer of mud

⬤ Mud volcanoes

Scale 1 : 1 500 000

Devil's Woodyard mud volcano has been active for over 150 years and is a major tourist attraction. It is surrounded by a number of smaller mud volcanoes.

## Caroni Swamp

- Caroni Swamp is located on the west coast of Trinidad where the Caroni river enters the Gulf of Paria
- The wetland consists of marshes, mangrove swamp and tidal mudflats giving a rich variety of habitats for both marine and freshwater plants and animals
- From the 1920s rice and sugar cane cultivation gradually encroached on the swamp affecting the water quality
- As agricultural activity gradually declined in the 1960s, salt water moved further inland and the coverage of mangrove forest steadily increased
- The swamp is constantly threatened by flood-control measures, industrial pollution from nearby factories and the development of housing and roads for Trinidad's growing population

This large protected swampland is laced with many navigable channels and is a major attraction for ecotourists.

Within the swamp is the Caroni Bird Sanctuary. Of the many nesting birds, the scarlet ibis is the most notable and is the national bird of Trinidad.

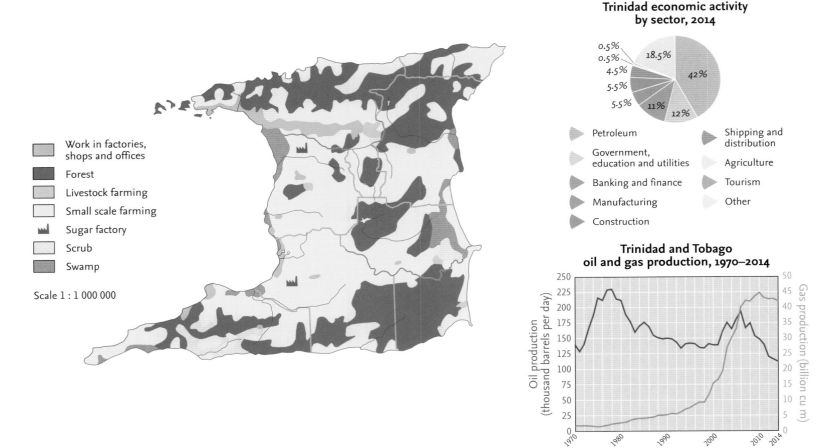

## Trinidad economic activity by sector, 2014

- 42% Petroleum
- 18.5% Government, education and utilities
- 12% Banking and finance
- 11% Manufacturing
- 5.5% Construction
- 5.5% Shipping and distribution
- 4.5% Agriculture
- 0.5% Tourism
- 0.5% Other

Work in factories, shops and offices
Forest
Livestock farming
Small scale farming
Sugar factory
Scrub
Swamp

Scale 1 : 1 000 000

## Trinidad and Tobago oil and gas production, 1970–2014

Oil production (thousand barrels per day)
Gas production (billion cu m)
Year

# Mining and manufacturing

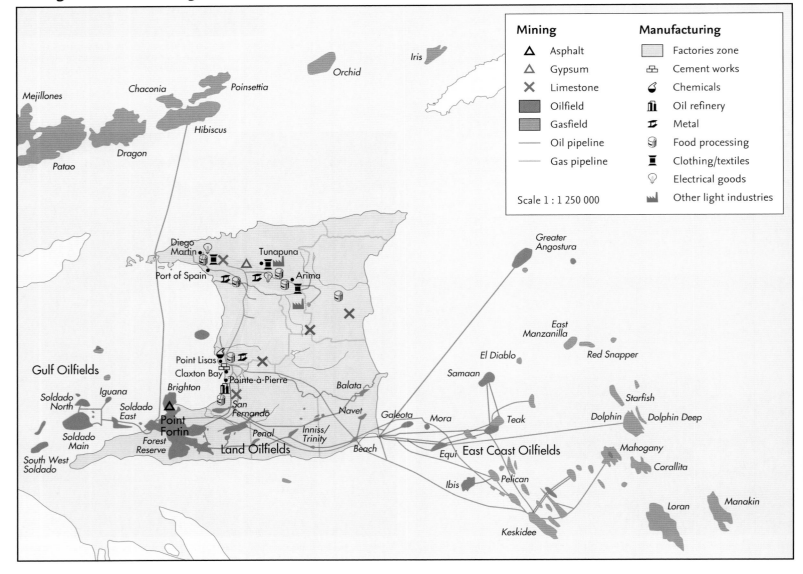

## Mining
- △ Asphalt
- △ Gypsum
- ✕ Limestone
- Oilfield
- Gasfield
- Oil pipeline
- Gas pipeline

Scale 1 : 1 250 000

## Manufacturing
- Factories zone
- Cement works
- Chemicals
- Oil refinery
- Metal
- Food processing
- Clothing/textiles
- Electrical goods
- Other light industries

## History

- Before European settlement Trinidad was inhabited by indigenous Arawak and Carib peoples
- Christopher Columbus explored the islands on his third voyage in **1498**
- Trinidad remained under Spanish rule until **1797** when it passed to the British, but was mainly colonised by French settlers
- From the late **17th** century the British, French, Dutch and Courlanders fought to control Tobago with the island eventually ending up under British rule
- In the late **18th** century African slaves were brought in to work on the sugar and cotton plantations
- When slavery was abolished in **1838** there were not enough freed Africans to work the plantations. After **1845** contract labourers were hired from India, China, and Madeira, and these were supplemented by freed slaves from many of the nearby Caribbean islands
- In **1889** the two islands became a single British crown colony
- Trinidad and Tobago gained independence from the British in **1962** and became a republic in **1976**

## Carnival

- Carnival originated with the French celebration of Lent in the 1700s
- The African slaves matched this with a festival celebrating the harvesting of the sugar cane
- After emancipation, and despite opposition from the colonial rulers, Carnival (known locally as 'Mas') went on to develop into the massive and spectacular event it is today
- The Trinidad carnival is one of the biggest in the world held annually on the Monday and Tuesday before Ash Wednesday
- As well as being the main social and cultural event of the year, Carnival now has great economic significance, currently attracting about an additional 10 000 visitors from all over the world
- The tourist industry benefits by over US$100 million each year from both domestic and foreign tourist expenditure

### Migration to Trinidad and Tobago

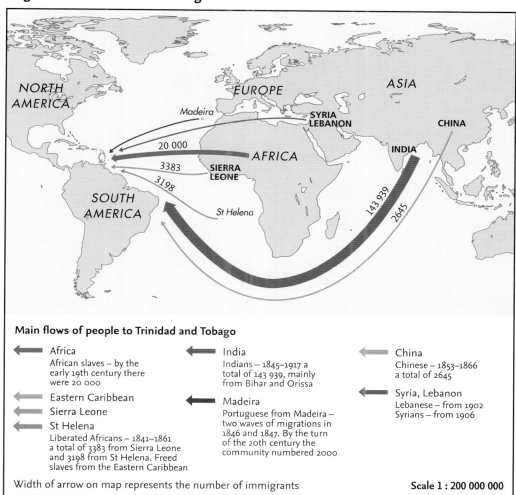

**Main flows of people to Trinidad and Tobago**

**Africa**
African slaves – by the early 19th century there were 20 000

**Eastern Caribbean**
**Sierra Leone**
**St Helena**
Liberated Africans – 1841–1861 a total of 3383 from Sierra Leone and 3198 from St Helena. Freed slaves from the Eastern Caribbean

**India**
Indians – 1845–1917 a total of 143 939, mainly from Bihar and Orissa

**Madeira**
Portuguese from Madeira – two waves of migrations in 1846 and 1847. By the turn of the 20th century the community numbered 2000

**China**
Chinese – 1853–1866 a total of 2645

**Syria, Lebanon**
Lebanese – from 1902
Syrians – from 1906

Width of arrow on map represents the number of immigrants

Scale 1 : 200 000 000

A performer at the Carnival celebrations on 11 February 2012, in Port of Spain.

A steelband plays for the judges at a competition in St Clair, Trinidad, in 2011.

## Tourism

### Stop-over visitor arrivals, 1995–2014

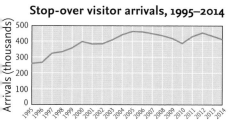

### Stop-over visitor arrivals by month, 2014

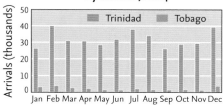

### Stop-over visitor arrivals by country of origin, 2014

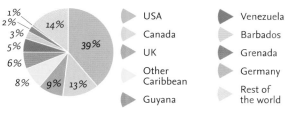

USA 39%
Canada 13%
UK 9%
Other Caribbean 8%
Guyana 6%
Venezuela 5%
Barbados 3%
Grenada 2%
Germany 1%
Rest of the world 14%

### Stop-over visitor arrivals by purpose of visit, 2010

Leisure/beach vacation 45%
Visiting friends and relatives 25%
Business/convention 18%
Wedding/honeymoon 9%
Study 2%
Other 1%

### Cruise passenger arrivals, 2001–2014

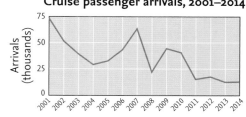

### Cruise passenger arrivals by month, 2014

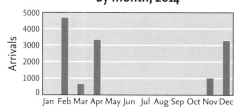

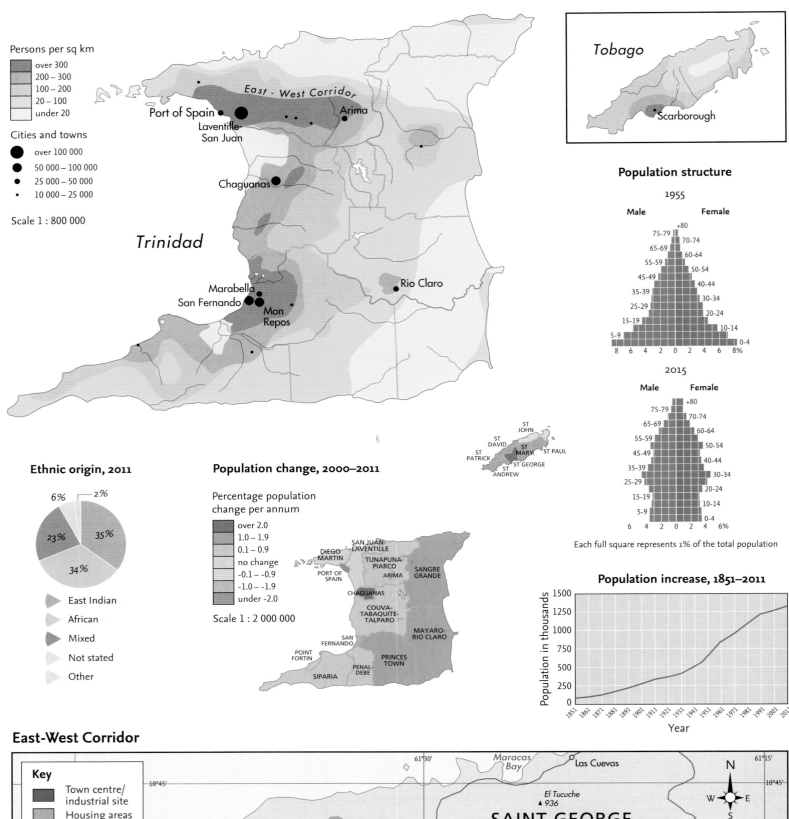

**Persons per sq km**
- over 300
- 200 – 300
- 100 – 200
- 20 – 100
- under 20

**Cities and towns**
- over 100 000
- 50 000 – 100 000
- 25 000 – 50 000
- 10 000 – 25 000

Scale 1 : 800 000

*Trinidad*

Port of Spain
Laventille
San Juan
East - West Corridor
Arima

Chaguanas

Marabella
San Fernando
Mon Repos
Rio Claro

*Tobago*
Scarborough

## Population structure

### 1955
Male | Female
+80, 75-79, 70-74, 65-69, 60-64, 55-59, 50-54, 45-49, 40-44, 35-39, 30-34, 25-29, 20-24, 15-19, 10-14, 5-9, 0-4
8 6 4 2 0 2 4 6 8%

### 2015
Male | Female
+80, 75-79, 70-74, 65-69, 60-64, 55-59, 50-54, 45-49, 40-44, 35-39, 30-34, 25-29, 20-24, 15-19, 10-14, 5-9, 0-4
6 4 2 0 2 4 6%

Each full square represents 1% of the total population

## Ethnic origin, 2011

6%   2%
23%   35%
34%

- East Indian
- African
- Mixed
- Not stated
- Other

## Population change, 2000–2011

Percentage population change per annum
- over 2.0
- 1.0 – 1.9
- 0.1 – 0.9
- no change
- -0.1 – -0.9
- -1.0 – -1.9
- under -2.0

Scale 1 : 2 000 000

SAN JUAN-LAVENTILLE
DIEGO MARTIN
PORT OF SPAIN
TUNAPUNA-PIARCO
ARIMA
SANGRE GRANDE
CHAGUANAS
COUVA-TABAQUITE-TALPARO
MAYARO-RIO CLARO
SAN FERNANDO
POINT FORTIN
PENAL-DEBE
PRINCES TOWN
SIPARIA

ST JOHN
ST DAVID
ST PATRICK
ST MARY
ST PAUL
ST GEORGE
ST ANDREW

## Population increase, 1851–2011

Population in thousands (0 to 1500)
Year: 1851, 1861, 1871, 1881, 1891, 1901, 1911, 1921, 1931, 1941, 1951, 1961, 1971, 1981, 1991, 2001, 2011

## East-West Corridor

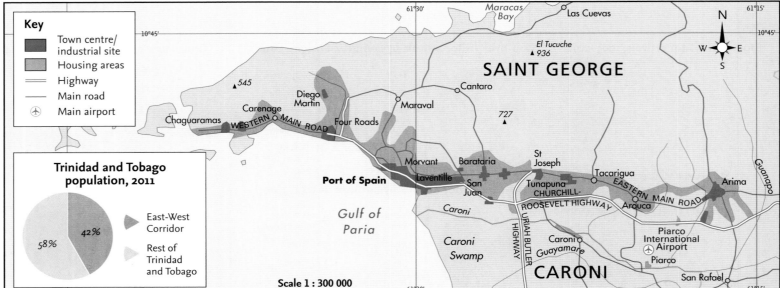

**Key**
- Town centre/industrial site
- Housing areas
- Highway
- Main road
- Main airport

**Trinidad and Tobago population, 2011**
42% East-West Corridor
58% Rest of Trinidad and Tobago

Maracas Bay
Las Cuevas
El Tucuche ▲ 936
SAINT GEORGE
▲ 545
Cantaro
Diego Martin
Maraval
Chaguaramas   WESTERN MAIN ROAD   Four Roads
Carenage
727 ▲
Morvant
Barataria
St Joseph
Tacarigua
Arima
Port of Spain
Laventille
San Juan
Tunapuna   CHURCHILL-ROOSEVELT HIGHWAY
Arauca
EASTERN MAIN ROAD
Guanapo
Gulf of Paria
Caroni
URIAH BUTLER HIGHWAY
Caroni
Caroni Swamp
Guayamare
Piarco International Airport
Piarco
San Rafael
CARONI

Scale 1 : 300 000

## Main Map

Tobago

St Giles Island

Bloody Bay · L'Anse Fourmi · Man of War Bay · Charlotteville

Parlatuvier · ST JOHN · Man of War Hill 560 · Little Tobago

Castara · Main Ridge · Centre Hill 565 · Speyside · Tyrrell Bay

ST DAVID · ST PAUL · Roxborough · Delaford · King's Bay

ST MARY · Belle · Roxborough

Moriah · Courland · Sandy · Hillsborough Dam · Belle Garden · Carapuse Bay

Plymouth · Mason Hall · Great · Pembroke

Great Courland Bay · Black Rock · 180 · ST GEORGE

Mount Irvine Bay · Patience Hill · ST ANDREW · Scarborough · Hillsborough Bay · Granby Point

Buccoo Bay · Buccoo · Bacolet

Pigeon Point · ST PATRICK · Rockly Bay · Bacolet Point

Store Bay · Canaan · Lowlands

Crown Point · A. N. R. Robinson International Airport

Columbus Point

Scale 1 : 250 000

0 2 4 6 8 km

### Key

- over 500 m
- 200 – 500 m
- 100 – 200 m
- 0 – 100 m
- 565 ▲ Mountain height (in metres)
- River
- Parish boundary
- ⊙ Important town
- ○ Other town
- Main road
- ✈ Main airport

## Features

- ● Forest reserve
- ★ Point of interest
- □ Major resort
- ✈ Main airport
- ⚓ Port
- 🚢 Cruise ships
- ⚓ Major marina
- 🐟 Fishing port

Pirate's Bay · Fort Campbleton · Hummingbird Gallery

Englishman's Bay · Tobago Forest Reserve · Little Tobago Bird Sanctuary

Arnos Farm and Nature Reserve · King's Bay Waterfall

Arnos Vale Waterwheel and Nature Park · Argyle Waterfalls

Fort James · Highland Waterfall · Tobago Cocoa Estate

Fort Bennett · Grafton Caledonia Wildlife Sanctuary · Richmond Great House

Mount Irvine Beach · Kimme Museum · Genesis Nature Park

Buccoo Reef and Nylon Pool · Fort Granby

Store Bay · Pigeon Point Heritage Park

Fort Milford

**Scarborough:**
Tobago House of Assembly
Fort King George and Tobago Museum
Botanical Gardens

Scale 1 : 350 000

## Rainfall

Average annual rainfall
- more than 2000 mm
- 1000 – 2000 mm
- less than 1000 mm

Scale 1 : 700 000

## Resources

- Work in factories, shops and offices
- Forest
- Crop farming

Scale 1 : 500 000

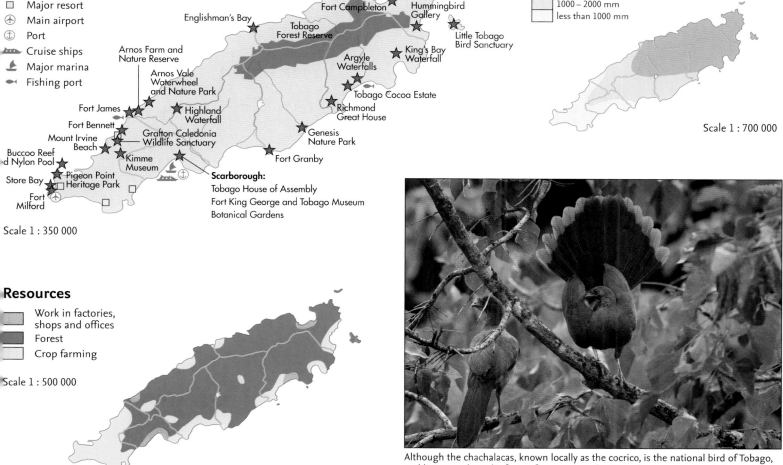

Although the chachalacas, known locally as the cocrico, is the national bird of Tobago, and lives mainly in the forest, farmers consider it a nuisance when it eats their crops.

**GUYANA**

| | |
|---|---|
| **Population** (2012) | 747 884 |
| **Capital city** | Georgetown |
| **Area** | 214 969 sq km |
| **Languages** | English, creole, Amerindian |
| **National flower** | Victoria Regia Lily |
| **National bird** | Hoatzin or Canje Pheasant |
| **National animal** | Jaguar |

Original inhabitants included coastal Arawaks and inland Caribs, and other Amerindian tribes

Sighted by Columbus in **1498**

Settled by Dutch from **1616** in three separate colonies

Also settled by British from **1746**, and ceded by Netherlands to Britain in **1814**

Became a British colony named British Guiana in **1831**

Became independent on 26 May **1966** and renamed Guyana

Declared a Cooperative Republic on 23 February **1970**

### Economic activity

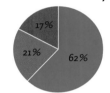

- Services 62%
- Agriculture, fishing and forestry 21%
- Manufacturing 17%

### Average rainfall

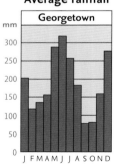

**Georgetown**

mm
300
250
200
150
100
50
0
J F M A M J J A S O N D

### Provinces

ESSEQUIBO
DEMERARA
BERBICE

Scale 1 : 14 000 000

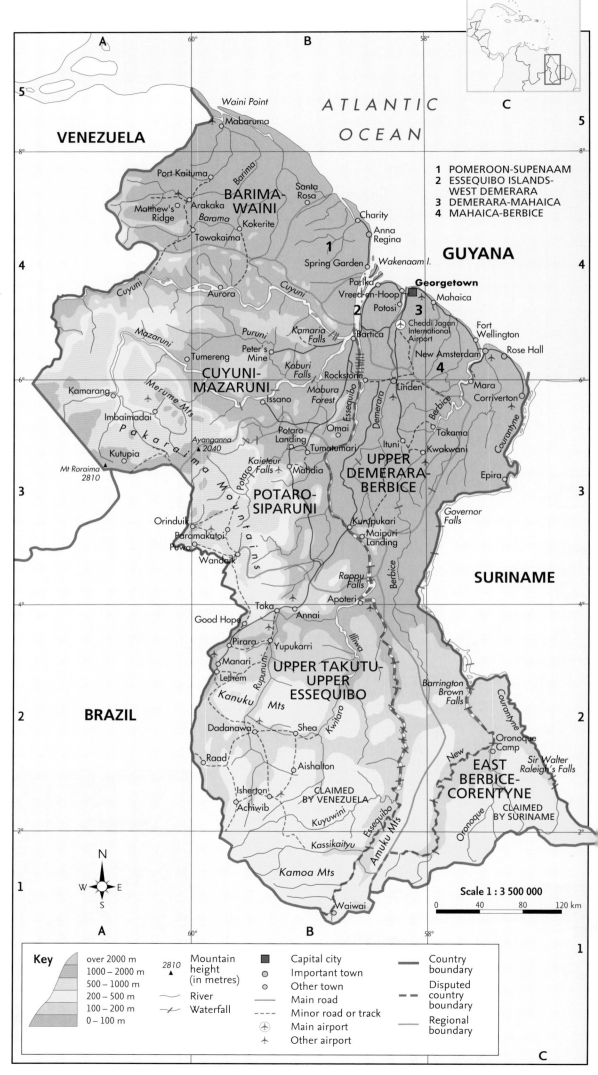

1 POMEROON-SUPENAAM
2 ESSEQUIBO ISLANDS-WEST DEMERARA
3 DEMERARA-MAHAICA
4 MAHAICA-BERBICE

**Scale 1 : 3 500 000**
0     40     80     120 km

**Key**

| | |
|---|---|
| over 2000 m | |
| 1000 – 2000 m | |
| 500 – 1000 m | |
| 200 – 500 m | |
| 100 – 200 m | |
| 0 – 100 m | |

2810 ▲ Mountain height (in metres)
~ River
Waterfall
✈ Main airport
✈ Other airport

■ Capital city
◉ Important town
○ Other town
— Main road
- - - Minor road or track

━━ Country boundary
- - - Disputed country boundary
— Regional boundary

## Features

- ● National park
- ★ Point of interest
- ▢ Major resort
- ⊕ Main airport
- ⚓ Port
- 🚢 Cruise ships
- 🐟 Fishing port

**Georgetown:**
St George's Cathedral
National Museum
Promenade Gardens
Parliament Building
Guyana Zoo and Botanical Gardens
Walter Roth Museum of Anthropology
Museum of African Heritage
International Conference Centre
Providence Cricket Stadium

Shell Beach
Saxacalli Beach
Salto Oshi (King George VI Falls)
Kamarang Meru (Great Falls)
Amaila Falls
King Edward VIII Falls
Kumaka Falls
Kaieteur Falls
Kaieteur National Park
Orinduik Falls
Iwokrama Forest Reserve
Barrington Brown Falls
King George V Falls

Scale 1 : 7 000 000

## Minerals

- ▢ Bauxite
- ■ Diamonds
- ▪ Oil
- ○ Gold
- ◉ Manganese
- ● Clay

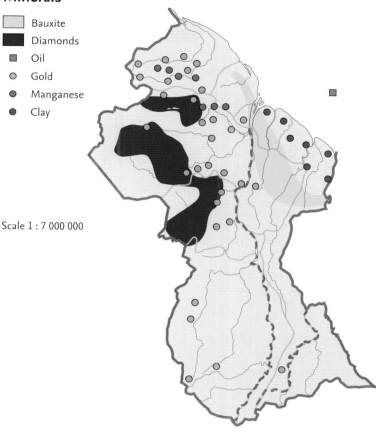

Scale 1 : 7 000 000

### Bauxite mining in Guyana

- Guyana has the oldest bauxite industry in the Caribbean, started in 1916 south of Georgetown
- A settlement named Mackenzie grew up and the workers excavated the bauxite (aluminium ore) by hand, and later with steam-powered machinery
- The ore was loaded into barges and sent down the Demerara River where it was transferred to ships at Georgetown
- The ore then travelled to smelters in Canada for refining into metal. Guyana (then British Guiana) did not have the energy to run smelters, but Canada had developed very cheap HEP on its large rivers
- Over the years more companies came to Guyana and bauxite is still the country's main export

Mashramani, often abbreviated to 'Mash', takes place on 23 February each year to celebrate Republic Day when Guyana gained independence. There are float parades, spectacular costumes and masquerade bands and dancing in the streets.

Gold and diamond mining is widespread in the interior of Guyana. Unfortunately the widely-used system of alluvial mining (panning, or sifting the river sediment) is very destructive.

## BELIZE

| | |
|---|---|
| **Population** (2010) | 312 971 |
| **Capital city** | Belmopan |
| **Area** | 22 965 sq km |
| **Languages** | English, Spanish, Mayan, creole |
| **National flower** | Black Orchid |
| **National bird** | Keel-billed Toucan |
| **National animal** | Baird's Tapir |

Occupied by the Mayans until conquest and settlement

Progressively conquered and partially occupied by the Spanish from **1544** onwards

From the early **1600s** British settlers cut and exported logwood, and later mahogany

In **1787** some 2000 British refugees from the Mosquito Coast of Nicaragua settled in Belize, and by **1854** the British had total possession

In **1862** the British declared Belize a colony which it named British Honduras

The name was changed to Belize in **1973**, and Belize became independent on 21 September **1981**

## Features

- ● National park
- ★ Point of interest
- ☐ Major resort
- ✈ Main airport
- ⚓ Port
- 🚢 Cruise ships
- 🐟 Fishing port

**Belize City:**
Museum of Belize
Maritime Museum
Baron Bliss Lighthouse

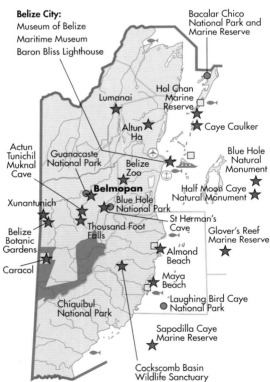

Scale 1 : 3 000 000

## Chewing gum

- Chewing gum was originally made from chicle, the sap of the sapodilla tree
- The sapodilla tree is common throughout the Caribbean, commonly called the 'Dilly' tree. It is widespread in Belize
- In the 1880s American companies, including Wrigley's and Beechnut, bought large amounts from local sap collectors, known as 'chicleros'
- In the 1960s chewing gum began to be made from a cheaper chemical product related to synthetic rubber, and the chicle industry collapsed
- Chewing gum is a worldwide pollution agent (it is banned in Singapore). It cannot be cleaned up easily as it does not dissolve in water

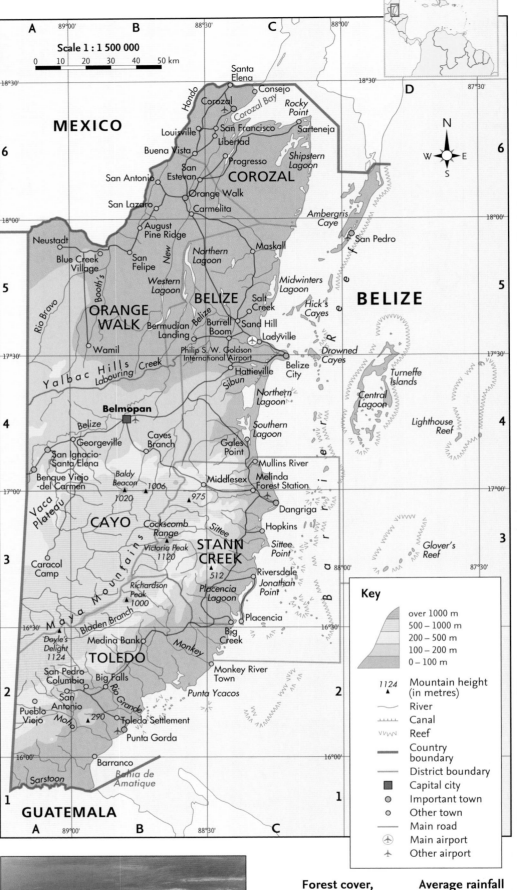

Scale 1 : 1 500 000

### Key

- over 1000 m
- 500 – 1000 m
- 200 – 500 m
- 100 – 200 m
- 0 – 100 m
- ▲ 1124 Mountain height (in metres)
- River
- Canal
- Reef
- Country boundary
- District boundary
- ■ Capital city
- ⊙ Important town
- ○ Other town
- Main road
- ✈ Main airport
- ✈ Other airport

The Great Blue Hole is a large solution hole (315 m wide and 124 m deep), now flooded since sea level rose after the ice ages. It is surrounded by coral reefs which are a World Heritage site popular with tourists.

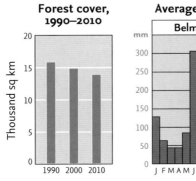

**Forest cover, 1990–2010**

Thousand sq km

1990  2000  2010

**Average rainfall**

**Belmopan**

J F M A M J J A S O N D

## Facts about Central America

**Population** (2015)
45 723 000

**Largest country**
Nicaragua 130 000 sq km

**Country with most people** (2015)
Guatemala 16 343 000

**Largest city** (2015)
San Salvador 1 740 000

### Key
— Country boundary
■ Capital city
○ Important city / town

Scale 1 : 11 000 000

0   100   200   300   400 km

## Facts about Central America

**Area**
523 166 sq km

**Highest peak**
Volcán de Tajamulco 4210 m

**Longest river**
Coco 750 km

**Largest lake**
Lake Nicaragua 8150 sq km

### Key
over 5000 m
3000 – 5000 m
2000 – 3000 m
1000 – 2000 m
500 – 1000 m
200 – 500 m
0 – 200 m

▲ 4210  Mountain height (in metres)

Scale 1 : 11 000 000

0   100   200   300   400 km

Lambert Conformal Conic projection

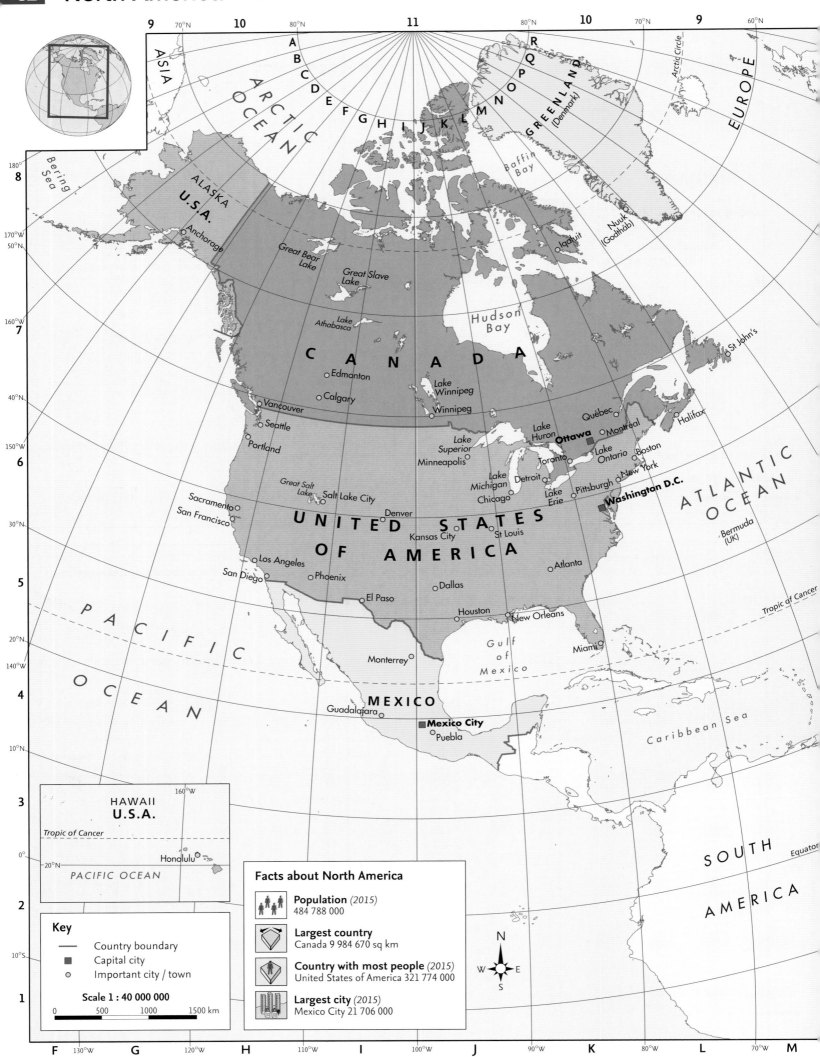

ASIA

9  70°N  10  80°N  11  N  R  80°N  10  70°N  9  60°N  EUROPE

ARCTIC OCEAN

GREENLAND (Denmark)

Arctic Circle

180°  8

Bering Sea

ALASKA U.S.A.

Anchorage

170°W  50°N

Great Bear Lake

Great Slave Lake

Baffin Bay

Nuuk (Godthåb)

160°W  7

Lake Athabasca

Hudson Bay

C A N A D A

Iqaluit

St John's

150°W  6

Edmonton

Calgary

Vancouver

Seattle

Portland

Lake Winnipeg

Winnipeg

Lake Superior

Minneapolis

Lake Huron

Toronto

Lake Michigan

Detroit

Chicago

Lake Erie

Québec

Ottawa  Montréal

Lake Ontario  Boston

Pittsburgh  New York

Halifax

ATLANTIC OCEAN

140°W

Sacramento

San Francisco

Great Salt Lake  Salt Lake City

U N I T E D   S T A T E S

Denver

O F   A M E R I C A

Kansas City

St Louis

Washington D.C.

Bermuda (UK)

30°N

130°W  5

Los Angeles

San Diego

Phoenix

El Paso

Dallas

Atlanta

Houston

New Orleans

Miami

Tropic of Cancer

20°N

Monterrey

Gulf of Mexico

Caribbean Sea

140°W  4

PACIFIC

OCEAN

MEXICO

Guadalajara

Mexico City

Puebla

10°N

3

HAWAII U.S.A.

160°W

Tropic of Cancer

Honolulu

20°N

PACIFIC OCEAN

SOUTH

Equator

2

AMERICA

**Facts about North America**

**Population** (2015)
484 788 000

**Largest country**
Canada 9 984 670 sq km

**Country with most people** (2015)
United States of America 321 774 000

**Largest city** (2015)
Mexico City 21 706 000

**Key**

— Country boundary

■ Capital city

○ Important city / town

Scale 1 : 40 000 000

0   500   1000   1500 km

N
W  E
S

F  130°W  G  120°W  H  110°W  I  100°W  J  90°W  K  80°W  L  70°W  M

Lambert Azimuthal Equal Area projection

**ARCTIC OCEAN**

Greenland

Iceland

Denmark Strait

Ellesmere Island
Queen Elizabeth Islands
Parry Islands
Baffin Bay
Baffin Island
Davis Strait
Labrador Sea
Cape Farewell

Wrangel I.
Point Barrow
Beaufort Sea
Banks Island
Victoria Island
Great Bear Lake
Foxe Basin
Southampton Island
Hudson Strait
Labrador

Bering Strait
Brooks Range
Yukon
Mackenzie Mts
Mackenzie
Great Slave Lake
Hudson Bay
Belcher Islands
Newfoundland

St Lawrence Island
Numivak I.
Bristol Bay
Alaska Range
Denali (Mt McKinley) 6190
Mt Logan 5959
Gulf of Alaska
Kodiak Island
Alaska Peninsula
Alexander Archipelago
Haida Gwaii (Queen Charlotte Islands)
Coast Mountains
Peace
Lake Athabasca
Churchill
Nelson
Severn
Lake Winnipeg
Canadian Shield
Gulf of St Lawrence
Cape Breton Island

Bering Sea

Vancouver Island
Fraser
Columbia
Missouri
Yellowstone
Snake
Rocky Mountains
Great Plains
Lake Superior
Lake Huron
Lake Michigan
Lake Ontario
Niagara Falls
Lake Erie
Cape Sable
Cape Cod

**PACIFIC OCEAN**

Cascade Range
Sierra Nevada
Great Salt Lake
Great Basin
Gannett Peak 4202
Mount Elbert 4398
Mississippi
Missouri
Ohio
Appalachian Mountains
Chesapeake Bay
Cape Hatteras

**ATLANTIC OCEAN**

Mount Whitney 4418
Death Valley
Colorado
Colorado Plateau
Grand Canyon
Arkansas
Ozark Plateau
Red
Cape Fear
Bermuda

Guadalupe
Rio Grande
Edwards Plateau
Mississippi
Cape Canaveral
Tropic of Cancer

Baja California
Gulf of California
Sierra Madre Occidental
Altiplano Mexicano
Sierra Madre Oriental
Mississippi Delta
Gulf of Mexico
Str. of Florida
Bahamas
Cuba
Greater Antilles
Hispaniola
Puerto Rico
Lesser Antilles

Cabo Falso
Volcán Popocatépetl 5452
Bahía de Campeche
Yucatán
Yucatán Channel
Jamaica
Caribbean Sea
Curaçao

Sierra Madre del Sur
Sierra Madre
G. of Honduras
Lake Nicaragua
Golfo del Darién
Isthmus of Panama
Orinoco
Cordillera Occidental
Cordillera Central
Cordillera Oriental
Guaviare

Île Clipperton
Isla de Coco
Islas Galapagos
Coquetá
Equator
Amazon
Marañón
Selvas
Cordillera Central
Cordillera Oriental
Cordillera Occidental
Lake Titicaca
Andes

**Hawaiian Islands** (inset)

Kure Atoll
Midway Is
Laysan I.
Tropic of Cancer
Necker I.
Kauai
Oahu
Maui
Hawaii
Johnston Atoll
PACIFIC OCEAN

## Key

- over 5000 m
- 3000 – 5000 m
- 2000 – 3000 m
- 1000 – 2000 m
- 500 – 1000 m
- 200 – 500 m
- 0 – 200 m
- land below sea level
- Ice cap
- ▲ 6190 Mountain height (in metres)

**Scale 1 : 40 000 000**

0    500    1000    1500 km

## Facts about North America

**Area**
24 680 331 sq km

**Highest peak**
Denali 6190 m

**Lowest point**
Death Valley -86 m

**Longest river**
Mississippi-Missouri 5969 km

**Largest lake**
Lake Superior 82 100 sq km

Lambert Azimuthal Equal Area projection

**Facts about South America**

**Population** (2015)
418 449 000

**Largest country**
Brazil 8 514 879 sq km

**Country with most people**
Brazil 207 848 000 (2015)

**Largest city** (2015)
São Paulo 21 028 000

**Key**

——— Country boundary
- - - - Disputed boundary
◼ Capital city
○ Important city / town

**Scale 1 : 35 000 000**

0    400    800    1200 km

Lambert Azimuthal Equal Area projection

**Key**

over 5000 m
3000 – 5000 m
2000 – 3000 m
1000 – 2000 m
500 – 1000 m
200 – 500 m
0 – 200 m
land below sea level

Ice cap

6961 ▲ Mountain height (in metres)

**Scale 1 : 35 000 000**

0    400    800    1200 km

**Facts about South America**

**Area**
17 815 420 sq km

**Highest peak**
Cerro Aconcagua 6961 m

**Lowest point**
Laguna del Carbón -105 m

**Longest river**
Amazon 6516 km

**Largest lake**
Lake Titicaca 8340 sq km

Lambert Azimuthal Equal Area projection

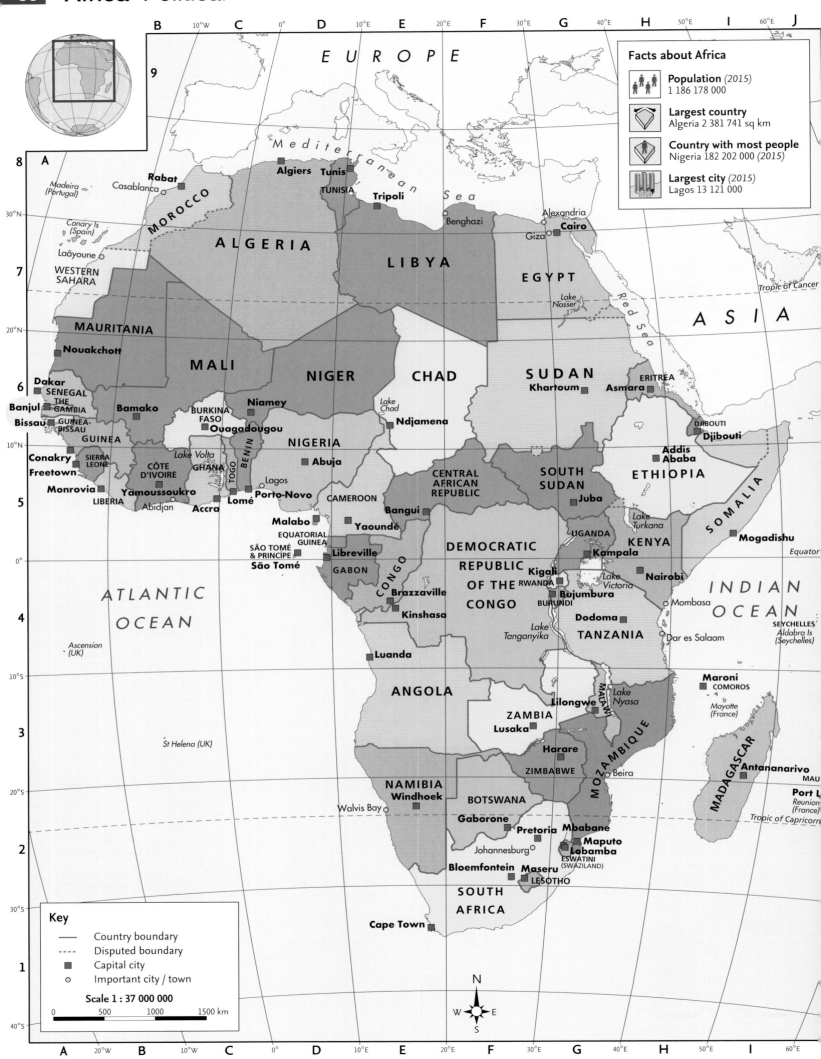

E U R O P E

**Facts about Africa**

**Population** (2015)
1 186 178 000

**Largest country**
Algeria 2 381 741 sq km

**Country with most people**
Nigeria 182 202 000 (2015)

**Largest city** (2015)
Lagos 13 121 000

Mediterranean Sea

Rabat
Casablanca
Madeira (Portugal)
MOROCCO
Algiers
Tunis
TUNISIA
Tripoli
Benghazi
Alexandria
Giza
Cairo

Canary Is (Spain)
Laâyoune
WESTERN SAHARA
ALGERIA
LIBYA
EGYPT
Lake Nasser
Tropic of Cancer

Red Sea
A S I A

MAURITANIA
Nouakchott
MALI
NIGER
CHAD
SUDAN
Khartoum
ERITREA
Asmara

Dakar
SENEGAL
THE GAMBIA
Banjul
Bissau
GUINEA-BISSAU
Bamako
BURKINA FASO
Niamey
Ouagadougou
Lake Chad
Ndjamena
DJIBOUTI
Djibouti

Conakry
SIERRA LEONE
GUINEA
Lake Volta
CÔTE D'IVOIRE
GHANA
BENIN
TOGO
NIGERIA
Abuja
Addis Ababa
ETHIOPIA

Freetown
Monrovia
LIBERIA
Yamoussoukro
Abidjan
Accra
Lomé
Porto-Novo
Lagos
CAMEROON
CENTRAL AFRICAN REPUBLIC
SOUTH SUDAN
Juba
SOMALIA

Malabo
EQUATORIAL GUINEA
Yaoundé
Bangui
UGANDA
KENYA
Mogadishu

SÃO TOMÉ & PRÍNCIPE
São Tomé
Libreville
GABON
CONGO
DEMOCRATIC REPUBLIC OF THE CONGO
Kampala
Kigali
RWANDA
Lake Turkana
Lake Victoria
Nairobi
INDIAN OCEAN
Equator

ATLANTIC OCEAN
Brazzaville
Kinshasa
Bujumbura
BURUNDI
Dodoma
Mombasa
SEYCHELLES
Aldabra Is (Seychelles)

Ascension (UK)
Luanda
Lake Tanganyika
TANZANIA
Dar es Salaam

St Helena (UK)
ANGOLA
Lilongwe
MALAWI
Lake Nyasa
Maroni
COMOROS
Mayotte (France)

ZAMBIA
Lusaka
Harare
ZIMBABWE
MOZAMBIQUE
Beira
MADAGASCAR
Antananarivo
MAU

NAMIBIA
Windhoek
Walvis Bay
BOTSWANA
Gaborone
Pretoria
Mbabane
Maputo
Lobamba
ESWATINI (SWAZILAND)
Johannesburg
Port L
Reunion (France)
Tropic of Capricorn

Bloemfontein
Maseru
LESOTHO
SOUTH AFRICA
Cape Town

**Key**
— Country boundary
--- Disputed boundary
■ Capital city
○ Important city / town

**Scale 1 : 37 000 000**
0    500    1000    1500 km

N
W E
S

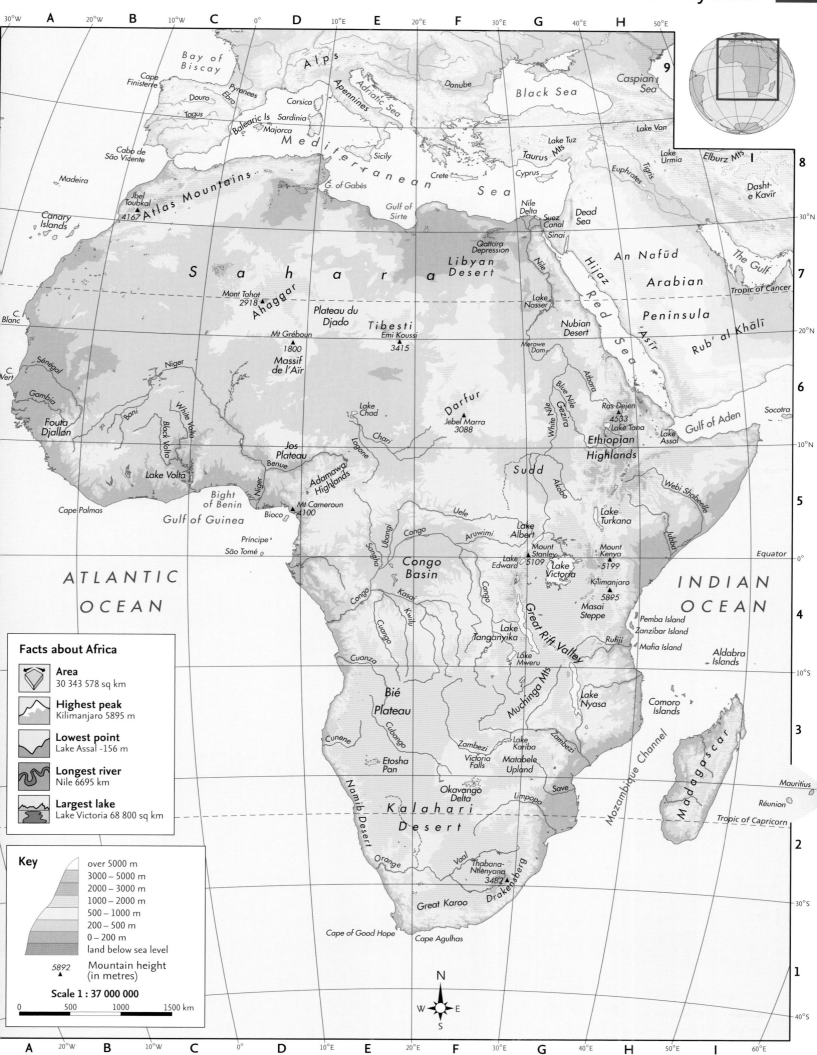

**Facts about Africa**

**Area**
30 343 578 sq km

**Highest peak**
Kilimanjaro 5895 m

**Lowest point**
Lake Assal -156 m

**Longest river**
Nile 6695 km

**Largest lake**
Lake Victoria 68 800 sq km

**Key**

over 5000 m
3000 – 5000 m
2000 – 3000 m
1000 – 2000 m
500 – 1000 m
200 – 500 m
0 – 200 m
land below sea level

5892 ▲ Mountain height
(in metres)

**Scale 1 : 37 000 000**

0　　500　　1000　　1500 km

Lambert Azimuthal Equal Area projection

ICELAND
Reykjavik
Arctic Circle
ATLANTIC OCEAN
Norwegian Sea
Barents Sea
RUSSIA
Faroe Islands (Denmark)
NORWAY
SWEDEN
FINLAND
Oslo
Helsinki
St Petersburg
Stockholm
Tallinn
ESTONIA
North Sea
Edinburgh
LATVIA
Riga
Belfast
DENMARK
LITHUANIA
Moscow
IRELAND
UNITED KINGDOM
Copenhagen
Vilnius
RUSSIA
Dublin
The Hague
NETH.
Berlin
Minsk
BELARUS
London
Amsterdam
POLAND
Cardiff
Brussels
BEL.
GERMANY
Warsaw
Luxembourg
LUX.
Prague
Kiev
UKRAINE
Paris
CZECHIA
Volgograd
SLOVAKIA
Bay of Biscay
Munich
Vienna
Bratislava
MOLDOVA
Bern
L.
AUSTRIA
Budapest
Chișinău
Odesa
FRANCE
SW.
HUNGARY
Lyon
Ljubljana
SL
ROMANIA
Milan
Zagreb
Caspian Sea
CROATIA
Belgrade
Bucharest
SAN MARINO
B.H.
SERBIA
Crimea: Administered by Russia
Andorra la Vella
MONACO
Sarajevo
MO.
Pristina
BULGARIA
Black Sea
A.
ITALY
K.
Sofia
PORTUGAL
V.C.
Podgorica
Skopje
Lisbon
Madrid
Rome
Tirana
N. MAC.
Istanbul
Barcelona
ALBANIA
TURKEY
SPAIN
ASIA
Gibraltar (UK)
GREECE
Mediterranean Sea
Athens
Valletta
MALTA
AFRICA

Country abbreviations
A. ANDORRA
BEL. BELGIUM
B.H. BOSNIA AND HERZEGOVINA
K. KOSOVO
L. LIECHTENSTEIN
LUX. LUXEMBOURG
MO. MONTENEGRO
NETH. NETHERLANDS
N. MAC. NORTH MACEDONIA
SL. SLOVENIA
SW. SWITZERLAND
V.C. VATICAN CITY

**Facts about Europe** (excluding Russia)

**Population** (2015)
594 823 000

**Largest country**
Ukraine 603 700 sq km

**Country with most people** (2015)
Germany 80 689 000

**Largest city** (2015)
Istanbul 12 459 000

Conic Equidistant projection

## Facts about Asia

**Population** (2015)
4 538 000 000

**Largest country** (in Asia and Europe)
Russia 17 075 400 sq km

**Country with most people** (2015)
China 1 383 925 000

**Largest city** (2015)
Tōkyō 38 197 000

ATLANTIC OCEAN

EUROPE

AFRICA

ARCTIC OCEAN

PACIFIC OCEAN

INDIAN OCEAN

Aleutian Islands

Bering Sea

Sea of Okhotsk

Sakhalin

Sapporo

JAPAN
**Tōkyō**
Osaka
Kobe
Fukuoka

Sea of Japan (East Sea)

East China Sea

Yellow Sea

Harbin

Shenyang

NORTH KOREA
**Pyongyang**

**Seoul**
SOUTH KOREA

**Beijing**
Tianjin

Shanghai

Nanjing

Wuhan

Xi'an

Lanzhou

Chongqing

Guangzhou

Hong Kong

**Taipei**
TAIWAN
Taiwan: China claims Taiwan as its 23rd province

Northern Mariana Islands

Saipan

Guam

Yap

Pohnpei

Caroline Islands

New Ireland

Bougainville

Guadalcanal

Bismarck Sea

New Guinea

Coral Sea

Arafura Sea

Banda Sea

Celebes Sea

Makassar Strait

Flores Sea

Java Sea

Sulu Sea

South China Sea

PHILIPPINES
**Manila**

Luzon

Luzon Strait

Mindanao

Davao

Halmahera

Serām

Celebes

Borneo

Sumatra

Java

**Jakarta**
Surabaya

INDONESIA

**Dili**
EAST TIMOR

PALAU

BRUNEI

MALAYSIA
**Putrajaya**
**Kuala Lumpur**
SINGAPORE

**Phnom Penh**
CAMBODIA

Gulf of Thailand

**Bangkok**
THAILAND

VIETNAM

Ho Chi Minh City

**Vientiane**
LAOS

**Hanoi**

**Nay Pyi Taw**
MYANMAR (BURMA)

Yangon

Bay of Bengal

Andaman Is (India)

Nicobar Is (India)

**Dhaka**
BANGLADESH

Kolkata

BHUTAN

NEPAL

**New Delhi**
Delhi

INDIA

Hyderabad

Chennai

SRI LANKA
**Sri Jayewardenepura Kotte**
Colombo

MALDIVES

Mumbai

Arabian Sea

Karachi

PAKISTAN
**Islamabad**
Lahore

AFGHANISTAN
**Kābul**

TAJIKISTAN

KYRGYZSTAN

Almaty

Ürümqi

C H I N A

M O N G O L I A
**Ulan Bator**

Irkutsk

Yakutsk

R U S S I A

Novosibirsk

Omsk

KAZAKHSTAN
**Astana**

UZBEKISTAN
**Tashkent**

TURKMENISTAN
**Ashgabat**

Caspian Sea

**Tehrān**
I R A N

**Muscat**
OMAN

UNITED ARAB EMIRATES

QATAR

BAHRAIN

The Gulf

**Kuwait**
KUWAIT

**Baghdād**
IRAQ

**Riyadh**
SAUDI ARABIA

**Sanaa**
YEMEN

Socotra (Yemen)

Gulf of Aden

Red Sea

JORDAN

ISRAEL

LEBANON

CYPRUS

SYRIA

**Ankara**
T U R K E Y

GEORGIA

ARMENIA

AZERBAIJAN

Black Sea

Mediterranean Sea

North Sea

Baltic Sea

Norwegian Sea

Barents Sea

St Petersburg

**Moscow**

Perm

Chelyabinsk

Volgograd

Tropic of Cancer

Arctic Circle

Equator

Lambert Azimuthal Equal Area projection

### Key

| | |
|---|---|
| —— | Country boundary |
| – – – | Disputed boundary |
| ······ | Ceasefire line |
| ■ | Capital city |
| ○ | Important city / town |

**Scale 1 : 50 000 000**

0   500   1000   1500   2000 km

N
W   E
S

## Facts about Asia

**Area**
45 036 492 sq km

**Highest peak**
Mt Everest 8848 m

**Lowest point**
Dead Sea -426 m

**Longest river**
Chang Jiang 6380 km

**Largest lake**
Caspian Sea 371 000 sq km

## Key

| | over 5000 m |
| | 3000 – 5000 m |
| | 2000 – 3000 m |
| | 1000 – 2000 m |
| | 500 – 1000 m |
| | 200 – 500 m |
| | 0 – 200 m |
| | land below sea level |
| | Ice cap |
| 8848 ▲ | Mountain height (in metres) |

**Scale 1 : 50 000 000**

0   500   1000   1500   2000 km

Lambert Azimuthal Equal Area projection

PACIFIC OCEAN

ARCTIC OCEAN

INDIAN OCEAN

ATLANTIC OCEAN

Equator
Tropic of Cancer
Arctic Circle

Bering Sea
Aleutian Islands
Kamchatka Peninsula
Mys Lopatka
Kuril Islands
Sakhalin
Sea of Okhotsk
Khrebet Kolymskiy
Wrangel Island
New Siberia Islands
Laptev Sea
Severnaya Zemlya
Franz Josef Land
Spitsbergen
Novaya Zemlya
Barents Sea
North Cape
Kola Peninsula
Norwegian Sea
Lake Onega
Lake Ladoga
White Sea
Northern Dvina
Pechora
Ural
Kama
Volga
Don
Dnieper
Vistula
Danube
Rhine
Pyrenees
Bay of Biscay
North Sea
Baltic Sea
Alps
Carpathian Mts
Central Russian Upland
North European Plain
Ural Mountains
Gora Narodnaya 1894
Ob
West Siberian Plain
SIBERIA
Central Siberian Plateau
Taymyr Peninsula
Yenisey
Nizhnyaya Tunguska
Lena
Lake Baikal
Angara
Selenga
Yablonovyy Khrebet
Stanovoy Khrebet
Verkhoyanskiy Khrebet
Khrebet Dzhugdzhur
Amur
Argun
Da Hinggan Ling
Manchuria
Amur
Irtysh
Ob
Lake Zaysan
Lake Balkhash
Aral Sea
Syr Darya
Amu Darya
Caspian Sea
Elburz Mts
Dasht-e Kavir
Iranian Plateau
Zagros Mts
Caucasus
El'brus 5642
Mount Ararat 5165
Black Sea
Tigris
Euphrates
Taurus Mts
Cyprus
Mediterranean Sea
The Gulf
Gulf of Oman
Jazirat Masirah
Makran
Hindu Kush
Helmand
Karakoram Ra.
K2 8611
Taklimakan Desert
Turpan Pendi
Lop Nur
Tien Shan
Altai Mountains
Gobi Desert
Plateau of Tibet
Kunlun Shan
Himalaya
Dhaulagiri 8167
Annapurna 8091
Mount Everest 8848
Ganges
Brahmaputra
Yamuna
Ghaghara
Sutlej
Indus
Thar Desert
Aravalli Range
Narmada
Godavari
Western Ghats
Eastern Ghats
Deccan
Cape Comorin
Sri Lanka
Laccadive Islands
Maldives
Chagos Archipelago
Arabian Sea
Bay of Bengal
Mouths of the Ganges
Arakan Yoma
Irrawaddy
Salween
Mekong
Gulf of Thailand
Andaman Islands
Nicobar Islands
Andaman Sea
Strait of Malacca
Kepulauan Mentawai
Sumatra
Peninsular Malaysia
Borneo
Palawan
Java Sea
Java
Bali
Lombok
Flores
Flores Sea
Celebes
Celebes Sea
Sulu Sea
Mindanao
Philippines
Luzon
Samar
Luzon Strait
Taiwan
Hainan
Xi Jiang
Nan Ling
Chang Jiang
Gongga Shan 7514
North China Plain
Huang He
Hai He
Yellow Sea
Korea Strait
East China Sea
Okinawa
Ryukyu Islands
Japan (East Sea)
Sea of Japan
Shikoku
Kyushu
Honshu
Hokkaido
Sikhote-Alin
North Cape
Scotra
Gulf of Aden
Red Sea
'Asir
Hijaz
An Nafud
Arabian Peninsula
Rub' al Khali
Nubian Desert
Eastern Desert
Western Desert
Ethiopian Highlands
New Guinea 4884
Arafura Sea
Timor
Timor Sea
Banda Sea
Seram
Buru
Halmahera
Palau Islands
Yap
Guam
Saipan
Northern Mariana Islands
Caroline Islands
Pohnpei
New Ireland
New Britain
Bougainville Island
Bismarck Sea
Cape York
Gulf of Carpentaria
Puncak Jaya
N E S W

ASIA

INDIAN OCEAN

PACIFIC OCEAN

Equator

Tropic of Capricorn

**Facts about Oceania**

**Population** (2015)
39 331 000

**Largest country**
Australia 7 692 024 sq km

**Country with most people** (2015)
Australia 23 969 000

**Largest city** (2015)
Sydney 4 844 000

FEDERATED STATES OF MICRONESIA

Baker Island (USA)

KIRIBATI

Bairiki

NAURU
Yaren

SOLOMON ISLANDS
Honiara

TUVALU
Vaiaku

Wallis and Futuna (France)

Tokelau (New Zealand)

American Samoa (USA)

SAMOA
Apia

FIJI
Suva

TONGA
Nuku'alofa

Niue (New Zealand)

Cook Islands (New Zealand)

VANUATU
Port Vila

New Caledonia (France)
Nouméa

Norfolk Island (Australia)

Lord Howe Island (Australia)

Kermadec Islands (New Zealand)

Chatham Islands (New Zealand)

NEW ZEALAND

Auckland
North Island (Te Ika-a-Māui)
Wellington
Christchurch
South Island (Te Waipounamu)
Dunedin

New Guinea

PAPUA NEW GUINEA
Lae
Port Moresby

Arafura Sea

Timor Sea

Ashmore and Cartier Islands (Australia)

Coral Sea

Coral Sea Islands Territory (Australia)

AUSTRALIA

Darwin
Alice Springs
Cairns
Townsville
Rockhampton
Brisbane
Gold Coast
Newcastle
Sydney
Canberra
Melbourne
Geelong
Adelaide
Kalgoorlie
Perth

Great Australian Bight

Tasman Sea

Tasmania
Hobart

N W E S

**Key**

— Country boundary
■ Capital city
○ Important city / town

**Scale 1 : 35 000 000**

0 500 1000 1500 km

Lambert Azimuthal Equal Area projection

Equator

20°S

20°S

40°S

40°S

120°E

140°E

160°E

180°

**Facts about Oceania**

**Area**
8 844 516 sq km

**Highest peak**
Puncak Jaya 4884 m

**Lowest point**
Kati Thanda–Lake Eyre -16 m

**Longest river**
Murray–Darling 3672 km

**Largest lake**
Kati Thanda–Lake Eyre 0–8900 sq km

Lambert Azimuthal Equal Area projection

**Key**
over 5000 m
3000 – 5000 m
2000 – 3000 m
1000 – 2000 m
500 – 1000 m
200 – 500 m
0 – 200 m
land below sea level

Mountain height
(in metres)

4884 ▲

**Scale 1 : 35 000 000**

0 500 1000 1500 km

Tropic of Capricorn

Equator

20°S

20°S

40°S

40°S

40°S

100°E

120°E

140°E

160°E

160°E

180°

160°W

140°W

**PACIFIC OCEAN**

**INDIAN OCEAN**

**ASIA**

Niue

Samoa

Tonga

Vanua Levu

Fiji

Viti Levu 1323
Tomanivi 1323

Gilbert Islands

Nauru

Santa Cruz Islands

Espíritu Santo

Loyalty Islands

New Caledonia

Chatham Islands

East Cape

Cook Strait

North Cape

Aoraki/
Mount Cook 3724
Southern Alps

Stewart Island

Auckland Islands

**Tasman Sea**

Admiralty Islands

New Ireland

Bougainville Island

New Britain

Bismarck Sea

Solomon Islands

Guadalcanal

**Coral Sea**

Mount Wilhelm 4509

Gulf of Papua

Puncak Jaya 4884 ▲

Cape York

Torres Strait

Cape York Peninsula

Gulf of Carpentaria

Great Barrier Reef

Great Dividing Range

Grey Range

Darling Downs

Darling

Lachlan

Murray

Blue Mts

Mount Kosciuszko 2228 ▲

Cape Howe

Flinders Island

Bass Str.

Mount Ossa 1617 ▲

Tasmania

South East Cape

Kangaroo Island

Spencer Gulf

Great Australian Bight

Lake Gairdner

Lake Torrens

Nullarbor Plain

Kati Thanda–Lake Eyre

Great Victoria Desert

Musgrave Ranges

Uluru/
Ayers Rock 863 ▲

Gibson Desert

Macdonnell Ranges

Lake Mackay

Lake Disappointment

Great Sandy Desert

Barkly Tableland

Arnhem Land

Kimberley Plateau

Melville Island

Pilbara

Mount Bruce 1235 ▲

North West Cape

Cape Leeuwin

**Timor Sea**

**Arafura Sea**

Equator

N
W E
S

## Manned bases in the Antarctic Peninsula

① Comandante Ferraz (Brazil)
② King Sejong (South Korea)
③ Artigas (Uruguay)
④ Eduardo Frei (Chile)
⑤ Bellingshausen (Russia)
⑥ Great Wall (China)
⑦ Carlini (Argentina)
⑧ Henryk Arctowski (Poland)
⑨ Bernardo O'Higgins (Chile)
⑩ San Martin (Argentina)

Ice shelf
Ice cap
Polar pack ice
Drifting ice
Glacier

Scale 1 : 35 000 000

0      500      1000      1500 km

Antarctic Circle

10°W  0°  10°E  20°W  20°E  30°W  30°E  40°W  40°E  50°W  50°E

Orcadas (Arg.)
South Orkney Is.

Neumayer III (Germany)
Troll (Norway)
Maitri (India)
Novolazarevskaya (Russia)
SANAE IV (South Africa)

South Shetland Is.

Esperanza (Arg.)
Marambio (Arg.)
Arturo Prat (Chile)
Palmer (USA)
Vernadskiy (Ukraine)
Rothera (UK)

Graham Land
Antarctic Peninsula
Palmer Land
Mount Jackson ▲ 3184
Alexander I.

Halley VI (UK)

Weddell Sea

Belgrano II (Arg.)

Berkner Subglacial I.

▲ Mt Wideroe 3180

Queen Maud Land

Syowa (Japan)

Enderby Land

Mawson (Australia)

SOUTHERN

3807 ▲

Mount Menzies 3355
Kemp Land

Prydz Bay

Bharati (India)
Zhongshan (China)
Progress III (Russia)
Davis (Australia)

60°E
70°E
80°E

**A N T A R C T I C A**

Transantarctic Mountains

South Pole ▶
Amundsen-Scott (USA)

4083 ▲

90°W
90°E

Bellingshausen Sea

**A**

Ellsworth Land
Mount Vinson ▲ 4892

Marie Byrd Land
Mount Sidley ▲ 4285
Amundsen Sea
Mount Siple ▲ 3100

SOUTHERN OCEAN

100°W
100°E

Queen Mary Land
Mount Amundsen ▲ 1445

**C**

Mirnyy (Russia)

Vostok (Russia)

Concordia (France/Italy)
3206 ▲

Casey (Australia)

Ross Ice Shelf
**B**
Roosevelt I.
80°S

McMurdo (USA)
Mount Erebus ▲ 3794
Scott Base (NZ)

Ross Sea

Jang Bogo (South Korea)

Mount Minto ▲ 4165

Wilkes Land

Oates Land

Dumont d'Urville (France)

110°W
120°W
130°W
140°W
150°W
160°W
170°W
180°
170°E
160°E
150°E
140°E
130°E
120°E
110°E

70°S

Under the Antarctic Treaty of 1959 all territorial claims are held in abeyance in the interest of international cooperation for scientific purposes.

## Cross-section

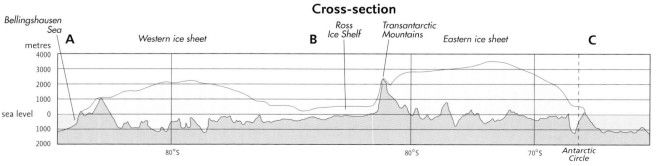

Bellingshausen Sea
metres
4000
3000
2000
1000
sea level 0
1000
2000

**A**  Western ice sheet  **B** Ross Ice Shelf  Transantarctic Mountains  Eastern ice sheet  **C**

80°S      80°S      70°S

Antarctic Circle

Polar Stereographic projection

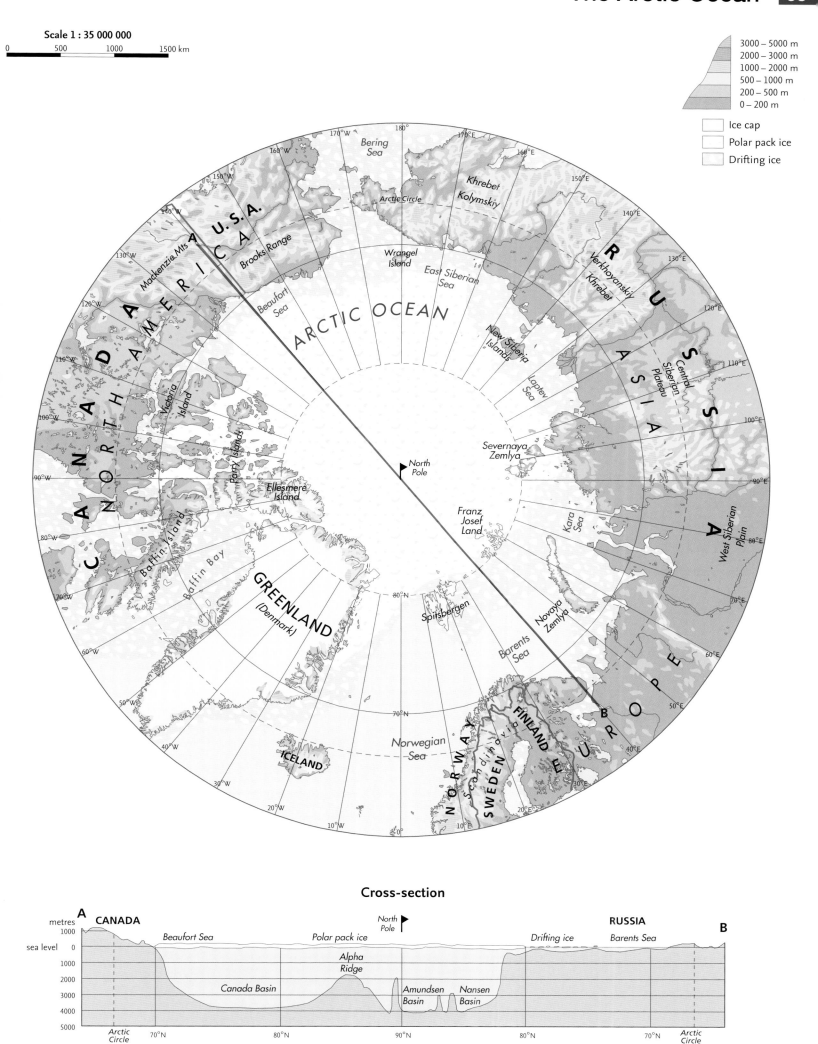

Scale 1 : 35 000 000

0   500   1000   1500 km

3000 – 5000 m
2000 – 3000 m
1000 – 2000 m
500 – 1000 m
200 – 500 m
0 – 200 m

Ice cap
Polar pack ice
Drifting ice

Bering Sea

Khrebet Kolymskiy

Arctic Circle

Wrangel Island

Brooks Range

Mackenzie Mts

U.S.A.

Beaufort Sea

East Siberian Sea

Verkhoyanskiy Khrebet

R U S S I A

ARCTIC OCEAN

New Siberia Islands

Laptev Sea

Central Siberian Plateau

C A N A D A

N O R T H   A M E R I C A

Victoria Island

Parry Islands

Severnaya Zemlya

A S I A

Ellesmere Island

North Pole

Baffin Island

Franz Josef Land

Kara Sea

West Siberian Plain

Baffin Bay

80°N

Spitsbergen

Novaya Zemlya

GREENLAND (Denmark)

Barents Sea

70°N

E U R O P E

NORWAY

Scandinavia

FINLAND

SWEDEN

Norwegian Sea

ICELAND

A

B

## Cross-section

A CANADA

metres 1000
sea level 0
1000
2000
3000
4000
5000

Beaufort Sea

Polar pack ice

North Pole

Drifting ice

Barents Sea

RUSSIA

B

Alpha Ridge

Canada Basin

Amundsen Basin

Nansen Basin

Arctic Circle

70°N

80°N

90°N

80°N

70°N

Arctic Circle

Polar Stereographic projection

- ■ Capital city
- ○ Other town/city

RUSSIA
U.S.A.
Arctic Circle
Anchorage
60°N
GREENLAND
(Denmark)
Nuuk
(Godthab)
AIR

C A N A D A
Edmonton
Winnipeg
Vancouver
Seattle
Ottawa
Montreal
Toronto
Chicago
Boston
Detroit
Pittsburgh
New York
40°N
UNITED
STATES
OF AMERICA
San Francisco
Washington
D.C.
Philadelphia
Azores
(Port.)
Rabat
MOROCCO
Los Angeles
7
Phoenix
Dallas
Houston
Laâyoune
WESTERN
SAHARA
Monterrey
Miami
THE
BAHAMAS
Tropic of Cancer
20°N
Nassau
MAURITANIA
Guadalajara
Havana
CUBA
DOMINICAN
REP.
San Juan
Nouakchott
MEXICO
Mexico City
Kingston
HAITI
PUERTO
RICO
(USA)
CAPE VERDE
SENEGAL
Dakar
Bamako
Belmopan
BELIZE
JAMAICA
SEE INSET FOR
MORE DETAIL
Bissau
THE GAMBIA
GUINEA-BISSAU
GUINEA
Ouagadou
GUATEMALA
HONDURAS
Guatemala City
Tegucigalpa
NICARAGUA
TRINIDAD & TOBAGO
Conakry
Freetown
SIERRA LEONE
C.D
Yamousso
EL SALVADOR
6
Managua
COSTA RICA
San José
Panama
City
Caracas
Port of Spain
Monrovia
LIBERIA
PANAMA
VENEZUELA
Georgetown
Paramaribo
Cayenne
GUY
SUR.
FR.G.
PACIFIC
Bogotá
COLOMBIA
Quito
ECUADOR
ATLANTIC
KIRIBATI
OCEAN
Equator
0°
Galapagos Is
(Ec.)
PERU
Recife
OCEAN
Marquesas
Is (Fr.)
B R A Z I L
5
SAMOA
French
Polynesia
Lima
Society Is
(Fr.)
Tuamoto Is
Brasília
Cook
Islands
(NZ)
Tahiti
La Paz
BOLIVIA
Belo Horizonte
20°S
TONGA
Sucre
PARAGUAY
Rio de Janeiro
Tropic of Capricorn
Pitcairn
Island (UK)
Easter I.
(Chile)
São Paulo
Asunción
4
ARGENTINA
CHILE
URUGUAY
Santiago
Buenos
Aires
Montevideo
40°S

3
ATLANTIC
OCEAN
Falkland Islands
(UK)
South Georgia
and South
Sandwich Islands
(UK)
60°S
Antarctic Circle
2

HAITI
Santiago
Port-au-
Prince
Santo
Domingo
DOMINICAN
REPUBLIC
Mona Passage
San
Juan
US
Virgin Is
(USA)
British
Virgin Is
(UK)
Anguilla
(UK)
St-Martin (Fr.)
St-Barthélemy (Fr.)
Mayagüez
PUERTO RICO
(USA)
Sint Maarten
(Neth.)
St Eustatius
(Neth.)
Basseterre
ANTIGUA AND
BARBUDA
ST KITTS AND NEVIS
St John's
Montserrat
(UK)
Guadeloupe
(Fr.)
Basse-Terre
C a r i b b e a n
Roseau
DOMINICA
S e a
Martinique
(Fr.)
Fort-de-France
Scale 1 : 15 000 000
ST LUCIA
Castries
Aruba
(Neth.)
Curaçao
(Neth.)
Bonaire
(Neth.)
ST VINCENT AND
THE GRENADINES
Kingstown
BARBADOS
Bridgetown
Willemstad
GRENADA
St George's
Scarborough
SOUTH AMERICA
Port of Spain
TRINIDAD
AND TOBAGO

### World facts

**Population** (2015)
7 349 472 000

**Largest country**
Russia 17 075 400 sq km

**Country with most people** (2015)
China 1 383 925 000

**Largest city** (2015)
Tōkyō 38 197 000

International boundaries in the sea shown on this map indicate ownership
of islands and island groups only. They do not infer the alignment of legal
maritime boundaries.
Not all countries are named on the map.

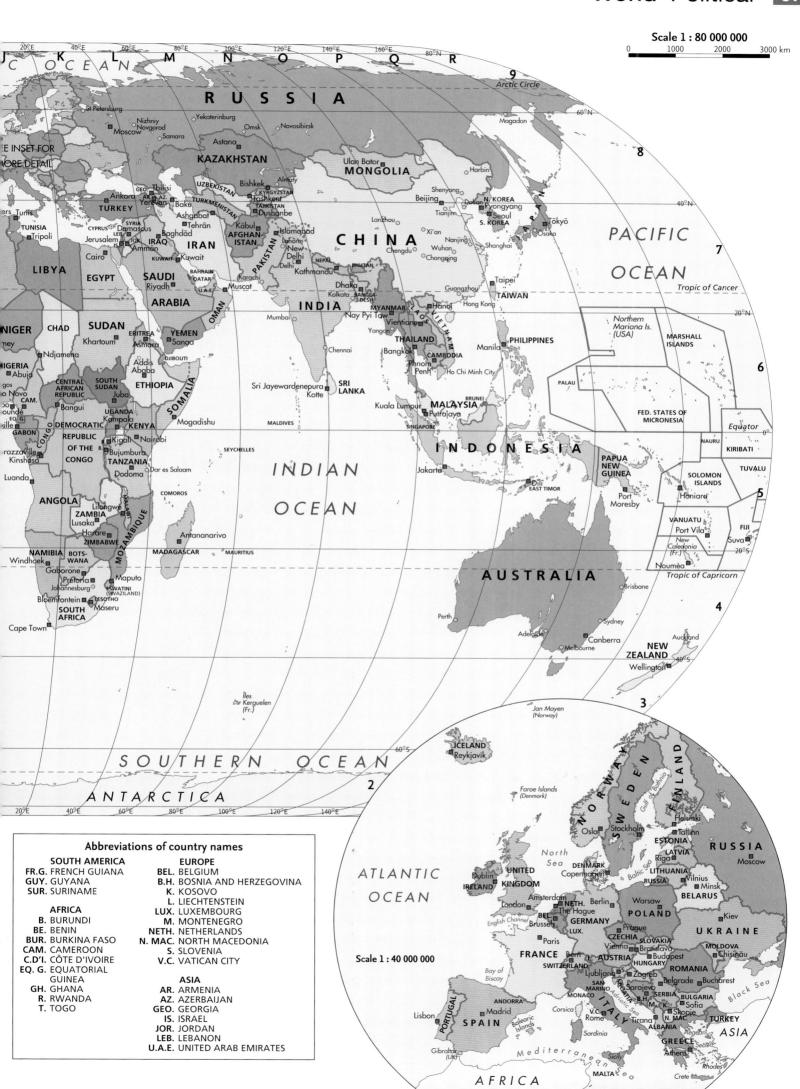

Scale 1 : 80 000 000

0     1000     2000     3000 km

## Abbreviations of country names

**SOUTH AMERICA**
FR.G. FRENCH GUIANA
GUY. GUYANA
SUR. SURINAME

**AFRICA**
B. BURUNDI
BE. BENIN
BUR. BURKINA FASO
CAM. CAMEROON
C.D'I. CÔTE D'IVOIRE
EQ. G. EQUATORIAL
          GUINEA
GH. GHANA
R. RWANDA
T. TOGO

**EUROPE**
BEL. BELGIUM
B.H. BOSNIA AND HERZEGOVINA
K. KOSOVO
L. LIECHTENSTEIN
LUX. LUXEMBOURG
M. MONTENEGRO
NETH. NETHERLANDS
N. MAC. NORTH MACEDONIA
S. SLOVENIA
V.C. VATICAN CITY

**ASIA**
AR. ARMENIA
AZ. AZERBAIJAN
GEO. GEORGIA
IS. ISRAEL
JOR. JORDAN
LEB. LEBANON
U.A.E. UNITED ARAB EMIRATES

Scale 1 : 40 000 000

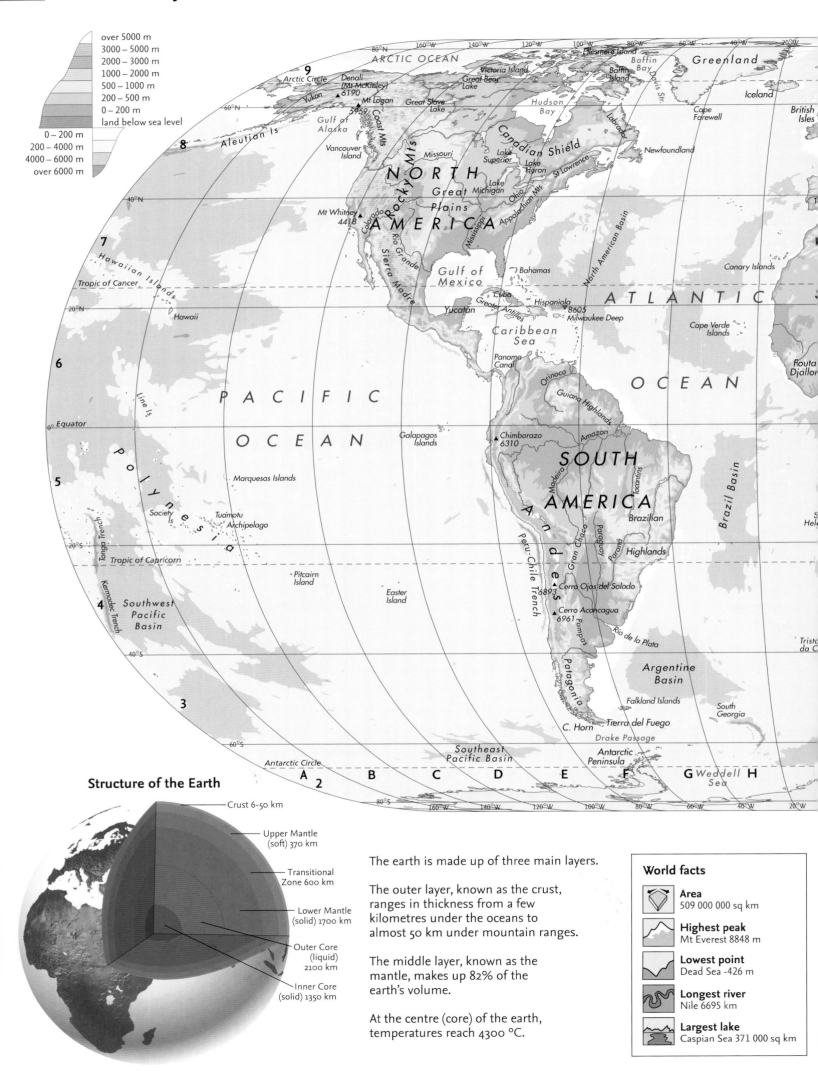

**Structure of the Earth**

- Crust 6-50 km
- Upper Mantle (soft) 370 km
- Transitional Zone 600 km
- Lower Mantle (solid) 1700 km
- Outer Core (liquid) 2100 km
- Inner Core (solid) 1350 km

The earth is made up of three main layers.

The outer layer, known as the crust, ranges in thickness from a few kilometres under the oceans to almost 50 km under mountain ranges.

The middle layer, known as the mantle, makes up 82% of the earth's volume.

At the centre (core) of the earth, temperatures reach 4300 °C.

**World facts**

| | |
|---|---|
| **Area** | 509 000 000 sq km |
| **Highest peak** | Mt Everest 8848 m |
| **Lowest point** | Dead Sea -426 m |
| **Longest river** | Nile 6695 km |
| **Largest lake** | Caspian Sea 371 000 sq km |

Scale 1 : 80 000 000

0  800  1600  2400  3200 km

Ice cap

8848 ▲ Mountain height (in metres)

▼ Ocean depth
10920 (in metres)

| Continents | Area (sq km) |
|---|---|
| Asia | 45 036 492 |
| Africa | 30 343 578 |
| North America | 24 680 331 |
| South America | 17 815 420 |
| Antarctica | 12 093 000 |
| Europe | 9 908 599 |
| Oceania | 8 844 516 |

| Oceans | Area (sq km) |
|---|---|
| Pacific Ocean | 166 241 000 |
| Atlantic Ocean | 86 557 000 |
| Indian Ocean | 73 427 000 |
| Arctic Ocean | 9 485 000 |

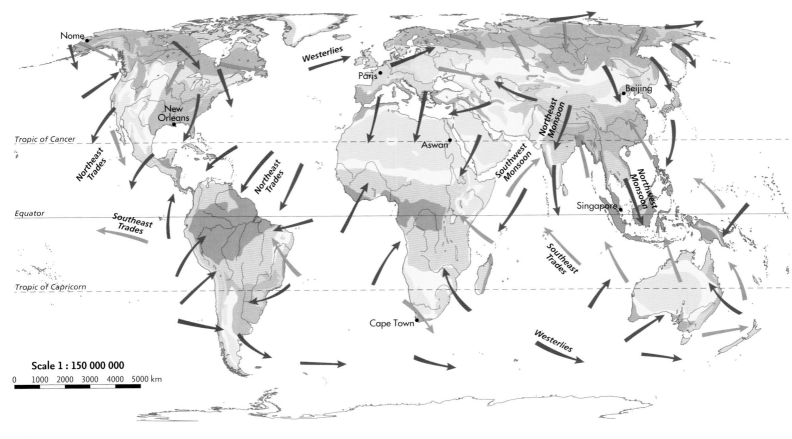

Scale 1 : 150 000 000

0 1000 2000 3000 4000 5000 km

## Climate types

**Ice cap**
Very cold and dry

**Tundra and mountain**
Very cold winters,
altitude affects climate

**Subarctic**
Rainy climate with
long cold winters

**Continental**
Rainy climate, cold winters,
mild summers

**Continental**
Rainy climate, cold winters,
warm summers

**Temperate**
Rainy climate, mild
winters, warm summers

**Subtropical**
Wet warm winters,
hot summers

**Mediterranean**
Rainy mild winters,
dry hot summers

**Semi-arid**
Hot and dry with
rainy season

**Desert**
Very hot and dry
all year

**Tropical**
Hot with wet and
dry seasons

**Tropical**
Hot and wet
all year

• Climate station

→ Wind direction
(January)

→ Wind direction
(July)

→ Wind direction
(all year)

## Rainfall

Average annual rainfall

- more than 3000 mm
- 2000 – 3000 mm
- 1000 – 2000 mm
- 500 – 1000 mm
- 250 – 500 mm
- less than 250 mm

• Climate station

Scale 1 : 250 000 000

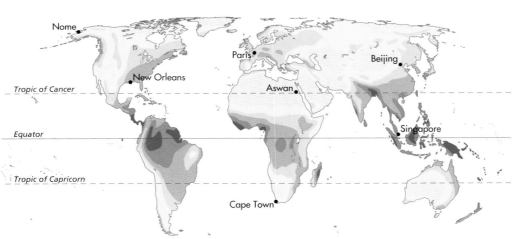

## Climate graphs

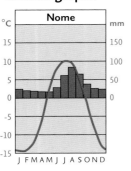

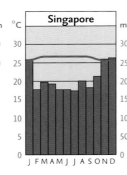

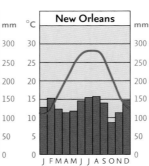

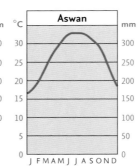

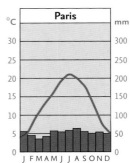

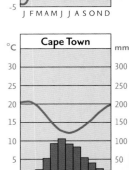

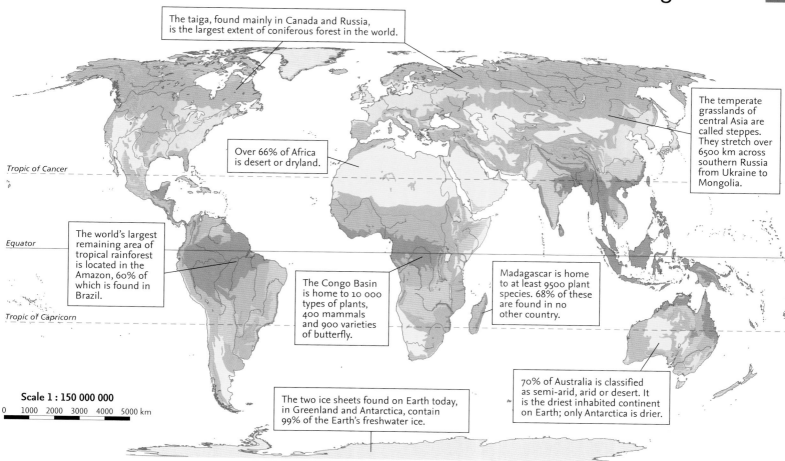

The taiga, found mainly in Canada and Russia, is the largest extent of coniferous forest in the world.

The temperate grasslands of central Asia are called steppes. They stretch over 6500 km across southern Russia from Ukraine to Mongolia.

Over 66% of Africa is desert or dryland.

*Tropic of Cancer*

*Equator*

The world's largest remaining area of tropical rainforest is located in the Amazon, 60% of which is found in Brazil.

The Congo Basin is home to 10 000 types of plants, 400 mammals and 900 varieties of butterfly.

Madagascar is home to at least 9500 plant species. 68% of these are found in no other country.

*Tropic of Capricorn*

70% of Australia is classified as semi-arid, arid or desert. It is the driest inhabited continent on Earth; only Antarctica is drier.

The two ice sheets found on Earth today, in Greenland and Antarctica, contain 99% of the Earth's freshwater ice.

**Scale 1 : 150 000 000**

0   1000   2000   3000   4000   5000 km

## Types of vegetation

**Ice cap and ice shelf**
Extremely cold.
No vegetation.

**Arctic tundra**
Very cold climate.
Simple vegetation
such as mosses,
lichens, grasses and
flowering herbs.

**Mountain/Alpine**
Very low night-time
temperatures. Only
a few dwarf trees and
small leafed shrubs
can grow.

**Mediterranean**
Mild winters and dry
summers. Vegetation
is mixed shrubs and
herbaceous plants.

**Savanna grassland**
Warm or hot climate.
Tropical grasslands with
scattered thorn bushes
or trees.

**Temperate grassland**
Grassland is the main
vegetation. Summers are
hot and winters cold.

**Desert**
Hot with little rainfall.
Very sparse vegetation
except cacti and grasses
adapted to the harsh
conditions.

**Boreal/Taiga forest**
Found between 50° and
70°N. Low temperatures.
Cold-tolerant evergreen
conifers.

**Coniferous forest**
Dense forests of pine, spruce
and larch.

**Mixed forest**
Broadleaf and coniferous forests.

**Tropical forest**
Dense rainforest found in areas
of high rainfall near the equator.

**Dry tropical forest**
Semi deciduous trees with low
shrubs and bushes.

**Sub tropical forest**
Rainfall is seasonal. Mainly
hard leaf evergreen forest.

**Monsoon forest**
Areas which experience
Monsoon rain. All trees are
deciduous.

Arctic tundra in Alaska.

Taiga forest in Siberia, Russia.

Savanna grassland in Tanzania, Africa.

The Sahara desert in Morocco, Africa.

## Earthquakes and volcanoes

- ● Earthquake
- ▲ Volcano
- —— Plate boundary
- ←→ Direction of movement

## Floods

- ⌇ Rivers that experience major flooding
- ▨ Country affected annually by severe flooding
- ⬤ Severe floods causing over 1000 deaths in 1 year (1985–2015)
- ⬤ Severe floods causing 500–1000 deaths in 1 year (1985–2015)

## Plates

The earth's crust is broken into huge plates which fit together like parts of a giant jigsaw. These float on the semi-molten rock below. The boundaries of the plates are marked by lines of volcanoes and earthquake activity.

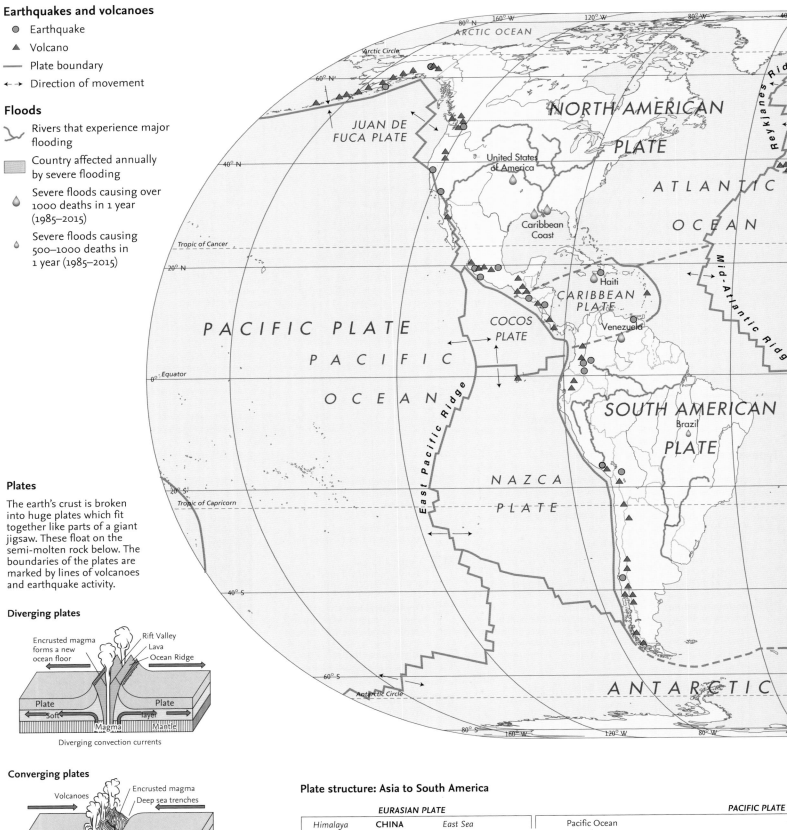

### Diverging plates

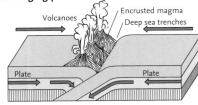

Diverging convection currents

### Converging plates

Converging convection currents

### Shearing plates

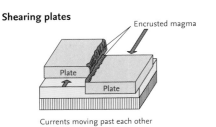

Currents moving past each other

**Plate structure: Asia to South America**

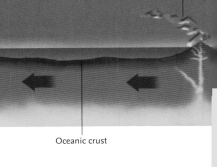

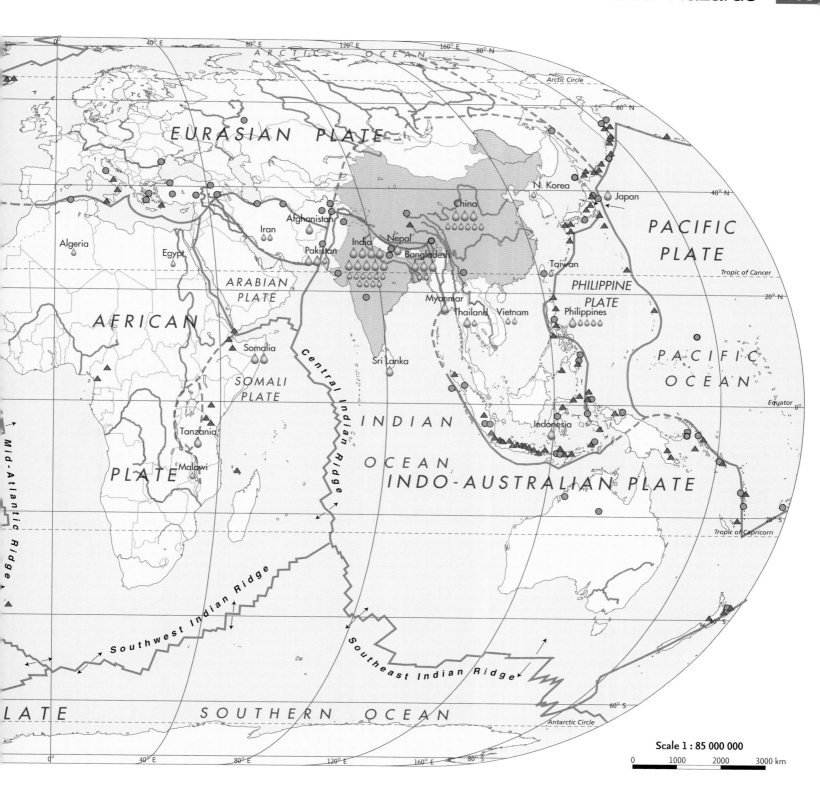

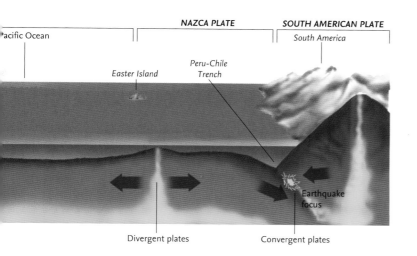

## Earthquakes

Earthquakes occur most frequently along the junction of plates which make up the earth's crust.

They are caused by the release of stress which builds up at the plate edges. When shock waves from these movements reach the surface they are felt as earthquakes which may result in severe damage to property or loss of lives.

## Volcanoes

The greatest number of volcanoes are located in the Pacific 'Ring of Fire'. Violent eruptions often occur when two plates collide and the heat generated forces molten rock (magma) upwards through weaknesses in the earth's crust.

See pages 16–17 for more on earthquakes and volcanoes in the Caribbean.

## Desertification

- [ ] Existing deserts
- [ ] Areas at risk of desertification

## Deforestation

- [ ] Existing tropical forests
- [ ] Forests cleared since 1940

## Forest fires

- ♦ Recent major forest fires

## Pollution

- Coastal pollution
- / River pollution
- • Major city with air pollution

The pink-boxed text on the map shows some of the signs of climate change.

**Desertification** is the transformation of fertile land into an arid or semi-arid region as a result of climatic change and human activities.

**Deforestation** is the clearance of forests so that the land can be used for other purposes – usually agriculture, but also urban expansion.

Forests are also lost through repeated **forest fires** that occur accidentally. These are also called wildfires or bushfires, and occur most often in forested regions that have a dry season.

**Ocean acidification**, due to increasing carbon dioxide levels, reduces the ability of marine life, such as coral, to extract calcium carbonate to make their shells and skeletons.

## The Greenhouse Effect

Greenhouse gases build up in the Earth's atmosphere, stopping heat bouncing back into space from the Earth's surface. Without these gases temperatures on Earth would be around 15°C lower.

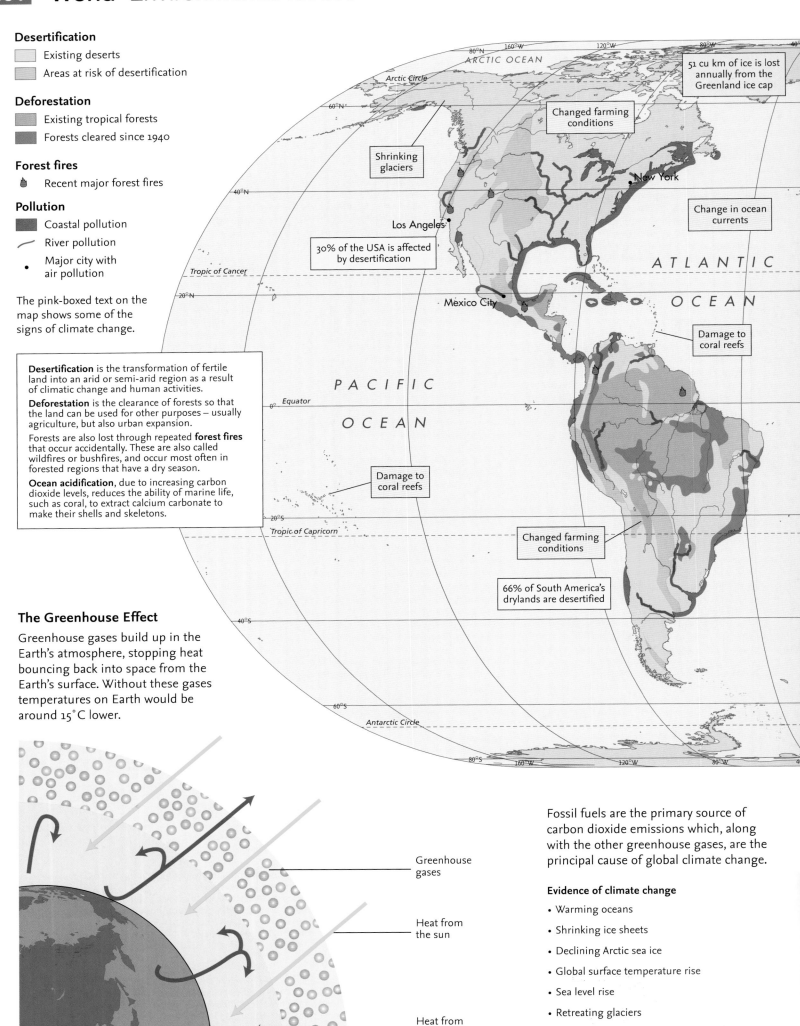

**51 cu km of ice is lost annually from the Greenland ice cap**

**Changed farming conditions**

**Shrinking glaciers**

**Change in ocean currents**

**30% of the USA is affected by desertification**

**Damage to coral reefs**

**Damage to coral reefs**

**Changed farming conditions**

**66% of South America's drylands are desertified**

New York
Los Angeles
Mexico City

ARCTIC OCEAN
Arctic Circle
ATLANTIC OCEAN
PACIFIC OCEAN
Equator
Tropic of Cancer
Tropic of Capricorn
Antarctic Circle

Greenhouse gases

Heat from the sun

Heat from the Earth

Fossil fuels are the primary source of carbon dioxide emissions which, along with the other greenhouse gases, are the principal cause of global climate change.

**Evidence of climate change**

- Warming oceans
- Shrinking ice sheets
- Declining Arctic sea ice
- Global surface temperature rise
- Sea level rise
- Retreating glaciers
- Ocean acidification
- Extreme events

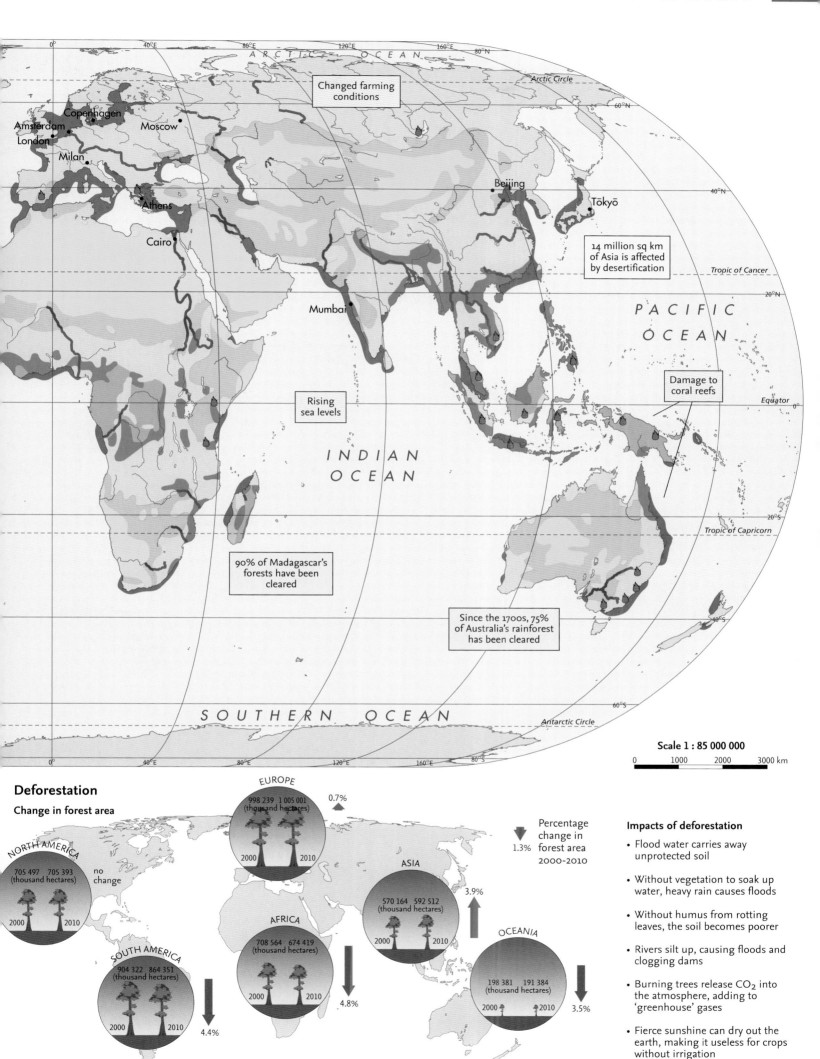

Changed farming conditions

14 million sq km of Asia is affected by desertification

Damage to coral reefs

Rising sea levels

90% of Madagascar's forests have been cleared

Since the 1700s, 75% of Australia's rainforest has been cleared

ARCTIC OCEAN

Arctic Circle

Amsterdam
London
Copenhagen
Moscow
Milan
Athens
Cairo

Beijing
Tōkyō

Mumbai

PACIFIC OCEAN

Tropic of Cancer

Equator

INDIAN OCEAN

Tropic of Capricorn

SOUTHERN OCEAN

Antarctic Circle

**Scale 1 : 85 000 000**

0   1000   2000   3000 km

## Deforestation

**Change in forest area**

NORTH AMERICA
705 497   705 393
(thousand hectares)
2000   2010
no change

SOUTH AMERICA
904 322   864 351
(thousand hectares)
2000   2010
4.4%

EUROPE
998 239   1 005 001
(thousand hectares)
2000   2010
0.7%

AFRICA
708 564   674 419
(thousand hectares)
2000   2010
4.8%

ASIA
570 164   592 512
(thousand hectares)
2000   2010
3.9%

OCEANIA
198 381   191 384
(thousand hectares)
2000   2010
3.5%

Percentage change in forest area 2000-2010
1.3%

### Impacts of deforestation

- Flood water carries away unprotected soil

- Without vegetation to soak up water, heavy rain causes floods

- Without humus from rotting leaves, the soil becomes poorer

- Rivers silt up, causing floods and clogging dams

- Burning trees release $CO_2$ into the atmosphere, adding to 'greenhouse' gases

- Fierce sunshine can dry out the earth, making it useless for crops without irrigation

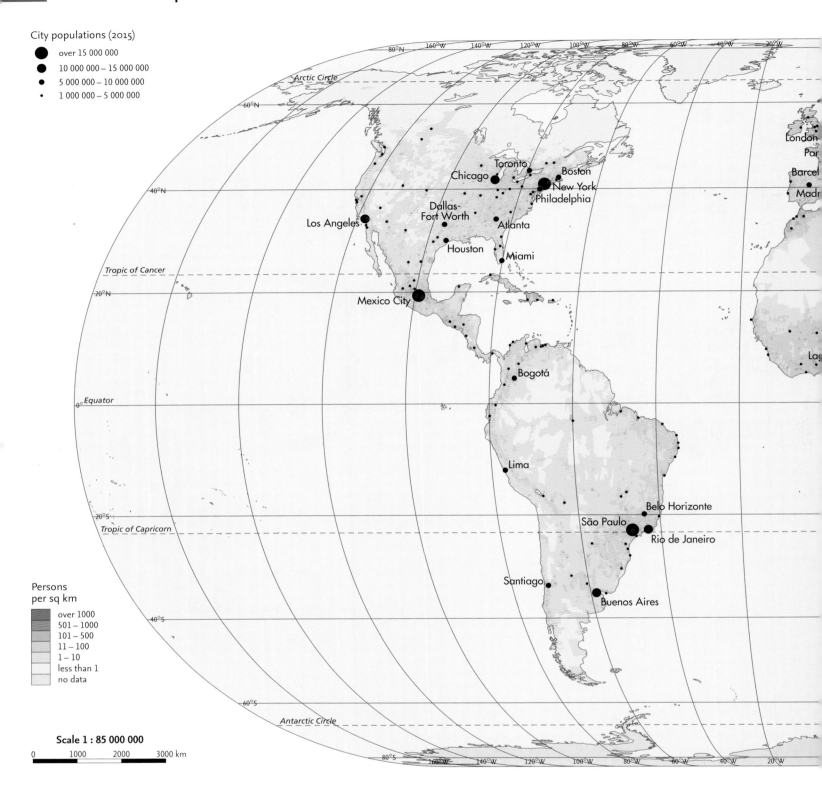

City populations (2015)
- ● over 15 000 000
- ● 10 000 000 – 15 000 000
- • 5 000 000 – 10 000 000
- · 1 000 000 – 5 000 000

Persons per sq km
- over 1000
- 501 – 1000
- 101 – 500
- 11 – 100
- 1 – 10
- less than 1
- no data

Scale 1 : 85 000 000

0    1000    2000    3000 km

## World population distribution by continent

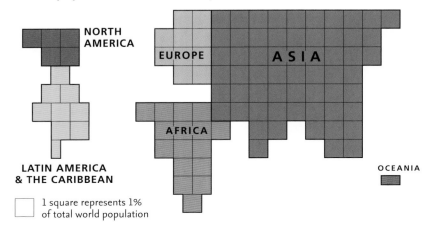

NORTH AMERICA

EUROPE

ASIA

AFRICA

OCEANIA

LATIN AMERICA & THE CARIBBEAN

☐ 1 square represents 1% of total world population

## Facts about world population

| | |
|---|---|
| World population, 2015 | 7 349 472 000 |
| World population, 2050* | 9 725 148 000 |
| Population 60 years and over, 2015 | 14.0% |
| Population 60 years and over, 2050* | 26.0% |
| Population under 15 years, 2015 | 26.1% |
| Population under 15 years, 2050* | 21.3% |
| Life expectancy, 2015-2020* | 72 |
| Male life expectancy, 2015-2020* | 69 |
| Female life expectancy, 2015-2020* | 74 |

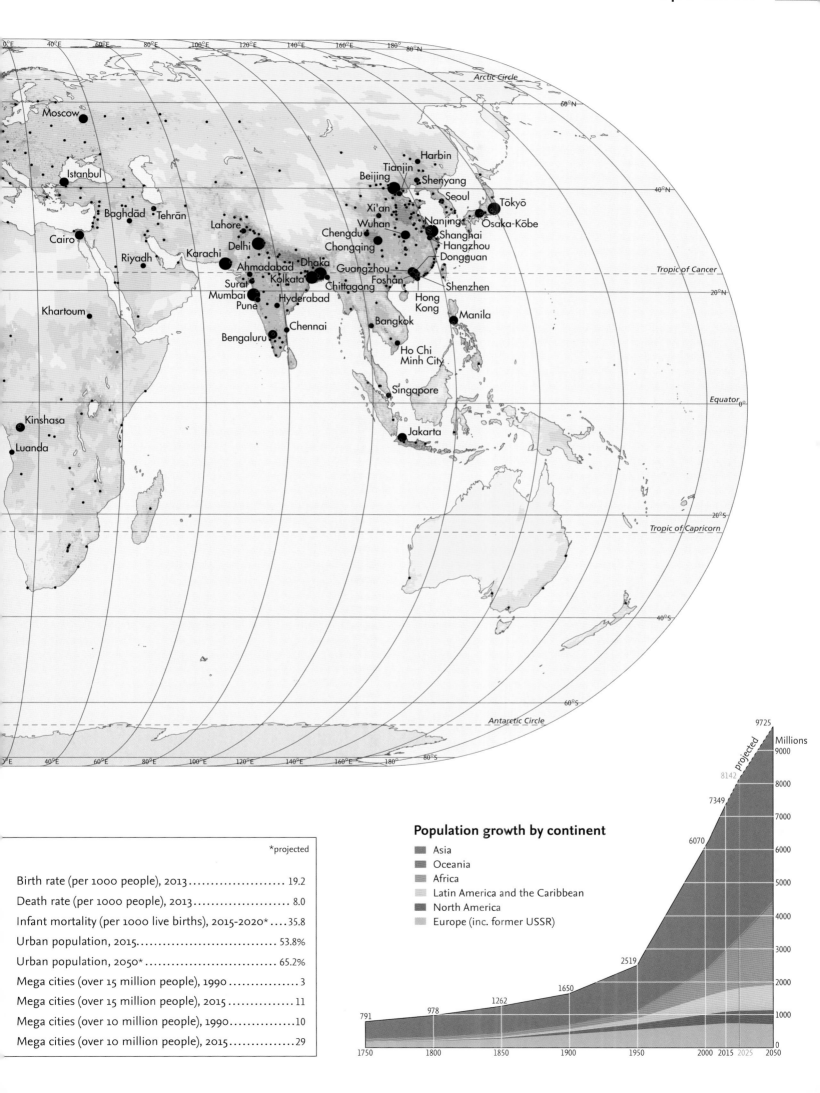

| | *projected |
|---|---|
| Birth rate (per 1000 people), 2013 | 19.2 |
| Death rate (per 1000 people), 2013 | 8.0 |
| Infant mortality (per 1000 live births), 2015-2020* | 35.8 |
| Urban population, 2015 | 53.8% |
| Urban population, 2050* | 65.2% |
| Mega cities (over 15 million people), 1990 | 3 |
| Mega cities (over 15 million people), 2015 | 11 |
| Mega cities (over 10 million people), 1990 | 10 |
| Mega cities (over 10 million people), 2015 | 29 |

## Population growth by continent

- Asia
- Oceania
- Africa
- Latin America and the Caribbean
- North America
- Europe (inc. former USSR)

| Flag | Country | Capital city | Area sq km | Total population 2015[†] |
|------|---------|--------------|-----------|--------------------------|
| | Afghanistan | Kābul | 652 225 | 32 527 000 |
| | Albania | Tirana | 28 748 | 2 897 000 |
| | Algeria | Algiers | 2 381 741 | 39 667 000 |
| | Andorra | Andorra la Vella | 465 | 70 000 |
| | Angola | Luanda | 1 246 700 | 25 022 000 |
| | Antigua & Barbuda | St John's | 442 | 81 799 |
| | Argentina | Buenos Aires | 2 766 889 | 43 417 000 |
| | Armenia | Yerevan | 29 800 | 3 018 000 |
| | Australia | Canberra | 7 692 024 | 23 969 000 |
| | Austria | Vienna | 83 855 | 8 545 000 |
| | Azerbaijan | Baku | 86 600 | 9 754 000 |
| | Bahamas, The | Nassau | 13 939 | 353 658 |
| | Bahrain | Manama | 691 | 1 377 000 |
| | Bangladesh | Dhaka | 143 998 | 160 996 000 |
| | Barbados | Bridgetown | 430 | 277 821 |
| | Belarus | Minsk | 207 600 | 9 496 000 |
| | Belgium | Brussels | 30 520 | 11 299 000 |
| | Belize | Belmopan | 22 965 | 312 971 |
| | Benin | Porto-Novo | 112 620 | 10 880 000 |
| | Bhutan | Thimphu | 46 620 | 775 000 |
| | Bolivia | La Paz/Sucre | 1 098 581 | 10 725 000 |
| | Bosnia and Herzegovina | Sarajevo | 51 130 | 3 810 000 |
| | Botswana | Gaborone | 581 370 | 2 262 000 |
| | Brazil | Brasília | 8 514 879 | 207 848 000 |
| | Brunei | Bandar Seri Begawan | 5 765 | 423 000 |
| | Bulgaria | Sofia | 110 994 | 7 150 000 |
| | Burkina Faso | Ouagadougou | 274 200 | 18 106 000 |
| | Burundi | Bujumbura | 27 835 | 11 179 000 |
| | Cambodia | Phnom Penh | 181 035 | 15 578 000 |
| | Cameroon | Yaoundé | 475 442 | 23 344 000 |
| | Canada | Ottawa | 9 984 670 | 35 940 000 |
| | Cape Verde | Praia | 4 033 | 521 000 |
| | Central African Republic | Bangui | 622 436 | 4 900 000 |
| | Chad | Ndjamena | 1 284 000 | 14 037 000 |
| | Chile | Santiago | 756 945 | 17 948 000 |
| | China | Beijing | 9 606 802 | 1 383 925 000 |
| | Colombia | Bogotá | 1 141 748 | 48 229 000 |
| | Comoros | Moroni | 1 862 | 788 000 |
| | Congo | Brazzaville | 342 000 | 4 620 000 |
| | Congo, Dem. Rep. of the | Kinshasa | 2 345 410 | 77 267 000 |
| | Costa Rica | San José | 51 100 | 4 808 000 |
| | Côte d'Ivoire | Yamoussoukro | 322 463 | 22 702 000 |
| | Croatia | Zagreb | 56 538 | 4 240 000 |
| | Cuba | Havana | 110 860 | 11 167 325 |
| | Cyprus | Nicosia | 9 251 | 1 165 000 |
| | Czech Republic | Prague | 78 864 | 10 543 000 |
| | Denmark | Copenhagen | 43 075 | 5 669 000 |
| | Djibouti | Djibouti | 23 200 | 888 000 |
| | Dominica | Roseau | 750 | 71 293 |

| Flag | Country | Capital city | Area sq km | Total populatio 2015[†] |
|------|---------|--------------|-----------|--------------------------|
| | Dominican Republic | Santo Domingo | 48 442 | 9 445 28 |
| | East Timor | Dili | 14 874 | 1 185 00 |
| | Ecuador | Quito | 272 045 | 16 144 00 |
| | Egypt | Cairo | 1 001 450 | 91 508 00 |
| | El Salvador | San Salvador | 21 041 | 6 127 00 |
| | Equatorial Guinea | Malabo | 28 051 | 845 00 |
| | Eritrea | Asmara | 117 400 | 5 228 00 |
| | Estonia | Tallinn | 45 200 | 1 313 00 |
| | Eswatini (Swaziland) | Mbabane/Lobamba | 17 364 | 1 287 00 |
| | Ethiopia | Addis Ababa | 1 133 880 | 99 391 00 |
| | Fiji | Suva | 18 330 | 892 00 |
| | Finland | Helsinki | 338 145 | 5 503 00 |
| | France | Paris | 543 965 | 64 395 00 |
| | French Guiana | Cayenne | 90 000 | 269 00 |
| | Gabon | Libreville | 267 667 | 1 725 00 |
| | Gambia, The | Banjul | 11 295 | 1 991 00 |
| | Georgia | Tbilisi | 69 700 | 4 000 00 |
| | Germany | Berlin | 357 022 | 80 689 00 |
| | Ghana | Accra | 238 537 | 27 410 00 |
| | Greece | Athens | 131 957 | 10 955 00 |
| | Grenada | St George's | 348 | 103 32 |
| | Guatemala | Guatemala City | 108 890 | 16 343 00 |
| | Guinea | Conakry | 245 857 | 12 609 00 |
| | Guinea-Bissau | Bissau | 36 125 | 1 844 00 |
| | Guyana | Georgetown | 214 969 | 747 88 |
| | Haiti | Port-au-Prince | 27 750 | 10 320 00 |
| | Honduras | Tegucigalpa | 112 088 | 8 075 00 |
| | Hungary | Budapest | 93 030 | 9 855 00 |
| | Iceland | Reykjavík | 102 820 | 329 00 |
| | India | New Delhi | 3 166 620 | 1 311 051 00 |
| | Indonesia | Jakarta | 1 919 445 | 257 564 00 |
| | Iran | Tehrān | 1 648 000 | 79 109 00 |
| | Iraq | Baghdād | 438 317 | 36 423 00 |
| | Ireland | Dublin | 70 282 | 4 688 00 |
| | Israel | Jerusalem* | 22 072 | 8 064 00 |
| | Italy | Rome | 301 245 | 59 798 00 |
| | Jamaica | Kingston | 10 991 | 2 697 98 |
| | Japan | Tōkyō | 377 727 | 126 573 00 |
| | Jordan | 'Ammān | 89 206 | 7 595 00 |
| | Kazakhstan | Astana | 2 717 300 | 17 625 00 |
| | Kenya | Nairobi | 582 646 | 46 050 00 |
| | Kiribati | Bairiki | 717 | 112 00 |
| | Kosovo | Pristina | 10 908 | 1 805 00 |
| | Kuwait | Kuwait | 17 818 | 3 892 00 |
| | Kyrgyzstan | Bishkek | 198 500 | 5 940 00 |
| | Laos | Vientiane | 236 800 | 6 802 00 |
| | Latvia | Rīga | 64 589 | 1 971 00 |
| | Lebanon | Beirut | 10 452 | 5 851 00 |
| | Lesotho | Maseru | 30 355 | 2 135 00 |

| Flag | Country | Capital city | Area sq km | Total population 2015[†] |
|---|---|---|---|---|
| | Liberia | Monrovia | 111 369 | 4 503 000 |
| | Libya | Tripoli | 1 759 540 | 6 278 000 |
| | Liechtenstein | Vaduz | 160 | 38 000 |
| | Lithuania | Vilnius | 65 200 | 2 878 000 |
| | Luxembourg | Luxembourg | 2 586 | 567 000 |
| | Madagascar | Antananarivo | 587 041 | 24 235 000 |
| | Malawi | Lilongwe | 118 484 | 17 215 000 |
| | Malaysia | Kuala Lumpur/Putrajaya | 332 965 | 30 331 000 |
| | Maldives | Male | 298 | 364 000 |
| | Mali | Bamako | 1 240 140 | 17 600 000 |
| | Malta | Valletta | 316 | 419 000 |
| | Marshall Islands | Dalap-Uliga-Darrit | 181 | 53 000 |
| | Mauritania | Nouakchott | 1 030 700 | 4 068 000 |
| | Mauritius | Port Louis | 2 040 | 1 273 000 |
| | Mexico | Mexico City | 1 972 545 | 127 017 000 |
| | Micronesia, Fed. States of | Palikir | 701 | 526 000 |
| | Moldova | Chişinău | 33 700 | 4 069 000 |
| | Mongolia | Ulan Bator | 1 565 000 | 2 959 000 |
| | Montenegro | Podgorica | 13 812 | 626 000 |
| | Morocco | Rabat | 446 550 | 34 378 000 |
| | Mozambique | Maputo | 799 380 | 27 978 000 |
| | Myanmar | Nay Pyi Taw | 676 577 | 53 897 000 |
| | Namibia | Windhoek | 824 292 | 2 459 000 |
| | Nauru | Yaren | 21 | 10 000 |
| | Nepal | Kathmandu | 147 181 | 28 514 000 |
| | Netherlands | Amsterdam/The Hague | 41 526 | 16 925 000 |
| | New Zealand | Wellington | 270 534 | 4 529 000 |
| | Nicaragua | Managua | 130 000 | 6 082 000 |
| | Niger | Niamey | 1 267 000 | 19 899 000 |
| | Nigeria | Abuja | 923 768 | 182 202 000 |
| | North Korea | Pyongyang | 120 538 | 25 155 000 |
| | North Macedonia | Skopje | 25 713 | 2 078 000 |
| | Norway | Oslo | 323 878 | 5 211 000 |
| | Oman | Muscat | 309 500 | 4 491 000 |
| | Pakistan | Islamabad | 881 888 | 188 925 000 |
| | Palau | Ngerulmud | 497 | 21 000 |
| | Panama | Panama City | 77 082 | 3 929 000 |
| | Papua New Guinea | Port Moresby | 462 840 | 7 619 000 |
| | Paraguay | Asunción | 406 752 | 6 639 000 |
| | Peru | Lima | 1 285 216 | 31 377 000 |
| | Philippines | Manila | 300 000 | 100 699 000 |
| | Poland | Warsaw | 312 683 | 38 612 000 |
| | Portugal | Lisbon | 88 940 | 10 350 000 |
| | Puerto Rico | San Juan | 9 104 | 3 725 789 |
| | Qatar | Doha | 11 437 | 2 235 000 |
| | Romania | Bucharest | 237 500 | 19 511 000 |
| | Russia | Moscow | 17 075 400 | 143 457 000[†] |
| | Rwanda | Kigali | 26 338 | 11 610 000 |
| | St Kitts & Nevis | Basseterre | 261 | 54 940 |

| Flag | Country | Capital city | Area sq km | Total population 2015[†] |
|---|---|---|---|---|
| | St Lucia | Castries | 617 | 173 765 |
| | St Vincent & the Grenadines | Kingstown | 389 | 109 991 |
| | Samoa | Apia | 2 831 | 193 000 |
| | San Marino | San Marino | 61 | 32 000 |
| | São Tomé & Príncipe | São Tomé | 964 | 190 000 |
| | Saudi Arabia | Riyadh | 2 200 000 | 31 540 000 |
| | Senegal | Dakar | 196 720 | 15 129 000 |
| | Serbia | Belgrade | 77 453 | 7 046 000 |
| | Seychelles | Victoria | 455 | 96 000 |
| | Sierra Leone | Freetown | 71 740 | 6 453 000 |
| | Singapore | Singapore | 639 | 5 604 000 |
| | Slovakia | Bratislava | 49 035 | 5 426 000 |
| | Slovenia | Ljubljana | 20 251 | 2 068 000 |
| | Solomon Islands | Honiara | 28 370 | 584 000 |
| | Somalia | Mogadishu | 637 657 | 10 787 000 |
| | South Africa | Pretoria / Cape Town Bloemfontein | 1 219 090 | 54 490 000 |
| | South Korea | Seoul | 99 274 | 50 293 000 |
| | South Sudan | Juba | 644 329 | 12 340 000 |
| | Spain | Madrid | 504 782 | 46 122 000 |
| | Sri Lanka | Sri Jayewardenepura Kotte | 65 610 | 20 715 000 |
| | Sudan | Khartoum | 1 861 484 | 40 235 000 |
| | Suriname | Paramaribo | 163 820 | 543 000 |
| | Sweden | Stockholm | 449 964 | 9 779 000 |
| | Switzerland | Bern | 41 293 | 8 299 000 |
| | Syria | Damascus | 184 026 | 18 502 000 |
| | Taiwan | Taipei | 36 179 | 23 462 000 |
| | Tajikistan | Dushanbe | 143 100 | 8 482 000 |
| | Tanzania | Dodoma | 945 087 | 53 470 000 |
| | Thailand | Bangkok | 513 115 | 67 959 000 |
| | Togo | Lomé | 56 785 | 7 305 000 |
| | Tonga | Nuku'alofa | 748 | 106 000 |
| | Trinidad & Tobago | Port of Spain | 5 128 | 1 328 019 |
| | Tunisia | Tunis | 164 150 | 11 254 000 |
| | Turkey | Ankara | 779 452 | 78 666 000 |
| | Turkmenistan | Ashgabat | 488 100 | 5 374 000 |
| | Tuvalu | Vaiaku | 25 | 10 000 |
| | Uganda | Kampala | 241 038 | 39 032 000 |
| | Ukraine | Kiev | 603 700 | 44 824 000 |
| | United Arab Emirates | Abu Dhabi | 77 700 | 9 157 000 |
| | United Kingdom | London | 243 609 | 64 716 000 |
| | United States of America | Washington D.C. | 9 826 635 | 321 774 000 |
| | Uruguay | Montevideo | 176 215 | 3 432 000 |
| | Uzbekistan | Tashkent | 447 400 | 29 893 000 |
| | Vanuatu | Port Vila | 12 190 | 265 000 |
| | Venezuela | Caracas | 912 050 | 31 108 000 |
| | Vietnam | Hanoi | 329 565 | 93 448 000 |
| | Yemen | Sanaa | 527 968 | 26 832 000 |
| | Zambia | Lusaka | 752 614 | 16 212 000 |
| | Zimbabwe | Harare | 390 759 | 15 603 000 |

The important names on the maps in the atlas are found in the index. The names are listed in alphabetical order. Each entry gives the country or region of the world in which the name is located followed by the page number, its grid reference and then its co-ordinates of latitude and longitude.

Some abbreviations have been used in the index; these are listed on the right.

| | | | |
|---|---|---|---|
| A&B | Antigua and Barbuda | mts. | mountains |
| Austa. | Australasia | N. America | North America |
| b. | bay | Oc. | Ocean |
| C. America | Central America | r. | river |
| Cr. | Creek | S. Africa | South Africa |
| des. | desert | S. America | South America |
| Dom. Rep. | Dominican Republic | StK&N | St Kitts and Nevis |
| f. | physical feature e.g. valley, plain | StV&G | St Vincent and the Grenadines |
| g. | gulf | str. | strait |
| i. | island | T&C Is. | Turks and Caicos Islands |
| Is. | Islands | T&T | Trinidad and Tobago |
| l. | lake | U.K. | United Kingdom |
| mtn. | mountain | U.S.A. | United States of America |

**Photo credits**

**front cover** Sergey Uryadnikov/SS (fish), RJ22/SS (flowers), Konstantin G/SS (flamingos), Ruth Peterkin/SS (photo); **back cover** NASA Earth Observatory (satellite image); **p3** NASA Earth Observatory (satellite image); **p5** glenda/SS (Haiti), Martin Mecnarowski/SS (scarlet ibis); **p8-9** Antony McAulay/SS; **p9** xfox01/SS (sun); **p12** Vilainecrevette/SS; **p13** Vyshnivskyy/SS; **p15** NASA Earth Observatory (satellite image), THONY BELIZAIRE/AFP/Getty Images (Red Cross); **p16** Jonathan Torgovnik/Getty Images; **p17** Christopher Pillitz/Getty Images; **p20** bayazed/SS (Taino village), Christopher Garrick/SS (Caguana Indigenous Ceremonial Park), Lorna Roberts/SS (basket weaving), Yatra/SS (cassava), Jeremy Beeler/SS (El Castillo), James L. Stanfield/National Geographic/Getty Images (archaeologists); **p21** Everett Historical/SS (Columbus), British Library (Ptolemy map); **p22** Everett Historical/SS (sugar plantation & cotton production), BOULENGER Xavier/SS (Goree); **p23** Trinimummy/SS (temple), Homo Cosmicos/SS (mosque), pansticks/SS (doubles), NICOLAS DERNE/AFP/Getty Images (shopkeeper), SEAN DRAKES/Alamy Stock Photo (Diwali), sad73ir/SS (sea sponges); **p24** Contraband Collection/Alamy Stock Photo (Empire Windrush), ALBERTO PIZZOLI/AFP/Getty Images (Baroness Scotland), Hulton Archive/Getty Images (Miami), Ms Jane Campbell/SS (carnival), Crush Rush/SS (Marco Rubio); **p25** Grey Villet/The LIFE Picture Collection/Getty Images (Adams), Popperfoto/Getty Images (Williams), Keystone Pictures USA/Alamy Stock Photo (Gairy), Allstar Picture Library/Alamy Stock Photo (Price); **p26-27** David Stringer/Getty Images; **p26** Broadbelt/SS (Climate change), Ethan Daniels/SS (Waste); © Sven Creutzmann/Mambo photo/Getty Images (Mining damage); © Robin Moore/Getty Images (Deforestation); **p27** Gillian Holliday/SS (cane toads), Pierre-Yves Babelon/SS (casuarina), Frolova_Elena/SS (lionfish), Ethan Daniels/SS (Endangered species), Steve Photography/SS (Wind power), Wild Horizon/Getty Images (Coral reef damage), Altin Osmanaj/SS (Carbon dioxide emissions); **p29** pics721/SS (seal), David Marten_House/SS (flamingo), kelldallfall/SS (blue marlin), Gowri Nagarajan/SS (yellow elder), songsak/SS (Lignum Vitae); **p31** NASA Earth Observatory; **p32-33** North Wind Picture Archives/Alamy Stock Photo (Acklins image), Everett Historical/SS (San Salvador), Everett Historical/SS (Blackbeard); **p35** Sara Kendall/SS (fruit), theCarolynWitt/SS (fisherman); **p36-37** Thomas Lorenz/SS (diver), Henner Damke/SS (parrot), Alexander Chaikin/SS (iguana), Sergey Uryadnikov/SS (flamingos), Shane Gross/SS (turtle), alphaborhjarding/Alamy Stock Photo (fish); **p40-41** nicolasvoisin44/SS (shark), Miami2youPhoto/SS (hotel resort), Nenad Basic/SS (garden); **p42-43** Nazar Skladanyi/SS (cruise ships), dnaveh/SS (Government House); **p44** Maddie Benavent/SS; **p45** BlueOrange Studio/SS (Glass Window Bridge), Zoe Esteban/SS (Harbour Island); **p46** Matt A. Claiborne/SS; **p47** Tosh Brown/Alamy Stock Photo (airport), Wikimedia Commons (police station); **p48** MJ Photography/Alamy Stock Photo (admin building), Alexander Chaikin/SS (Yacht Club); **p49** Ramunas Bruzas/SS (Duke Street), jpbarcelos/SS (Grace Bay); **p50** Wikimedia Commons; **p51** Frontpage/SS; **p52** twiggyjamaica/SS, Paul_Brighton/SS; **p53** UniversalImagesGroup/Getty Images; **p54** Robert S. Patton/Getty Images (Cockpit Country), Ruth Peterkin/SS (Ocho Rios); **p55** delafow/SS; **p56** Ian Cumming/Getty Images (coffee), Education Images/Getty Images (Port Kaiser); **p57** jiawangkun/SS (Falmouth Courthouse), Joseph Okpako/Getty Images (Chronixx), Aspen Photo/SS (Fraser-Pryce); **p58** glenda/SS (Haiti), hessbeck/SS (Santo Domingo); **p59** Sean Pavone/SS; **p60** R.A.R. de Bruijn Holding BV/SS; **p62** PlusONE/SS; **p63** OkFoto/SS; **p64** T photography/SS; **p65** Paul Wishart/SS; **p66** Salim October/SS; **p67** Qin Xie/SS; **p68** NASA Earth Observatory; **p69** CJG - Caribbean/Alamy Stock Photo (Oistins), LOOK Die Bildagentur der Fotografen GmbH/Alamy Stock Photo (festival); **p70** timsimages/SS (Port of Spain), Anton_Ivanov/SS (Pitch Lake), John de la Bastide/SS (Maracas Bay); **p73** Chad Mohammed/Wikipedia (mud volcano), John de la Bastide/SS (Caroni Swamp), Martin Mecnarowski/SS (carnival); **p75** Salim October/SS (carnival), John de la Bastide/SS (steelband); **p77** Martin Mecnarowski/SS; **p79** ZUMA Press, Inc/Alamy Stock Photo (carnival), Nature Picture Library/Alamy Stock Photo (mining); **p80** Tami Freed/SS; **p101** George Burba/SS (tundra), Serg Zastavkin/SS (taiga), Oleg Znamenskiy/SS (savanna), oleandra/SS (Sahara). [SS = Shutterstock]

**Acknowledgements**

**p19** Center for International Earth Science Information Network - CIESIN - Columbia University, International Food Policy Research Institute - IFPRI, The World Bank, and Centro Internacional de Agricultura Tropical - CIAT. 2011. Global Rural-Urban Mapping Project, Version 1 (GRUMPv1): Population Density Grid. Palisades, NY: NASA Socioeconomic Data and Applications Center (SEDAC). http://sedac.ciesin.columbia.edu/data/set/grump-v1-population-density. Accessed 18 11 2013 (population data); **p35** Food and Agriculture Organization of the United Nations, The Bahamas Ministry of Agriculture and Marine Resources, Citation: MCD12Q1.A2017001.h10v06.006, NASA EOSDIS Land Processes DAAC, USGS Earth Resources Observation and Science (EROS) Center, Sioux Falls, South Dakota (https://lpdaac.usgs.gov), accessed January 11th, 2019, at https://earthexplorer.usgs.gov/; **p36-37** The Bahamas Ministry of Tourism; **p38-48** The Bahamas Department of Statistics.